Humor
and Children's Development:
A Guide
to Practical Applications

The *Journal of Children in Contemporary Society* series:

Humor and Children's Development: A Guide to Practical Applications

Paul E. McGhee, PhD
Editor

The Haworth Press
New York • London

Humor and Children's Development: A Guide to Practical Applications has also been published as *Journal of Children in Contemporary Society*, Volume 20, Numbers 1/2 1988.

The Haworth Press, Inc., 12 West 32 Street, New York, NY 10001
EUROSPAN/Haworth, 3 Henrietta Street, London WC2E 8LU England

Library of Congress Cataloging-in-Publication Data

Humor and children's development : a guide to practical applications / edited by Paul E. McGhee.
    p. cm.
    "Also . . . published as Journal of children in contemporary society, volume, 20, numbers 1/2, 1988"—Verso t.p.
    Includes bibliographical references and index.
    ISBN 0-86656-681-3
    1. Humor in children. I. McGhee, Paul E.
BF723.H85H86 1989
155.4—dc 19

88-37931
CIP

Humor and Children's Development: A Guide to Practical Applications

CONTENTS

PART VI: CHAPTER COMMENTARY

ABOUT THE EDITOR

Paul E. McGhee, PhD, one of the world's foremost authorities on humor development, is Professor of Human Development at Texas Tech University and Research Fellow at the Laboratoire de Psychologie Différentielle, Université de Paris V. Since earning his doctorate degree in developmental psychology from Ohio State University in 1968, the majority of his research has been concerned with the development of humor in children. He has also, however, completed studies on humor among adults and the elderly. A prolific writer on humor, Dr. McGhee's publications include *Humor: Its Origin and Development* (Freeman; San Francisco, 1979) a highly readable textbook on the development of children's humor. He is also an editorial board member of the *International Journal of Humor Research* and the co-editor of five volumes on humor published during the past 16 years.

Preface

This volume stands as a testimony to the change in attitude toward humor which has taken place over the past 10 to 15 years. We knew very little about humor at any age level in the early 1970s, and the general public showed few signs of interest in the subject. If anything, there was a stronger interest in leaving humor unstudied than in learning more about it. Many seemed to feel that we might lose our sense of humor if we started to "seriously" study it. Not only do we take the fun out of humor by "analyzing" it, according to this view, but we also risk spending the rest of our days limited to a serious approach to the world.

Now, however (in the late 1980s), there are many signs of interest in understanding humor better — both among the general public and among scholars in a broad range of academic disciplines. It is very common these days to pick up a magazine and find an article on humor or laughter. Such articles have appeared recently in *Newsweek, Penthouse, Parent's Magazine, Redbook*, airline magazines, and numerous others. Newspaper articles featuring the topic are also common now. In academic fields, researchers have published a steadily increasing number of books and articles on humor over the past 15 years (see Part I of this volume).

I was aware of these developments, but was honestly surprised when Mary Frank, editor of the *Journal of Children in Contemporary Society*, contacted me with the request to produce a volume devoted to practical applications of humor with children. She indicated that there was a strong interest in having such a volume available for consultation, and that many people had become convinced of the value of humor, and wanted to know more about how to effectively incorporate it into children's lives. I initially declined the request because I knew that we had only begun to understand children's humor, and there was much more that we did not understand about it than that we did understand. With the passage of several months and periodic prompting from Mary, I gradually realized that even if most of the important scientific questions related to children's humor remained unresolved, most of us who study children's humor have no doubts about its potential benefits for children (as well as adults). Thus, if researchers are convinced of the value of humor and laughter for children, and if parents and members of various professions having daily contact with children are expressing a growing interest in how to use humor effectively with children, a volume like the present one is very timely. A considerable amount of humor research with an applied focus has been completed at the same time that investigators have studied fundamental cognitive, social, emotional and physiological aspects of humor. Thus, we have a good starting point for making recommendations regarding the application of humor in several different areas.

Part I of this volume documents the major research trends and other important events (such as conferences, publication of books, development of a professional journal devoted to humor research, etc.) which have given rise to (or resulted from) the renewed interest in humor and its development. The remaining chapters examine the potential benefits of humor and laughter for children's functioning and development in various cognitive, social, and emotional domains.

In Part II, the potential uses of humor and metaphor in promoting learning in the classroom are discussed along with humor's potential capacity to foster higher levels of creative thinking. Part III examines the importance of humor for children's social and emotional development. Humor's effectiveness in facilitating adaptation to stressful situations provides the basis for the three chapters in Part IV which discuss potential uses of humor as an intervention technique. Separate attention is given in this section to the use of humor with children in hospital settings, the dentist's office, and in therapy. Part V considers the value of humor in mass media productions especially geared toward children, including both educational television and children's literature. Finally, Part VI provides a commentary on key issues, theories, and research findings advanced in each chapter, and on points of view taken by the writers of these chapters.

This volume should hold special interest for teachers, social workers, pediatricians, nurses, and other medical staff, counselors, therapists, dentists, those involved in mass communication, and any other groups having frequent contact with children. It is also a valuable book for parents; for those who had no idea that humor could be important in their children's lives; for those who sensed its importance, but simply never knew what to make of their children's silliness (which often accompanies their humor and laughter); or for those who never realized the importance of their own adoption of a playful style of interaction with their children. The volume will also prove to be interesting reading for any other individuals keen on understanding children's behavior and development.

Finally, this volume can be effectively used as a text in courses on child development. In the case of courses which have a general text on child development, but where the instructors seek to provide the opportunity to examine a single aspect of children's behavior and development in detail, the topic of children's humor is ideal. Students invariably have a high level of interest in the topic to begin with, and their initial reading generally stimulates the desire to learn more. The volume is also an excellent resource for seminars devoted exclusively to humor.

Paul E. McGhee, PhD
Paris

Introduction: Recent Developments in Humor Research

Paul E. McGhee, PhD

The present volume is a direct reflection of the steadily growing interest in the study of humor during the past 15 years. Philosophers have speculated about the nature and significance of humor since at least the time of Aristotle. While psychologists began to study humor at the turn of the century, the topic never became a popular one for research. Goldstein and McGhee (1972) systematically reviewed all of the articles in English focusing on psychological theory and research on humor published in the 1900s and found only 376 articles. Of these, only 47 focused on children's humor. That volume was designed to draw attention to the importance of humor as an area of research and to provide new research directions outside of a psychoanalytic framework. To that point, Freud's (1905) seminal work on humor continued to provide the major theoretical focus for research. Levine's (1969) *Motivation and Humor*, for example, deals almost exclusively with issues related to Freudian theory.

BUT SERIOUSLY NOW . . .

The increase in humor research in the 1970s reflected the arrival (finally) of a frame of mind in psychology and other disciplines that allowed humor research a certain respectability. This same trend led

Paul E. McGhee is affiliated with the Laboratoire de Psychologie Différentielle, Université de Paris V, Paris, France, and the Department of Human Development and Family Studies, Texas Tech University, Lubbock, TX.

1

to an increase in research on play. By the mid 1970s, there was even an interdisciplinary organization (TAASP, the Association for the Anthropological Study of Play — now TASP, the Association for the Study of Play), holding annual meetings focusing on a broad range of issues related to play.

In spite of this generally increased receptiveness to studying humor, creating a domain that might legitimately be called "humor research" has not been an easy task. As Rodney Dangerfield used to say, humor research just "never got any respect." For those of us who have been committed to a better understanding of humor for a number of years, there was always an awareness that humor is somehow viewed as different from other research areas. For example, people tend to think that those of us who are humor researchers must be constantly telling jokes, anecdotes, witticisms, or otherwise being funny. In fact, some of us do and some of us do not. We may be funnier on the average than those who study other topics (we are definitely funnier than those who study AIDS or cancer), but most of us would die within 30 seconds as stand-up comedians. The important point here is that until recently, the desire to be entertained in any discussion of issues related to humor heavily outweighed the desire to really understand humor. Following research presentations on humor, there was — if we failed to keep the audience laughing — the inevitable question about how we could defend such a serious approach to humor. When we countered that those who study aggression or human sexuality are not expected to be especially hostile or sexy, the person asking the question was rarely convinced. Humor is different! If we were very funny, but offered little real substance in our talk, most people seemed to be very content.

Even researchers themselves have only slowly overcome the tendency not to take humor research seriously. My first experience with this phenomenon (duplicated endlessly) occurred in 1971. James McConnel had organized a day-long humor symposium at the annual meeting of the American Association for the Advancement of Science. The morning session was intended to be a "serious" look at issues related to humor research — a session like all of the other AAAS sessions. The afternoon session, on the other hand, was supposed to be a "spoof" session in which social scientists poked fun at themselves, their disciplines and their research methods. In the morning session, the only paper that seemed to be well-received was a presentation which consisted mainly of jokes along with an accompanying psychodynamic commentary. The papers by Arthur Koestler and myself focused on basic issues in humor theory and research with only a limited sprinkling of real humor. These papers were roundly criticized for their failure to be amusing, and there was virtually no discussion of the substantive points made. This example is described in detail because it captures the essence of an ongoing conflict in humor research; namely, should humor research also be humorous research? Also, to what extent should presentations of humor research be humorous?

THE EMERGENCE OF CONFERENCES AND BOOKS ON HUMOR

One of the most important events for the establishment of humor as a legitimate topic for research was the organization of an International Conference on Humor and Laughter in Cardiff by Tony Chapman and Hugh Foot in 1976. Subsequent international conferences have been held in Los Angeles (1979), Washington, D.C. (1982), Tel Aviv (1984), Cork, Ireland (1985) and Phoenix (1987). In 1980, the Nilsens organized the first WHIM (Western Humor and Irony Membership—now called the World Humor and Irony Membership) conference in Arizona. This conference continues to be held every April. Humor conferences with a very specialized focus (e.g., humor and therapy) have also been organized. There are now even special weekend conferences/workshops designed to acquaint the general public with the value of humor—and to increase their humor skills! These conferences have played an important role in spurring on the development of humor research by bringing researchers and others with active interests in humor into personal contact with one another, and by increasing receptiveness to the mere idea of studying humor (both among our colleagues and the general public).

There was great excitement at the Cardiff conference. An entire conference devoted to studies of humor was unimaginable to those of us who had difficulty defending research on humor in our academic department (there was usually an implicit understanding that the others were studying *important* topics). The conference gave us a certain credibility. The mass media and the general public, however, found the idea of a few hundred scholars settling down in the outskirts of Cardiff to talk seriously about humor quite comical. Most of the major British newspapers carried daily reports of one or another aspect of the conference, usually underscoring the absurdity of doing research on humor. (The BBC filmed many sessions and produced a special program based on the conference — aired the following April 1, of course.)

Part of the general public interest in the Cardiff conference was undoubtedly due to the following common assumption: "Everyone knows that you can't analyze humor; if you try, you just destroy it." And to be honest, "aren't some things — like humor and love — best left unstudied and not understood?" At this point (the mid 1970s), it was not unusual to find AP or UPI write-ups following special symposia (e.g., within a conference devoted to psychological research in general) on humor which ran somewhat like the following: "In the midst of threats of nuclear war, poverty, hunger, cancer and other sources of stress in contemporary life, at least we have our sense of humor to carry us through; but now they're trying to take that away from us." Such articles presumably reflected a genuine concern that we could possibly lose our sense of humor if we allow it to be exposed to intellectual scalpels. I have not seen such an article in any newspaper or magazine in the 1980s, a sure sign of a shift of attitude toward the value of a better understanding of humor.

Chapman and Foot's (1976) book *Humor and Laughter: Theory, Research and Applications* appeared at about the same time as the Cardiff conference, and was followed by the conference proceedings book, *It's a Funny Thing, Humour*, in 1977. In combination, these events suddenly created the feeling that humor research finally had a future, and that it would soon have a present and a past. Prior to the mid 1970s, entire volumes devoted to research and theory on humor were a rarity. Jeff Goldstein and I had a difficult time even finding potential contributors for *The Psychology of Humor* in 1972. Now we have the opposite problem; it is difficult to keep up with all of the work being published. The number of research articles being published has increased to the point that a new humor journal has been created, and is scheduled to appear in 1988 (*International Journal of Humor Research*, published by Mouton de Gruyter). The following (incomplete) list of books on humor published in the social sciences in the past decade attests to both the sharply increased amount of research on the topic and the growing diversity of that research. (Numerous other volumes on humor with a weaker link to humor research were also published.)

1977
Playfulness: Its Relation to Imagination and Creativity, by Lieberman.
Humor and the Health Professions, by Robinson.

1978
Understanding Laughter: The Workings of Wit and Humor, by Gruner.
Laugh After Laugh: The Healing Power of Humor, by Moody.

1979
Jokes: Form, Content, Use and Function, by Wilson.

1980
Mathematics and Humor, by Paulos.

1981
Pretend the World Is Funny and Forever: A Psychological Analysis of Comedians, Clowns and Actors, by Fisher and Fisher.

1982
Laughing: A Psychology of Humor, by Holland.

1983
Handbook of Humor Research. Vol. 1, *Basic Issues*, and Vol. 2, *Applied Studies*, by McGhee and Goldstein.
Taking Laughter Seriously, by Morreal.

1984
Humor: A Sociological Perspective, by Koller.

Humor and Psychotherapy, by Kuhlman.
Personality and Sense of Humor, by Ziv.

1985
Humor and Laughter: An Anthropological Approach, by Apte.
Semantic Mechanisms of Humor, by Raskin.

1986
Humor and Life Stress: Antidote to Adversity, by Lefcourt and
  Martin.

1987
*Handbook of Humor in Psychotherapy: Advances in the Clinical
  Use of Humor*, by Fry and Salameh.

From the point of view of the general public, Norman Cousin's
book *Anatomy of an Illness* (1979) clearly contributed to an enhanced awareness of the value of laughter and humor. Many have
long held the belief (in the absence of any real research support, but
in the presence of Freudian theory) that humor contributes to good
mental health, but there was never any reason to think that humor
could contribute to physical health as well. In his book, Cousins
claimed to have cured himself of a normally terminal disease using
heavy doses of laughter and vitamin C. While most people have
accepted this view as already established, it is only in the past few
years that researchers have *begun* to systematically test it. (See
Goldstein, 1987, for a discussion of the history of views on the
impact of humor on health.)

RESEARCH ON CHILDREN'S HUMOR

The study of children's humor and of humor development also
sharply increased in the 1970s. McGhee and Chapman's (1980)
bibliography of children's humor includes the following frequency
of publication by decade: 1900-1910 = 2; 1910-1919 = 2; 1920-
1929 = 9; 1930-1939 = 12; 1940-1949 = 13; 1950-1959 = 8;
1960-1969 = 14; 1970-1979 = 115. (This bibliography includes
some publications not included in the Goldstein and McGhee,
1972, bibliography.) Thus, the limited rate of research on chil-

dren's humor remained very stable throughout the century—until the 1970s. In comparison with the 1960s, the 1970s marked an 800% increase in number of published articles, chapters and books on the topic. No comparable data are available for the 1980s. While much remains to be learned about children's humor, we have learned enough to realize that humor has an important role to play in children's development. The purpose of this volume is to help those who work with children in a broad range of disciplines capitalize on what we have learned in order to enhance children's intellectual, social and emotional development.

The first volume on children's humor, *Children's Humor: A Psychological Analysis*, was published in 1954 by Wolfenstein (and subsequently reprinted in 1978). This book was completed before the resurgence of research on humor, but remains an excellent summary of the psychoanalytic perspective on children's humor. McDowell's (1979) *Children's Riddling* presents a detailed analysis of children's spontaneous riddling, using observational techniques in a naturalistic setting. The first general text on the development of children's humor, *Humor: It's Origin and Development* (by McGhee), also appeared in 1979. In 1980, McGhee and Chapman's edited volume, *Children's Humour*, was geared toward researchers; it summarized research findings and discussed a broad range of research issues with the goal of stimulating new directions of research. In France, Bariaud's (1983) *La genese de l'humour chez l'enfant* provided an in-depth examination of individual differences in children's comprehension and appreciation of humor, and it helped generate interest in the topic in that country.

Virtually all of the research and theory concerning humor development has been restricted to preadolescents. The great majority of work completed up to 1988 used elementary school-aged children as subjects, with preschoolers being the second most frequently studied group. College students have been used for many humor studies, but only a tiny fraction of these have focused on developmental issues. Thus, in spite of all the attention given to the study of humor since 1970, we understand humor development in adolescence no better than we did 80 years ago. While we have learned a great deal about the humor of adolescents, we have learned nothing about its development.

Surprisingly, a volume has already been published dealing with humor among the elderly (*Humor and Aging*, by Nahemow, Mc-Cluskey-Fawcett, & McGhee, 1986). Again, however, little attention was given to developmental issues. Similarly, no attempt has yet been made to study humor development during the adult years (although many studies of humor have used adults as subjects). McGhee (1983, 1986) has recently taken steps to rectify this situation by calling for a life-span approach to studies of humor development, and suggesting possible starting points for undertaking life-span developmental studies.

THE STUDY OF CHILDREN'S PLAY

Most researchers studying children's humor agree that there is an important link between play and humor. Many of the same issues that arise in studies of humor also arise in studies of play. The notion of playfulness as a prerequisite for genuine humor enjoyment or production is especially important. That is, both children and adults are more likely to initiate humor themselves or to appreciate the humor of others when in a playful frame of mind. As with humor (and play in general), studies of children's play have increased enormously in the past decade. The present volume does not focus on play, but given the close connection between children's play and children's humor, the following (non-exhaustive) list of volumes on children's play is provided as a means of helping interested readers familiarize themselves with that area as well.

1977
Play, by Garvey.
Playfulness: Its Relation to Imagination and Creativity, by Lieberman.
Partners in Play: A Step by Step Guide to Imaginative Play in Children, by Singer and Singer.

1978
Activity and Play of Children, by Ellis and Scholtz.
Transformation: The Anthropology of Children's Play, by Schwartzman.

1979
Children's Play and Playgrounds, by Frost and Klein.
Play and Learning, by Sutton-Smith.

1982
The Play of Children: Current Theory and Research, by Pepler and Rubin.
Children's Play, by Rubin.
Learning is Child's Play, by Yawkey and Trostle.

1984
Symbolic Play: The Representation of Social Understanding, by Bretherton.
Text and Context in Imaginative Play: New Directions for Child Development, by Kessel and Goncu.
Child's Play: Developmental and Applied, by Yawkey and Pellegrini.

1985
When Children Play, by Frost and Sunderlin.

1987
School Play, by Block and King.
Curiosity, Imagination and Play: On the Development of Spontaneous Cognitive and Motivational Processes, by Gorlitz and Wohlwill.
Play and Early Child Development, by Johnson, Christie, and Yawkey.

CONCLUDING NOTE

This introduction was intended to provide a general overview of recent developments in research on humor. No attempt has been made to summarize actual research findings in any area of humor or play. For the topics covered in this volume, a detailed discussion of pertinent research findings is presented within each chapter. Readers should refer to the volumes cited here for summaries of research not discussed in this volume.

REFERENCES

Apte, M.L. (1985). *Humor and laughter: An anthropological approach*. Ithaca, N.Y.: Cornell University Press.

Bariaud, F. (1983). *La genese de l'humour chez l'enfant*. Paris: Presses Universitaires de France.

Block, J., & King, N. (1987). *School play*. New York: Garland.

Bretherton, I. (Ed.). (1984). *Symbolic play: The representation of social understanding*. Orlando, Fla.: Academic Press.

Chapman, A.J., & Foot, H.C. (Eds.). (1976). *Humour and laughter: Theory, research and application*. London: Wiley.

Chapman, A.J., & Foot, H.C. (Eds.). (1977). *It's a funny thing, humour*. London: Pergamon.

Cousins, N. (1979). *Anatomy of an illness as perceived by a patient*. New York: Norton.

Ellis, M.J., & Scholtz, G.J.L. (1978). *Activity and play of children*. Englewood Cliffs, N.J.: Prentice-Hall.

Fisher, S., & Fisher, R.L. (1981). *Pretend the world is funny and forever: A psychological analysis of comedians, clowns, and actors*. Hillsdale, N.J.: Erlbaum.

Freud, S. (1960). *Jokes and their relation to the unconscious*. New York: Norton. (Originally *Der witz und seine beziehung zum ubewussten*. Leipzig: Deuticke, 1905.)

Frost, J.L., & Klein, B.L. (1979). *Children's play and playgrounds*. Boston: Allyn & Bacon.

Frost, J.L., & Sunderlin, S. (Eds.). (1985). *When children play*. Wheaton, Md.: Association for Childhood Education Int.

Fry, W.F., & Salameh, W.A. (Eds.). (1987). *Handbook of humor and psychotherapy: Advances in the clinical use of humor*. Sarasota, Fla.: Professional Resource Exchange, Inc.

Garvey, C. (1977). *Play*. Cambridge, Mass.: Harvard Univ. Press.

Goldstein, J.H. (1987). Therapeutic effects of laughter. In W.F. Fry & W.A. Salameh (Eds.), *Handbook of humor and psychotherapy: Advances in the clinical uses of humor*. Sarasota, Fla.: Professional Resource Exchange, Inc.

Goldstein, J.H., & McGhee, P.E. (1972). An annotated bibliography of published papers on humor in the research literature, and an analysis of trends: 1900-1971. In J.H. Goldstein & P.E. McGhee (Eds.), *The psychology of humor: Theoretical perspectives and empirical issues*. New York: Academic Press.

Goldstein, J.H., & McGhee, P.E. (Eds.). (1972). *The psychology of humor: Theoretical perspectives and empirical issues*. New York: Academic Press.

Gorlitz, D., & Wohlwill, J.F. (Eds.). (1987). *Curiosity, imagination, and play: On the spontaneous development of cognitive and motivational processes*. Hillsdale, N.J.: Erlbaum.

Gruner, C.R. (1978). *Understanding laughter: The workings of wit and humor*. Chicago: Nelson-Hall.

Holland, N.M. (1982). *Laughing: A psychology of humor*. Ithaca, N.Y.: Cornell University Press.

Johnson, J.E., Christie, J.F., & Yawkey, T.D. (Eds.). (1987). *Play and early childhood development*. Glenview, Ill.: Scott Foresman.

Kessel, F.S., & Goncu, A. (Eds.). (1984). *Text and context in imaginative play: New directions for child development*. San Francisco: Jossey-Bass.

Koller, M. (1984). *Humor: A sociological perspective*. Houston: Cap and Gown Press.

Kuhlman, T. (1984). *Humor and psychotherapy*. Homewood, Ill.: Dow Jones-Irwin.

Lefcourt, H.M., & Martin, R.A. (1986). *Humor and life stress: Antidote to adversity*. New York: Springer-Verlag.

Levine, J. (Ed.). (1969). *Motivation in humor*. New York: Atherton.

Lieberman, J.N. (1977). *Playfulness: Its relation to imagination and creativity*. New York: Academic Press.

McDowell, J.H. (1979). *Children's riddling*. Bloomington: Indiana University Press.

McGhee, P.E. (1979). *Humor: Its origin and development*. San Francisco: Freeman.

McGhee, P.E. (1983). Humor development: Toward a lifespan approach. In P.E. McGhee & J.H. Goldstein (Eds.), *Handbook of humor research*. Vol. I. *Basic issues*. New York: Springer-Verlag.

McGhee, P.E. (1986). Humor across the lifespan: Sources of developmental change and individual differences. In L. Nahemow, K. McCluskey-Fawcett, & P.E. McGhee (Eds.), *Humor and aging*. New York: Academic Press.

McGhee, P.E., & Chapman, A.J. (Eds.). (1980). *Children's humour*. Chichester, England: Wiley.

McGhee, P.E., & Goldstein, J.H. (Eds.). (1983). *Handbook of humor research*. Vol. I. *Basic issues*. New York: Springer-Verlag.

McGhee, P.E., & Goldstein, J.H. (Eds.). (1983). *Handbook of humor research*. Vol. II. *Applied studies*. New York: Springer-Verlag.

Moody, R.A. (1978). *Laugh after laugh*. Jacksonville, Fla.: Headwaters Press.

Morreal, J. (1983). *Taking laughter seriously*. Albany: SUNY Press.

Nahemow, L., McCluskey-Fawcett, K., & McGhee, P.E. (Eds.). (1986). *Humor and aging*. New York: Academic Press.

Paulos, J.A. (1980). *Mathematics and humor*. Chicago: University of Chicago Press.

Pepler, D.J., & Rubin, K.H. (Eds.). (1982). *The play of children: Current theory and research*. Basel: Karger, Ag.

Raskin, V. (1985). *Semantic mechanisms of humor*. Boston: D. Reidel.

Robinson, V.M. (1977). *Humor and the health professions*. Thorofare, N.J.: Charles B. Slack.

Rubin, K.H. (Ed.). (1982). *Children's play*. San Francisco: Jossey-Bass.

Schwartzman, H.B. (1978). *Transformation: The anthropology of children's play*. New York: Plenum.

Singer, D.G., & Singer, J.L. (1977). *Partners in play: A step by step guide to imaginative play in children*. New York: Harper & Row.

Sutton-Smith, B. (Ed.). (1979). *Play and learning*. New York: Gardner Press.

Wilson, C.P. (1979). *Jokes: Form, content, use and function*. London: Academic Press.

Wolfenstein, M. (1954). *Children's humor: A psychological analysis*. Glencoe, Ill.: Free Press. (Reissued in 1978 by Indiana University Press.)

Yawkey, T.D., & Pellegrini, A.D. (Eds.). (1984). *Children's play: Developmental and applied*. Hillsdale, N.J.: Erlbaum.

Yawkey, T.D., & Trostle, S.L. (1982). *Learning is child's play*. Provo, Utah: Brigham Young University Press.

Ziv, A. (1984). *Personality and sense of humor*. New York: Springer.

PART I: DEVELOPMENTAL CHANGES IN CHILDREN'S HUMOR

Introduction

Part I is designed to provide a foundation for the remainder of the volume by reviewing theories and research related to our present understanding of children's humor and its development. Bariaud discusses the problem of defining humor along with the problems associated with studying humor. The special importance of incongruity (and its resolution) and a playful frame of mind is noted, but it is concluded that there are neither any necessary nor sufficient conditions for humor. After discussing issues related to the initial appearance of humor in children, she examines in detail theoretical models and research findings related to the humor of preschool and elementary school aged children. Attention is given to individual differences in the humor produced or enjoyed within a given age level as well as to differences between the humor of different age groups.

13

Chapter 1

Age Differences in Children's Humor

Francoise Bariaud, PhD

SUMMARY. Developmental changes in humor between age two and about eleven years are reviewed here. Problems in defining humor are noted, but the special importance of incongruity, resolution of incongruity, and a playful frame of mind are emphasized. Divergent viewpoints regarding the onset of humor are reviewed, and cognitively- and affectively-oriented models of humor development are presented. Detailed discussion of theoretical views and research findings is provided separately for preschool and school-aged children. Separate sections suggest that the cognitive contribution to humor is greatest when the difficulty level of the humor matches the child's cognitive level, but full appreciation of the humor depicted in cartoons or jokes requires an emotional identification with the humorist and a sharing of his perceived intent.

This chapter concentrates on what research can tell us about the development of humor in children: humor they produce and humor they appreciate. It will provide adults who are in daily contact with children (parents, teachers, social workers, medical staff, etc.) with the means of better recognizing the simpler forms of humor in children and what children attempt to convey by this mode of communication. Perhaps it will also encourage adults to take an interest in children's humor, to reinforce it through their understanding, and even actively solicit this playful behavior which is so valuable for learning and for coping with stressful situations (see other chapters in this volume). Secondly, from the standpoint of research, the de-

---

Francoise Bariaud is affiliated with C. N. R. S., Laboratoire de Psychologie Differentielle, Université Rene Descartes, Paris, France.

velopmental study of children's humor (in the Piagetian sense) can be used to improve our understanding of the complexity of the higher forms of humor found in adolescence and adulthood, through an analysis of the simpler forms and a reconstruction of their progressive complexification during the course of childhood.

Naturally, any attempt at tracing developmental paths and identifying qualitative changes implies starting with a definition of humor with all the arbitrariness and tentativeness this entails (future research should help refine current definitions). I will begin with this point, before dealing chronologically with the evolution of children's humor from age 2 to preadolescence.

WHAT IS HUMOR?

Humor generally makes people laugh or smile, but not all laughs or smiles are manifestations of humor. Laughter and smiling are ambiguous in terms of meaning, and they may derive from highly varied types of emotional experiences. Numerous situations which produce laughter or smiling in children have been observed (e.g., Blurton Jones, 1967; Ding and Jersild, 1932; Justin, 1932; Kenderdine, 1931; Nichol, 1981; Valentine, 1942; Wilson, 1931). As early as 1923, Dumas stressed the importance of differentiating between "laughter which indicates a state of general excitement of pleasure" and "laughter which indicates the pleasure of comic experience." The present article focuses on the latter form which often (but not necessarily always: children can be deadpan) arises from the specific experience engendered by the perception or the evocation of a "funny" or "amusing" event.

Since laughter and smiling are "polysemic" (multiply determined) and thus risky indicators, researchers take the precaution of validating them by the "feeling" of amusement expressed in verbalizations, such as "It's funny!" A situation can be funny accidentally because of the circumstances or because of "distractedness" (as in accidentally tripping and slips of the tongue, analyzed, for example, by Bergson, 1900). An event can also be funny deliberately, when it is produced to amuse, either arising spontaneously in the fleeting context of a repartee or drawn from the storehouse of the comic universe composed of witticisms, gags, caricatures and treasures of humorous "folklore." A situation can also be funny if one experiences it in a playful mood (Eastman, 1936) while the others take it in a serious vein. But everything that belongs to the universe of funniness is not humor (tripping, jack in the box, etc.) because humor is only one of its variants, doubtless one of the most complex. Numerous authors in fields such as literature, philosophy (Bergson, 1900; Jankelevitch, 1964, among others), and also psychoanalysis (Freud, 1928) have put forward definitions of humor. However, until now psychologists studying the development of humor have devoted little attention to these distinctions and have based their work on a broad definition of humor.

Incongruity, the Basic Component

There is almost total consensus among researchers that humor is related to comprehending (humor reaction) or producing (humor creation) an "incongruity." Incongruity refers to the simultaneous, or almost simultaneous, occurrence of normally incompatible elements (i.e., elements which are not ordinarily associated with each other in a given context). The originality of this creation by the humorist is attributed to an ability to see things on two levels at once ("the bisociation phenomenon" in Koestler's, 1964, terms), but little research has been devoted to this process itself, a process which reflects a specific form of mental gymnastics linked to more general measures of creativity.

In terms of the humor reaction, which has received much more attention from researchers, "incongruity" designates the way in which the humorous situation "works psychologically" in the individual who encounters it; certain features that the individual identifies activate familiar schemas (verbal or imaginal mental representations) and create expectations about how these features should relate to each other which are dependent upon prior experience of the environment and internalized representations of that experience. However, the quasi-simultaneous input of other situational elements suddenly clashes with these expectations, generating a sort of cognitive contradiction which produces surprise. In this way, it can be said that through its structure, humor creates a momentary imbalance in the organization of familiar schemas whether this is on a perceptual level, or a more abstract one involving a sequence of ideas. But here the main issue is why individuals' emotional reaction is not perplexity, fear, or simple astonishment, but laughter, smiling, or (even when these are not present), the feeling of funniness. In other words, incongruity, although it is necessary to describe the humor experience, is not sufficient in itself to account for it and must be accompanied by other components.[1]

The Playful Framework

Both adults and children laugh at times at incongruities in outward appearances or behaviors which are unintentionally funny (for example, inappropriate conduct in others and the ridicule attributed to it). But in my opinion, this form of laughter is related to a comic feeling and not to a sense of humor. For humor implies that there has been creation, including an awareness of the incongruity, and its power to amuse in the person who generates it. Humor supposes this dual awareness, even if it seems to arise from an unconscious mechanism. Moreover, humor transcends this awareness through its intent to amuse. Whereas, humor can occasionally make someone smile "mentally," inwardly to himself (which is already an interaction with the "socius," the "other" integrated in ourselves),[2] it is only complete when it is set in social communication whose aim is to make others laugh. Humor cannot be really understood without placing it in the framework of social exchange, an exchange based on mutual complicity and not on exclusion (as is the case in mockery, or the "badgering" laugh discussed in Bergson, 1900).

People are usually cued to the intent to amuse through certain communicative signals which are invitations to take the incongruous event in a playful mode:. "It's not serious, it's for a laugh." Drawing style in comic illustrations, the identity of the characters in action, standard introductory lead-ins to jokes, the framework of the exchange . . . are all cues which help the receiver define the intent of the situation and foster in him, if his mood is favorable, the frame of mind to "take things in a joking fashion," or what has been termed by McGhee (1972) "fantasy assimilation." In its most subtle forms, adult humor can bypass these cues and sneak surreptitiously into the midst of serious discourse. But even in this case, the identity of the humorist, the glint in his eye, the hints of his smile are there to guide us and confirm the presence of humorous intent.

Children need these cues more than adults in order to be sure that they are encountering humor and not something bizarre. Children's ability to recognize such cues apparently has its roots in early experience, in the first play-exchanges with familiar adults. Ten- or twelve-month-olds are able to perceive the playful, non-threatening character of unexpected or incongruous scenes which, in other circumstances, would provoke fear rather than laughter (Sroufe and Wunsch, 1972; Sroufe, Waters and Matas, 1974). On the basis of this early "social intelligence," children gradually familiarize themselves with humor in a variety of partners and a range of institutionalized forms (TV commercials, cartoons, pictures in books, etc.) and in this way learn to decode the rules behind what is humorous.

When these contextual cues are difficult for the child to identify, or when they are not sufficient to generate the affective distance necessary for a playful attitude to take place (Bariaud, 1983), incongruity will not produce laughter, but rather other diametrically opposed emotional reactions. For example, younger children can be frightened of what older ones find very funny (see observations by Leroy-Boussion, 1955).

Resolution of Incongruity

In their descriptions of the humor reaction (in different theoretical frameworks), Freud (1905a), Maier (1932), Bateson (1953), and Berlyne (1960) all suggest that a second process involving the reassessment of the situation as a whole takes place after incongruity has been grasped. Wit, for Freud, starts by puzzling, and subsequently becomes intelligible, thus allowing the initial surprise to give way to clarity. This produces the comic effect. In the psychology of humor, this notion is central to the theory of incongruity-resolution put forward by Schultz (1970, 1972), Jones (1970) and Suls (1972). Following an initial phase of contradiction between what the individual encounters and his original expectations, the receiver of humor engages in a second phase of "resolution" of incongruity in which the two initially incompatible elements are reconciled. Thus, resolution gives a certain coherency to incongruity without, however, rendering it more serious. This process implies finding an explanation for the incongruity, discovering some "justification for the simultaneous presence of the incompatible elements or extracting some new meaning from their co-occurrence" (Shultz, 1972).

For example, in a humorous drawing, a patient is seen from the back and getting up from the operating table after the surgery; the surgeons around him burst into laughter. This is definitely incongruous behavior on the part of the medical profession, but their behavior can be accounted for by the sign on the wall stating "cosmetic surgery." Here lies "the element of resolution" (which cannot in all cases be identified so clearly) which enables comprehension to overcome the initial reaction of surprise. Similar examples could be given for verbal humor (see Suls, 1972).

Resolution is the complement of identification of incongruity, and they together make up comprehension, the intellectual part of the humor reaction which is an indispensable basis for amusement. Debate between researchers has centered on whether there is always resolution in humor. Shultz (1977), in an analysis of verbal jokes and riddles across very different cultures (e.g., Western culture, non-literate cultures, China, Japan), concluded that most of these forms are consistent with the incongruity-resolution structure. Other researchers, in particular Nerhardt (1977) and Rothbart (1973, 1976), investigating other situations, posit that incongruity alone is enough to provoke laughter, provided that it is perceived in a "secure" environment. This may be the case for gags, tricks, caricatures, and certain "comic situations." Because there are multiple humors, and not only *one* humor, the "incongruity alone in a secure context" model and the "incongruity followed by resolution" model are both useful as Suls (1983) points out.

However, I would like to stress that although both are useful, they are still not sufficient to fully account for the appreciation of humor. Obviously, one needs to understand to find something funny. But understanding does not necessarily mean one will think it is funny. Appreciation requires a certain mutual complicity with the creator, a sharing of his underlying playful intention and what is implied through his incongruity (Bariaud, 1983). The experience of humor cannot be reduced to a purely cognitive process, be it a one- or two-stages process. It is also an affective experience.

THE ORIGINS OF HUMOR

Malrieu (1967), McGhee (1977a, 1979), and Tower and Singer (1980) argue that humor has its origin in pretend play which develops at about the age of 18 months as a manifestation of a significant change in cognitive development: the emergence of capacities for symbolic thought through which individuals can mentally represent objects, people, or events they have had prior experience with. In make-believe play, the object towards which an action is directed is often temporarily utilized in a way that differs from the ordinary one (i.e., it is used in an incongruous manner). The child is perfectly aware of the real identity of the object that he is pretending with. But he situates it in the universe of fantasy, and this provides an opportunity for (often intense) enjoyment. "There is a form of trickery the child amuses himself with," wrote Wallon in 1949, "he feels he is manipulating reality at will. If an adult pretends to fall into the trap, the child is delighted because he enjoys thinking that the adult has been fooled, and this type of collusion increases his joy."

There are theoretical reasons for linking later forms of humor with these early forms of make-believe play. In humor, also, we momentarily free ourselves from the fetters of reality and accept, in fantasy, incongruities which we do not take literally because we are aware that they are erroneous. "Playing the game" in humor as in pretend play amounts to acting "as if" these incongruities were not erroneous. In humor, as in pretend play, there is a certain "distancing" from the norms of reality, and a combination of being fooled and complicity required from the other. This suggests that there may be a positive relationship between humor and pretend play, but empirical research has yet to provide clearcut evidence for this.[3]

If this point of view is accurate, the question which logically follows is how humor, if it shares common roots with symbolic play, branches off from it and differentiates itself at a certain point in development such that enjoyment from play and from humor are experienced as being different. From a psychoanalytical perspective, Wolfenstein (1954) distinguished between two types of pretend play which are governed by different drives: serious make-believe and joking make-believe. Her remarks concern the forms of play which develop at about the age of three where the distortions invented by the child are related to his identity, the identity of his partners, the nature of the situation, and are expressed through multiple roles. Serious pretend play, although it breaks with reality, in fact draws on known forms of behavior and emotions, and its aim is to create the illusion of a compensatory universe: the child is different from what he is really, lives the experiences of others, masters what normally defeats him ("I'm Superman!") or frightens him ("I'm a lion"). But in this imaginary world, incongruity is not in the forefront. In fact, incongruity is only central to the outside observer who is uninvolved in the play activity. The child is carried away by illusion, although knowing that it is nothing more than illusion. In joking make-believe, in contrast, the emphasis remains on the distortion of reality, on incongruity which in this case is consciously used to serve another purpose: to make fun of both the constraints that weigh too heavily in real life and the negative feelings these constraints engender such as anxiety, suffering, and the need for compensation. Joking pretend play involves inventing fictitious deformations of the world, of others and of oneself. This fiction is not there for purposes of reverie, but to trigger laughter. The comic hero distances himself in two ways: through fantasy and through discordance with the known world.

An important issue along these lines concerns how children acquire the feeling that their creations are funny. For McGhee (1979), the child would be capable of first experiencing humor in his own fantasy productions in playing alone. For Singer (1973) and Bariaud (1983), the child builds up this feeling via social learning experiences, in particular through adults' laughter and his desire to reproduce these positive interactions. On an observational level, laughter and smiling in the child engaged in solitary play are ambiguous since they may only indicate enjoyment of playing. But the feeling of funniness is more apparent when the child, using language, becomes able to exploit his personal incongruous invention to fool others and at the same time to lead them into an upsidedown world with their complicity. Intent of this type was observed in a 23-month-old girl who, with both a clever and embarrassed look which expressed her playful mood, said to her father: "Daddy, (d)oggie — miaow," before bursting into laughter (Chukovsky, cited by McGhee, 1979). This was this child's first joke, at least the first that the father recognized as such.

McGhee (1972, 1979) used the term "fantasy assimilation" to refer to the child's manner of adapting his thinking to incongruous events without "really" changing his corresponding mental schemas. That is, the incongruity is momentarily treated "as if it were really like that," but the child doesn't walk away believing it to be like that. While this mechanism is inherent to his humor creation, however, the child has more difficulty interpreting things at a fantasy level when the incongruity is produced by others (McGhee, 1979). This is because, to do so, he must be sure of the contradiction with reality, and aware of the playful intent of the partner so as not to take his behavior as an error or something strictly bizarre. In other words, the child must have constructed a sufficiently firm knowledge of the events in question to recognize the incongruity, and must be able to detect the verbal and nonverbal cues provided indicating that "it's for laughs." These cues are paramount factors for children of about 3 or 4 years of age when mastery of reality is still uncertain. All of this is a matter of intelligence (i.e., of cognitive acquisitions and social intelligence in the sense of the ability to understand situations as a function of subtle cues and previous experience with the partner). Adults vary in the extent to which they enjoy laughing with children. As early as 2 1/2, a child is perfectly able to distinguish between those who do and do not in his familiar environment. "Did you put your shoes under the Christmas tree?" I asked to a little girl of this age who I know well. Answer: "Yes." "And Mommy's?" "Yes." "And Daddy's?" "Yes" And Jaffa's?" (the name of the dog) "No," immediately followed by a burst of laughter and the statement "You make me laugh!" This is clearly an example of an early form of humor reaction.

PRESCHOOL HUMOR

Relationship of Humor to Intellectual and Emotional Development in the Child: Two Theoretical Frameworks

The cognitive point of view: the McGhee model. As the child develops, he shows an increasing capacity for creation and appreciation of humor. This capacity to produce and enjoy more and more complex forms of humor, progressively approaching what adults consider to be "humor," is concomitant with the development of his intellectual abilities. By definition, humor requires possession of the referents it distorts. Humor is thus necessarily dependent upon the acquisitions which are progressively made over the course of childhood. This includes the integration of increasingly richer knowledge (of the features of the physical world, norms of social conduct, rules of the language, etc.) and the development of more and more complex cognitive mechanisms of thought (concept formation, logical operations, etc.). To understand the funniness of a flying cow with blue wings (either in producing the image or reacting to it with a laugh), the child evidently must have a clearcut concept of "cow" in his repertoire, specifying its salient features. To laugh at the stupidity of the four men who carry their car that weighs 1200 pounds across a wooden bridge because the signs says "no access to vehicles over 1000 pounds," the child must have acquired conservation of weight, which is dependent upon complex logical operations and appears much later in the development than the concept of "cow" (see Piaget and Inhelder, 1941). Without these cognitive acquisitions, which are situated on very different levels, the child is not in a position to understand the incongruities which in both examples form the basis of the humor. Thus, the development of cognitive tools is a prerequisite for the progress in humor, and these can be described in parallel.

For McGhee (1977a, 1979), humor is essentially a "cognitive experience." That is, while one's emotional state can influence his experience of humor, and while there are normally predictable emotional reactions associated with humor (e.g., pleasure and laughter), it is a cognitive insight that triggers humor. The model he puts forward to account for its development in preschoolers and older children (the latter will receive attention in the next section) is composed of several phases which are tightly linked to the Piagetian stages of intellectual development. Transitional ages from one stage to another can vary across individuals, but the sequence is thought to be identical for all. As we have already seen, *the first stage*, at the foundations of humor, is characterized by incongruities in pretend play behaviors. The emergence of language at the end of the second year of life opens up new and broad perspectives for humor:

the child can now share his incongruous actions with others by substituting one object designation for another, thus discovering the social enjoyment involved in these exchanges.

In the *second stage* of the McGhee model, "incongruous labels for objects or events" may be combined with incongruous actions directed toward objects, or the child may also create purely verbal incongruities. As Aimard (1984) has suggested, perhaps it is the same impetus which governed the transformation of the identity of objects in the first stage which now governs the transformation of the identity of words in the second. When a child has mastered a word (the phonetic sequence and its relationship with a specific referent), he plays with it, having it mean something else: a dog is called a cat, a fork is called a knife or other terms (McGhee, 1979; Shinn, cited by Piret, 1940; Sully, 1902). The phase of enjoyment derived from incorrect labelling may extend over several years with great differences between children, depending on their personalities and the reaction of those around them. Not all cultures, and not all social classes in a single culture have the same reactions to "fractured language." Some parents are unwilling to accept deviations from standards from their children, feeling them as detrimental to learning, or perhaps unconsciously having a hard time accepting the image of a "retarded" offspring. Their disapproval ("don't talk like that") discourages further such attempts. In contrast, other parents are entertained by the same verbal fantasies, and by not concealing their amusement, encourage their production. These parents intuitively grasp an inherent value in play of this type, which lies in the flexibility and pleasure it engenders in language use, and later in the flourishing of creativity and humor. The children can also share this enjoyment with their peers. Thus, in nursery schools, they can be observed imitating each other's language distortions, but at the same time adding their own "twist."

Although these forms of humor remain available for both creation and reaction (when the underlying knowledge of the elements related to the incongruities is sufficiently strong, and playful cues are discernible), a new advance in humor accompanies the emergence of conceptual thought at about age 3. At this age, children begin to understand that a word does not refer to a single object, but rather to a category of objects sharing common distinctive features that differentiate them from other objects. A "cow" (the class of cows) has four legs, a characteristic head, is big, eats grass, says "moo," etc. A cow thus neither resembles a human being nor a canary. Gradually, children structure knowledge acquired through previous experience via what they have seen and what they have been told into conceptual categories (e.g., the concept of "cow"). This development of conceptual categories makes children between the ages 3 to 6 particularly amused by incongruities which bear on distinctive category features such as a cartoon of a cow which scratches its back with a brush and whistles like a canary while taking a bath in a bathtub, or a picture of a man with a frog's head. The child also derives enjoyment when stories depicting such incongruities are told to him. The important point is the violation of conceptual representations. Note that in this *third stage*, the child's mode of thought is based exclusively on the perceptual characteristics of objects or events which is in striking contrast to the *fourth stage*. Thus, humor at this point is centered around incongruities related to appearance. In its verbal expression, it consists of the invention of nonsense words, enjoyment of rhymed sequences, and laughter when hearing words having unexpected pronunciations, as though what was the most important was the distortion of the "physical" aspect of the word (i.e., its sound, and not its meaning [McGhee, 1979]).

The affective point of view: the Wolfenstein model. The preceding section has shown the ways in which cognitive development determines comprehension of humor. In a very different theoretical framework, which conceives of humor essentially as an affective phenomenon, Wolfenstein's (1954) model enriches our understanding of its development through an emphasis on the deep-seated motivations and emotions which are expressed in connection with incongruity.

Humor is viewed by Wolfenstein as a procedure which turns a negative experience (for example, frustration or guilt when faced with all-powerful adults and the constraints they impose) into a positive one. The contents of humor over the course of childhood reflect the concerns which mark the successive steps of emotional development and which were at one time associated with worry or anxiety. Thus, the affirmation of gender-identity generates gender reversal play: calling a boy "a girl" at about age 3 and changing gender-linked proper names (calling John "Sally"). Sphincter control concerns produce "B.M." jokes at around 3 1/2-4 years of age. The amount of emotional investment needs to be attenuated for a child to create humor based on these themes. Humor implies "affective mastery," an emotional distancing which often is naturally established with the passing of time, but which some children achieve even in the presence of situations which can be very distressing to others of the same age (Wolfenstein, 1954, cites examples of this at age five).

Another of Wolfenstein's major contributions, aside from the analysis of dominant themes in humor at different stages of childhood, is her charting of children's acquisition of more and more complex ways of making jokes (i.e., of using the "joke facade" to conceal their sexual and aggressive tendencies which would be criticized if openly expressed). Humor is a way of subtly getting around a prohibition (Freud, 1905a) through the use of increasingly complicated disguises. This skill reflects underlying cognitive development as well as a need arising from the progressive internalization of morals. As a result of these developments, an important change in joking style takes place at about 6 years of age. Prior to this time, children's productions are spontaneous, original, and relatively crude: sexual, scatological, or aggressive motivation is very apparent (e.g., "pee-pee," "ka-ka," "Auntie B.M.," etc.). Children seem more prone to enjoying their own inventions than standard joking forms at this age. But, at about age 6 they begin to show a pronounced interest in ready-made jokes, and this interest will develop between the ages of 7 and 10 for reasons which will be discussed later.

Additional Research Findings

The two previous models, linked with more general theories of cognitive and affective development, are based on facts resulting from rigorous observations of children in natural or experimental situations. However, studies completed by other researchers have brought out other facts which are presented. The theories of McGhee and Wolfenstein can provide an interesting background for making sense out of these findings, but these data can also be seen as a means of enriching theorizing about humor development. First, however, some methodological problems confronting scientific research on humor in children must be briefly noted.

Problems in conducting humor research. As to humor creation, which at the age of 3 cannot be exercised in all domains of expression because of the child's limited abilities (intellectual, motor, verbal, social), one of the main difficulties lies in identifying what is humor and what is not. Many children's verbalizations which are amusing to adults are in fact mere mistakes of language or manifestations of innocence. Our criteria for humor are: (a) the presence of laughter or smiling revealing in the child an awareness of the incongruity, and (b) the evident possession of the cognitive representation which is distorted in the incongruous production (even when laughter and smiling are absent). This requires a great deal of knowledge about the particular child, not just knowledge of normal cognitive acquisitions typically associated with a given age category (i.e., the latter varies according to individual experience).

In order to study humor creation, not only at the age of 3 but through the whole course of childhood, the ideal would be to catch its products in their natural and spontaneous context (as in Aimard, 1975; Tessier, 1986). One can imagine the cost and difficulty of this procedure which implies close contact with the children in a setting conducive to the emergence of humor. Attempts to provoke humorous production in an experimental context resolve the problem of intention (the children are asked to make others laugh), but inevitably reduces the range of possible forms of humor. Thus, in a "made-to-measure" situation, I think only the most accessible ways of joking, the simplest and the most primitive ones, are gathered, and these are not representative of all the humorous outbursts that the child is capable of in the social contexts which are normally the source of his inspiration.

The study of humor reactions is easier than the study of the creation, lending itself to the experimental presentation of humorous products (drawings, riddles, jokes) in order to analyse how they are understood and appreciated. However, there are snags here too such as a possible absence of a playful mood in the experimental setting (for example, when the child interprets the situation as a school test), the inappropriateness of a great deal of humorous material for the youngest children, and the inability of preschoolers to provide explanations of the reasons for their amusement. Such explanations are of central importance to the researcher, however, because of the possible absence of laughter and smiling, the ambiguous nature of these expressions when they do occur, and the fact that the source of amusement can be in other elements than the supposed ones.

Humor in actions. In observing children during free play at nursery school, we can see that laughter and smiling often accompany the joyful excitement of intense motor activity in group games: running, jumping, chasing, climbing, etc. This type of laughter has its roots in infancy, and is linked with a general state of heightened arousal. It does not involve the cognitive processes which we have defined as characteristic of the experience of humor. Mocking laughter at another's inept behavior (e.g., tripping) also has to be excluded because as we have seen, it belongs to a category of laughter-inducing events other than humor. The realm of "humor in actions" at this age involves clowning around, playing the fool, making faces, distorted imitations (such as mooing like a cow, but in a high pitch voice), and other tomfooleries which are based on the distortion of usual sounds and appearances (McGhee and Kach, 1981). We can also observe the laughter of 3-year-olds in reaction to behavior which deliberately violates social norms (Kenderdine, 1931) and to certain transformations of identities (e.g., the father putting on the child's hat).

Humor in pictures. It is not until the age of four that the child can draw funny pictures. Piret's (1940) work, which deserves to be extended with equal rigor to children of today who are more accustomed to the world of images, consisted of an analysis of 259 drawings ("comical, funny pictures, which would make one laugh") by Belgian children between 4 and 8 years of age. The aim was to identify the main comic themes of these drawings. Moreover, Piret's research contains a study of the reactions of children of the same ages and younger to graphic representations of these "primitive comic themes" in order to identify the origins and development of the perception of funniness in them. Based on his findings, Piret distinguished between two large categories of humor.

The "comical characteristics" category is composed of distortions which concern the physical aspect of objects, people, animals, etc. It consists of the addition or removal of elements (a three-legged man, an eyeless face), deformation (a man with a square head and stomach, matchstick legs), and above all, the following (which occur more frequently or are more effective at provoking laughter when presented to the child):

Distortion of sizes. This appears in children's own drawings starting at age four (e.g., making people very large, very small, very tall, and especially changing proportions); laughter or smiling in reaction to this form of distortion emerges even earlier (at age 3) for a drawing of a little boy wearing an enormous hat and very large shoes), and is very potent (more than half of the 4-year-olds and nearly all of the 5- and 6-year-olds found this drawing funny);

Transfer of features. Children transfer from one category of beings to another (giving humans animal qualities or giving animals human qualities (e.g., a little girl with rabbit's ears, or a duck wearing a hat). This is used as a comic technique in children's own drawings starting at the age of 5, and provokes amusement as early as age 3 (e.g., in drawings of a duck smoking a pipe, a dog-man, and a chair with four hands);

Disguises (clowns, carnival characters, masks, false noses, fancy hats, etc.). These appear in children's drawings at 5 years of age and probably owe their comic value to memories of the festive atmosphere and laughter associated with prior experiences of such situations.

"Comical situations and behaviors" compose the other major category illustrated in the drawings created by the children. These have a higher degree of complexity as they involve characters in action in situations whose incongruity is based on the relationship between several components (e.g., between a behavior and the context in which it occurs). This category includes:

Anomalous behaviors or situations. Sometimes these border on the absurd (e.g., a man astride a butterfly, a man standing on the roof with the sun in his hand). Such humor theme is found in drawings produced by children of about 6 years of age and above, and can provoke laughter or smiling in 4- or 5-year-olds when it is presented to them (as in the picture of a little girl pushing a pram with an old man in a top hat in it); these scenes are too difficult for younger children to interpret;

Mishaps and pranks. These are peculiarities of situations resulting from blunders, foolishness or bad luck in the former case, and from mischievousness in the latter. Being relatively complex, these are also found in drawings only from age 6 onwards (e.g., a man sits on a child by mistake, a man falls into a bucket, a small boy rings a doorbell and runs away). However, the child is likely to react positively to the mishaps depicted in drawings at a more precocious age provided that the event is quite easy to decode.

With increasing age, the category of "comical characteristics" becomes less frequent in children's drawings, yielding its place to "comical situations and behaviors," a category which is well represented in 7- and 8-year-olds' graphic productions. Funny drawings are not very effective in provoking laughter, and they are seldom used as a means of humorous expression in the youngest children, but they tend to strengthen their position with increasing age. Even among adults, cartoon humor borrows many of these primitive themes, although in more complex forms: distortions of size in caricatures, mishaps of others in cartoons, transfer of features of characters in cartoon films, etc.

Verbal humor. Language is a prominent vehicle for humor, and we have already mentioned several modes of verbal humor: recounting an incongruous situation, jokingly saying a taboo word with sexual or scatological connotations, etc. But language as a system also lends itself to humor by conscious violation of rules governing it on different linguistic levels (see Shultz and Robillard, 1980, regarding the acquisition of these rules in the course of development). This type of humor stems primarily from the child's extreme joy in language learning and in the affective exchanges with others now possible through language. In this context, the following forms of "play with words" can be observed, which seem to be the roots of puns and related forms of word play.

1. *Play with word sounds (phonological level).* This involves consciously distorted or childish pronunciations (Shultz and Robillard, 1980), substitutions, or pure inventions based on phonetic resemblance (Tessier, 1986). The young child purposely slips from one word to another similar one in terms of sound ("Mrs. Street is like sweet, she's a sheet"), or goes on to another nonexistent word resembling the previous one's sound ("He's really suntinned" for

suntanned). Another practice is to string together words, real or invented, without any logical sequence so that they seem to follow one another by virtue of a similarity in their sound ("What a flooty, what a flooto"). The pleasure in all these cases derives essentially from manipulating word sounds. Slipping into homonyms (words which are pronounced the same or nearly the same; e.g., "ate," "eight") and paronyms (words which are almost but not quite homonyms; e.g., "construct," "constrict") seems to be at the root of puns and the use of double meaning which emerge at about age 7. Tessier's (1986) observations show that homophonic play can appear very early, and appear earlier in spontaneous creation (3 years of age) and comprehension than in the context of ritualized games which have linguistic constraints. Moreover, Tessier (1988) states that the enjoyment of homophony is often based on proper nouns and is related either to the entire word or to its ending. The form of homophony which entails cutting up words does not appear until later, at about 7, with the development of reading skills, and it coincides with the emergence of a marked taste for charades and riddles involving this technique.

Certain forms of ritualized language games accessible to young children make use of the manipulation of sounds such as nursery rhymes or strings of nonsense words and rhyming games. When a 4 1/2-year-old child who intends to retort with a rhyme to the end of the adult's sentence fails to find an adequate word, he invents something which fits in phonetically, and he seems quite satisfied with it. In older children, tongue twisters are a more mature version of these first word sound games, but the procedure here is placed into a more complex structure since it adds the pleasure of getting another person to fall into the trap of mispronunciation at an age when he thinks himself to be far beyond such childish incompetence ("I slit a sheet, a sheet I slit, upon the slitted sheet I sit"). However, there were also other forms of traps in some of the ritualized rhyming games of the youngest children.

2. *Play with word shapes (morphological level)*. A young child who makes a mistake in formulating a word (e.g., constructing a plural or a verb tense) sometimes deliberately exploits the situation to provoke laughter. The mistake entails the intervention of an adult who corrects it. At the beginning the child was serious, but then he

is sidetracked into a game of reiterating, this time voluntarily, his inadequacy. His attention is at first centered on his speech but shifts to the expectation of others and to the amusement produced by not conforming. The initial mistake is thus transformed into a farce.

In the course of trial and error while learning language, children often produce strange creations. Sometimes their laughter or smiling shows that they are aware of their incongruity. Thus, they invent words when they do not know the appropriate ones (e.g., "boing, boing" for Jack-in-the-box). They make new words or expressions by association (see Aimard, 1984, and Tessier, 1986, for numerous examples in French). With their peers, they sometimes burst into laughter by using key words to create nonsense sequences ("boing boing to the moon," "boing boing to the window," "boing boing to . . ." etc.).

ELEMENTARY SCHOOL HUMOR

The majority of research has been done on this period and concentrates, for the most part, on humor reactions, and particularly on the cognitive aspects of such reactions (see reviews by McGhee, 1979; McGhee and Chapman, 1980).

Major Changes Around 6 to 7 Years of Age

Striking changes in cognitive abilities, the acquisition of knowledge, communication skills and the capacity to regulate one's emotions, mark the beginning of the school years. And these changes are associated with major qualitative progress in humor.

Wolfenstein's theory. In contrast with humor of 5-year-olds, which was mostly a spontaneous personal invention, the early elementary school years are characterized by a pronounced interest in ready-made forms of humor. How is one to explain this great pleasure that each of us has noticed in 8-year-olds' memorizing and endless repeating of riddles and jokes to others? Wolfenstein's (1954) analysis focuses on the structure and the thematic content of the more popular of these humorous forms at elementary school ages. During this "latency period" (Freud, 1905b), there is an increase in the personal inhibition of the direct expression of sexual and hostile impulses. Thus, the school-age child, unlike the younger one, in order to free these tendencies through humor, feels a need to hide them behind a "joke facade," and this facade becomes more and more sophisticated with increasing age. In doing so, he retreats into the security that this ready-made disguise offers him. He disclaims responsibility by displacing his own intentions onto an external person (the character of the joke), and the laughter of others is an indication of social acceptance. Hence, Wolfenstein demonstrates the progressive degrees of complexity that sexual and hostile jokes show up to adolescence.

Along with providing a means of disguising aggressive or sexual tendencies, verbal jokes and riddles also provide other benefits. In them, the child can discover the pleasure of escaping the frustration and anxiety produced by the heavy demands of that period, notably in school. Parents and teachers pressure the child to achieve: he must concentrate, learn, and answer correctly. This is, no doubt, the source of his liking for the riddle format which adopts the familiar question-answer pattern but with a surprising and incongruous answer, and also for the contents of riddles and jokes which, among 7- to 10-year-olds, concern the theme of success or failure. In France, they feature the incompetence of the fool, the stupidity of the idiot, the superiority of the child to the adults, and always, of course, the superiority of French in comparison to all others (a superiority which is obtained by incongruous means). In the United States, this tradition depicts the same ignorance and incompetence of the "moron" in the last generation (see Wolfenstein, 1954), and of "Pollocks," "Aggies" and others more recently.

Finally, by telling jokes, the child also obtains social benefits. He holds the attention of others (whether peers or adults), establishes positive relationships (it is enjoyable to laugh together), gains accomplices to his underlying intentions, and reverses the usual order of dominance. The latter is particularly marked in riddling for it is he who knows, he who has the right answer, however incongruous or unreasonable, and it is the adult or older child who will get trapped (Sutton Smith, 1975; Wolfenstein, 1954).

McGhee's theory. In McGhee's model, the age of 7 also corresponds to a major transition but for different reasons. It marks the attainment of another stage in humor (the fourth stage), thanks to the child's new abilities associated with the emergence of concrete operational thinking (Piaget, 1947). Thought at this point ceases to be dominated by perceptual appearances. The child can consider certain types of logical relationships between events regardless of the perceptual appearances associated with them. He can also keep two things in mind at the same time. The onset of concrete operational thinking has a remarkable influence on the child's humor. He becomes capable of understanding more abstract and implied incongruities and not just those that can be immediately perceived. Instead of simply keeping in mind the perceptual features of the event, he is also able to mentally reconstruct the successive actions that led up to it; this makes it possible to understand an incongruity which is not immediately obvious (McGhee, 1971 a and b, 1972). It is also at this age that he becomes capable of understanding verbal humor based on the double meaning of a word which not only involves the knowledge of both meanings of that word, but also the ability to keep one meaning in mind while shifting to the other. Finally, with his new cognitive capacities, the child is better able to explain the reason for his amusement (McGhee, 1979).

Shultz's theory of incongruity-resolution. A series of empirical studies led Shultz to suggest that the resolution process (discovering an explanation which makes sense of the incongruity) influences the appreciation of humor only from a particular point in the child's development and prior to that, the incongruity alone contributes to the feeling of funniness. Shultz's technique consists of constructing the several versions of the same cartoon or the same joke (the original form, a form with incongruity but without resolution, and a form without incongruity) and of assessing how they are understood and appreciated (of course, each child is confronted with only one of the versions). The first experiments, with cartoons (Shultz, 1970, 1972), were conducted with children between 7 and 12 years of age. The results of these studies support the incongruity-resolution theory in that the degree of appreciation followed this order: it was weaker when the cartoon had no incongruity, stronger when it contained one without the resolution information, and even stronger when the incongruity and resolution information were both available. However, the data failed to confirm the hypothesis concerning the two developmental stages. Indeed, while 11- to 12-year-olds were more likely to detect "pertinent" or intended resolutions, 7- to 8-year-olds also tended to find some other ways of resolving the incongruity. The preference for the incongruity with resolution form (as opposed to a form lacking incongruity and a form including incongruity but no resolution), was comparable in both age groups.

In another study with verbal jokes, Shultz and Horibe (1974) found the same order of appreciation of the three versions noted above among 8-, 10- and 12-year-olds. But 6-year-olds found the original form (containing both incongruity and the information necessary for its resolution) and the form with incongruity but without resolution equally funny, and found both more funny than the form without incongruity. Since the resolution-removed version of jokes was just as funny to these children as the original version, Shultz concluded that he had identified the transition age between the two stages that he assumed: first, before 7 years of age, there is a stage in which only the incongruity contributes to funniness; then, starting from about 7, a second stage emerges in which both incongruity and resolution are important. The transition is considered to be due to the acquisition of concrete operational thinking.

But Shultz's work related to this presumed transition has encountered several criticisms. McGhee (1979) noted that 6-year-olds are not able to grasp the linguistic ambiguity of the proposed jokes and that this is the real reason why they did not differentiate between the original jokes and the form without resolution. Pien and Rothbart (1976) used other techniques and easier material and concluded that 4- to 5-year-olds are already capable of appreciating the resolution information in humor. We can only conclude that this developmental issues has not yet been resolved. Nevertheless, it is a very interesting one. In order to resolve it, researchers will have to give more careful attention to the definition of "resolution" since it appears that explanations of incongruity can be provided at different levels of complexity, depending on the intellectual capacities of the child.

The Relationship Between Comprehension and Appreciation of Humor: The Cognitive Congruency Principle

Zigler, Levine and Gould (1966) were the first to suggest the idea that appreciation of humor in jokes or drawings should be greater if the material presents a challenge to the child's capacity for understanding; in other words, if it fits with "the complexity level of his cognitive apparatus." Presumably, the child experiences a sense of pleasure in mastery when some optimal moderate amount of cognitive effort is required to "get" the point of a joke. Zigler et al. (1967) empirically tested this hypothesis by using cartoons varying in difficulty level with 8- to 12-year-old children. Appreciation was clearly greatest of those cartoons which were neither too easy nor too difficult to understand. McGhee (1976, 1976b) criticised the measure of ease of understanding employed in this work and undertook another study whose results are more suggestive. The children varied in their degree of acquisition of conservation and class inclusion concepts, and they were presented jokes in which humor derived from the violation of these two concepts. The results obtained showed greater amusement by the children who had just acquired the concept in question than both by the children who had not yet acquired it (they did not possess the cognitive skills required to understand the humor) and the children who had possessed conservation or class inclusion skills for several years (they easily understood the humor). These findings suggest that adults working with children will be more effective in using humor when it matches the child's developmental level.

Changes in Humor Between the Ages of 7 and 11

The acquisition of humor conventions. In their contact with adults, children intuitively understand early that the art of humor involves breaking with normal behavior (they first play practical jokes at 2 1/2 or 3 years of age). However, when they are 6 or 7 years old, they still need to master this "principle" for the complex forms of institutionalized humor that they newly come into contact with at this age. Seven-year-olds may respond seriously to riddles, or tell jokes or riddles without a punch line (Sutton Smith, 1975; Wolfenstein, 1954). Some 7-year-olds also may be resistant to accept the incongruity of a cartoon in the playful fashion that is required for humor. For example, when presented with a drawing in which a horse is seen walking away in the distance, with a series of human footprints trailing behind it, some children say: "here are a man's footprints, and here is a horse, the horse can't have made those footprints" (Bariaud, 1983). Such reactions indicate that the child has not yet mastered the convention according to which such cartoons purposefully distort things in order to be funny.

The age of 7 is also an age of "realism," probably prompted by pressure from the school system to conform to the norms of reality: the world is the way it is, and the child must acquire knowledge about it. His realistic attitude contrasts with the fantasy found in 5-year-olds and interferes with the tendency to see incongruities as humorous. When 7-year-olds were shown cartoons of impossible events, some made comments such as: "It's not funny because it can't be like that," or "It's not funny because normally it's not like that" (Bariaud, 1983). The humor reaction involves just the opposite of these responses because it implies momentarily accepting the possibility that the incongruous event really can happen (pretending "as if" . . .). Not all 7-year-olds manifest this type of refusal to playfully accept the incongruity, but those that do not refuse do so for all impossible events that they see. With increasing age, this rejection of incongruity because of its incompatibility with reality disappears.

Older children easily perceive that humorous intent is indeed founded upon this incompatibility. When shown a cartoon, they immediately start looking for an incongruity. Ten- or 11-year-olds, because of their greater mastery of humor conventions and their better understanding of others' expectations in humorous situations, are able to enjoy and use "meta-incongruities": "What is the difference between a bowl and a chamber pot?" asked of me by one 10 1/2-year-old. "I don't know," I answered, expecting to encounter in the child's response some incongruity that would relate the two elements. "Well, I sure won't come to dinner at your house!" said the child. This joke is a trap which plays on the ordinary humorous convention which builds the expectation of the other that a certain kind of humorous answer is about to follow. It is illustrative of the complexities older children appreciate in jokes, in their structure as well as in the motivations they conceal (scatological in the previous case).

Humor in actions. Clowning, making faces, gestures, and exaggerated movements are still found in elementary schoolers (Nicol, 1981) but are more likely to take the form of imitation of other's social conduct (e.g., imitation of the teacher, his behavior, his typical facial expressions . . .).

Humor in words. With the development of cognitive capacities, and especially the increased understanding of how language works, qualitative changes take place in the type of verbal humor schoolchildren produce. Paronymy and homophony alone lose their power of entertainment: words are increasingly associated with each other not only because they have something in common structurally, but also because the shift from one word to the other includes a meaning. Puns begin to appear. For example, the substitution of a common noun to someone's surname, based on a phonological similarity, now suggests some characteristic of the person in a social situation. In the most successful cases, the allusion is subtly alluded to (see Tessier, 1986, 1988, for a series of examples in French and an analysis of changes in verbal creations up to the age of twelve).

The discovery of the ambiguity of words is also linked to the enjoyment of riddles and jokes which are based on double meanings (and there are many of them). When McGhee (1974) asked 6-year-olds to say whether a serious or a humorous ending to a riddle was the funniest, children chose one or the other indiscriminately. According to McGhee, this is because they were not cognitively equipped, in the "preoperational period," to appreciate what made the riddle funny (i.e., to alternately switch from one meaning to another).

Jokes and riddles exploit a range of linguistic ambiguity; some ambiguities are more difficult than others for the child to grasp. Shultz and Pilon (1973) describe four levels of difficulty. Phonological ambiguity, which is based on sounds and appears to be the first type of ambiguity understood, between six and seven years of age. Lexical ambiguity, which implies double meaning, can be appreciated at around the age of seven. The two remaining levels of difficulty, surface-structure ambiguity ("the fat sailor's wife likes to cook") and deep-structure ambiguity ("the duck is ready to eat"; see additional examples in Shultz and Pilon, 1973), which involves starting sentences in different ways and are thus based on syntactic effects, are apparently not understood before the age of 11 or 12.

Humor in pictures. In the elementary school years, the child is able to understand not only more complex cartoons, but also comic strips because of their capacity, from about 6 years of age, to comprehend temporal organization (Rodriguez-Tome and Bariaud, 1987). In a study we conducted with 7- to 11-year-olds (Bariaud, 1983), children were given a set of humorous drawings without captions. In this type of situation (as in all potentially funny ones), children may be entertained for reasons other than the central incongruity. Among the "irrelevant" features children found to be funny (irrelevant for us, but relevant for them), were a number of features which younger children laugh at. These include, principally at age seven, elements related to happiness (circuses, adventures), physical incongruities of the characters (disproportionality, etc.), strange behaviors or functioning (unfamiliar or impossible actions, objects working in a strange way), and misfortunes of others. Older children tend to notice more abstract incongruities such as inappropriate social conduct and faulty reasoning.

Identification of the "pertinent" incongruity in the drawings increases with age since the child has more complex cognitive tools at his disposal. But what is more important to note is that the period between the ages of 7 to 11 is characterized by a changeover from a "perceptual approach," based on a distortion of the perceptual aspects of reality that many 7-year-olds enjoy, to an "interpretative approach," which consists of going beyond appearances to find a meaning connected to social reality. For example, a picture of a two-seated-bicycle with two handlebars, each facing in the opposite direction, is funny to the older children not only because it is bizarre, but because they imagine what would happen to those trying to ride it: falling off, the inevitable conflict between the two, making the effort in vain, etc. Similarly, a man who greets another by taking off both his hat and his head (in the usual manner of tipping one's hat to someone) is not only funny because "it's not normally like that," as many 7-year-olds point out, but also because of the meaning it conveys in this incongruous gesture. Eleven-year-olds are able to verbalize this meaning, which is not the same for all: "He's lost his head (marbles)," "His hat is too small for his head," "Two men meet each other, one says hello and takes off his hat, the other one is even more polite and takes off his hat and his head." Adolescents, reaching the stage of abstract thought and having a greater knowledge of the social world, are even more likely to bring out the varied meanings that can make a cartoon funny (see Puthomme, 1984). However, in children of 9 to 11 years of age, grasping an allusion behind the incongruity already seems to be a crucial feature in the appreciation of humor.

In my own research, I have tried to highlight the fact that the "emotional tonality" linked to the meaning is a decisive factor, over and above comprehension, in determining amusement or its absence. Understanding involves providing a meaning for what one perceives. However, to fully appreciate humor, something richer than mere understanding is needed. Once the intent of the humorist is understood, we can say that the child (or adult) understands the cartoon or joke. But full appreciation requires that he shares this intention and adopts it as his own. Otherwise, it is not funny. For example, consider the case of a cartoon in which a zoo is depicted, but with a human in the cage and apes outside as visitors (see Bariaud, 1983). The emotional tonality of the event depicted here may be either negative or positive. On the negative side, some 11-year-olds did not enter into the game of humor because they clearly did not share the humorist's point of view: "It's not funny because the person is reduced to being an attraction or object of amusement, and I don't like that," "It's not funny, it's too bad, the person is just an animal to them, so it's not funny," or "It's not funny, I wouldn't want to be in that cage." In these reactions, the point of the humor seems clearly understood, but it is not shared as a basis for laughter. The child doesn't enter into the intent that he attributes to the humorist.

In contrast, other children of the same age have a positive emotional reaction to the same cartoon: "It's funny, the animals are taking their revenge on him," "It's funny, that shows us that man is not the king here on earth, that everything could change." These children take into consideration the aggression carried by the incongruity, and they use it to mock a particular value system. Appreciation of the humor arises from something over and above comprehension (the intellectual grasping of the incongruity and its underlying meaning); it results from the emotional complicity with the humorist regarding this underlying meaning. The previous examples show that this kind of sharing of the identified intent of a cartoon or a joke determines amusement and it is already present in the elementary school years. In our view, as soon as the child understands, this complicity is the most important factor in determining humor appreciation.

Thus, the changes in humor during the elementary school period, which are marked by the mastery of humor conventions and the search for an underlying meaning in both physical, verbal and pictorial humor, reveal a new type of humorous laughter: laughter not only at distortions of reality, but also at the derision of the social world. In adolescence this sense of social derision by humor will reach its full expression. But in studying the humor of adolescents, we enter the world of adult humor.

NOTES

1. The notion of "incongruity" is also central in theories of fear (Hebb, 1946), astonishment (Artemenko, 1972) and curiosity (Berlyne, 1960).
2. See Baldwin J.M. (1985). *Mental development in the child and the race.* New York: Macmillan.
3. There is only limited evidence that increased imaginative play skills in preschoolers is correlated with creativity and sense of humor at later stages (Tower and Singer, 1980).

REFERENCES

Aimard, P. (1975). *Les jeux de mots de l'enfant.* Villeurbane: SIMEP Editions.
Aimard, P. (1984). *L'enfant et la magie du langage.* Paris: Laffont.
Artemenko, P. (1972). *Recherches sur l'étonnement chez l'enfant.* Thèse pour le Doctorat es Lettres, Université de Bourdeaux II.
Bariaud, F. (1983). *La genèse de l'humour chez l'enfant.* Paris: P.U.F.
Bateson, G. (1953). The role of humor in human communication. In H. Von Foerster (Ed.) *Cybernetics.* New York: Macy Foundation.
Bergson, H. (1900). *Le rire. Essai sur la signification du comique.* Paris: Alcan.
Berlyne, D.E. (1960). *Conflict, arousal and curiosity.* New York: McGraw Hill.
Blurton Jones, N.G. (1967). An ethological study of some aspects of social behaviour of children in nursery schools. In D. Morris (Ed.), *Primate ethology* (pp. 347-368). London: Weidenfeld and Nicolson.
Ding, G.F., & Jersild, A.T. (1932). A study of the laughing and smiling of preschool children. *Journal of Genetic Psychology, 40,* 452-472.
Dumas, G. (1923). *Traité de Psychologie.* Paris: Alcan, Tome I, livre III, chap. 3: "Le rire et les larmes."
Eastman, M. (1936). *Enjoyment of laughter.* New York: Simon & Shuster.

Freud, S. (1905a). *Der Witz Und seine Beziehung zum Unbewussten.* Leipzig: Denticke.

Freud, S. (1905b). *Drei Abhandlungen zur Sexualtheorie.* French translation, *Trois essais sur la théorie de la sexualité.* Paris: Gallimard, 1962.

Freud, S. (1928). Humour. *International Journal of Psycho-Analysis, 9*(1), 1-6.

Hebb, D.O. (1946). On the nature of fear. *Psychological Review, 53,* 259-276.

Jankelevitch, V. (1964). *L'ironie.* Paris: Flammarion.

Jones, J.M. (1970). *Cognitive factors in the appreciation of humor: A theoretical and experimental analysis.* Unpublished Doctoral Dissertation, Yale University.

Justin, F. (1932). A genetic study of laughter-provoking stimuli. *Child Development, 3,* 114-136.

Kenderdine, M. (1931). Laughter in the preschool child. *Child Development, 2,* 228-230.

Koestler, A. (1964). *The act of creation.* London: Hutchinson.

Leroy-Boussion, A. (1955). De l'inquiétude au rire. *Enfance, 5,* 455-483.

Maier, N.R. (1932). A gestalt theory of humour. *British Journal of Psychology, 23,* 69-74.

Malrieu, P. (1967). *La construction de l'imaginaire.* Bruxelles: Dessart.

McGhee, P.E. (1971a). Cognitive development and children's comprehension of humor. *Child Development, 42,* 123-138.

McGhee, P.E. (1971b). Development of the humor response: A review of the literature. *Psychological Bulletin, 76,* 328-348.

McGhee, P.E. (1972). On the cognitive origins of incongruity humor: Fantasy assimilation versus reality assimilation. In J.H. Goldstein, & P.E. McGhee (Eds.), *The Psychology of Humor* (pp. 61-80). New York: Academic Press.

McGhee, P.E. (1974). Development of children's ability to create the joking relationship. *Child Development, 45,* 552-556.

McGhee, P.E. (1976). Children's appreciation of humor: A test of the cognitive congruency principle. *Child Development, 47,* 420-426.

McGhee, P.E. (1977a). A model of the origins and early development of incongruity-based humour. In A.J. Chapman, & H.C. Foot (Eds.), *It's a funny thing humour* (pp. 27-36). Oxford: Pergamon Press.

McGhee, P.E. (1977b). Children's humour: a review of current research trends. In A.J. Chapman, & H.C. Foot (Eds.), *It's a funny thing, humour* (pp. 199-209). Oxford: Pergamon Press.

McGhee, P.E. (1979). *Humor: Its origin and development.* San Francisco: Freeman.

McGhee, P.E., & Chapman, A.J. (Eds.) (1980). *Children's humour.* Chichester: Wiley.

McGhee, P.E., & Kach, J.A. (1981). The development of humor in black, Mexican-American and white preschool children. *Journal of Research and Development in Education, 14,* 81-90.

Nerhardt, G. (1977). Operationalization of incongruity in humour research: A critique and suggestions. In A.J. Chapman, & H.C. Foot (Eds.), *It's a funny thing, humour* (pp. 47-51). Oxford: Pergamon Press.

Nicol, E. (1981). *Les rires et les sourires à l'école, chez les enfants de 7 à 9 ans.* Mémoire de Maîtrise en Psychologie Génétique, Université de Paris X - Nanterre (sous la direction de F. Bariaud).

Piaget, J. (1947). *La psychologie de l'intelligence.* Paris: Leclerc et Cie.

Piaget, J., & Inhelder, B. (1941). *Le développement des quantités physiques chez l'enfant. Conservation et atomisme.* Neuchâtel: Delachaux et Niestlé.

Pien, D., & Rothbart, M.K. (1976). Incongruity and resolution in children's humour. *Child Development, 47*, 966-971.

Piret, R. (1940). *La genèse du sens du comique chez l'enfant.* Thèse de Doctorat en Sciences Pédagogiques, Université de Liège.

Puthomme, R. (1984). *La réaction d'humour de l'enfance à l'adolescence.* Mémoire de Maîtrise, Université de Paris X - Nanterre (sous la direction de H. Rodriguez-Tome).

Rodriguez-Tome, H., & Bariaud, F. (1987). *Les perspectives temporelles à l'adolescence.* Paris: P.U.F.

Rothbart, M.K. (1973). Laughter in young children. *Psychological Bulletin, 80*, 247-256.

Rothbart, M.K. (1976). Incongruity, problem-solving and laughter. In A.J. Chapman, & H.C. Foot (Eds.), *Humour and laughter: Theory, research and applications* (pp. 37-54). London: Wiley.

Shultz, T.R. (1970). *Cognitive factors in children's appreciation of cartoons: Incongruity and its resolution.* Unpublished Doctoral Dissertation, Yale University.

Shultz, T.R. (1972). The role of incongruity and resolution in children's appreciation of cartoon humor. *Journal of Experimental Child Psychology, 13*, 456-477.

Shultz, T.R. (1974). Development of the appreciation of riddles. *Child Development, 45*, 100-105.

Shultz, T.R. (1977). A cross-cultural study of the structure of humour. In A.J. Chapman, & H.C. Foot (Eds.), *Its a funny thing, humour* (pp. 175-179). Oxford: Pergamon Press.

Shultz, T.R., & Pilon, R. (1973). Development of the ability to detect linguistic ambiguity. *Child Development, 44*, 728-733.

Shultz, T.R., & Horibe, F. (1974). Development of the appreciation of verbal jokes. *Developmental Psychology, 10*, 13-20.

Shultz, T.R., & Robillard, J. (1980). The development of linguistic humour in children: incongruity through rule violation. In P.E. McGhee, & A.J. Chapman (Eds.), *Children's Humour* (pp. 55-96). Chichester: Wiley.

Singer, J.L. (1973). *The child's world of make-believe: Experimental studies of imaginative play.* New York: Academic Press.

Sroufe, L.A., & Wunsch, J.C. (1972). The development of laughter in the first year of life. *Child Development, 43*, 1326-1344.

Sroufe, L.A., Waters, E., & Matas, L. (1974). Contextual determinants of infant affective response. In M. Lewis, & L.A. Rosenblum (Eds.), *The origins of fear* (pp. 49-72). New York: Wiley.

Sully, J. (1902). *Essay on laughter*. New York: Longmans Green.

Suls, J.M. (1972). A two-stage model for the appreciation of jokes and cartoons: An information-processing analysis. In J.H. Goldstein, & P.E. McGhee (Eds.), *The Psychology of humor* (pp. 81-100). New York: Academic Press.

Suls, J.M. (1983). Cognitive processes in humor appreciation. In P.E. McGhee, & J.H. Goldstein (Eds.), *Handbook of humor research. Vol. 1, Basic issues* (pp. 35-57). New York: Springer Verlag.

Sutton-Smith, B.A. (1975). A developmental structural account of riddles. In B. Kirschenblatt-Gimblett (Ed.), *Speech, play and display*. Hague: Mouton.

Tessier, G. (1986). *Contribution à une étude de la créativité verbale chez l'enfant*. Thèse de Doctorat en Sciences de l'Education, Université de Tours.

Tessier, G. (1988). Le développement du comique verbal chez l'enfant à travers le traitement du nom propre. *Cahiers Comique et Communication*, CERCC Grenoble.

Tower, R.B., & Singer, J.L. (1980). Imagination, interest and joy in early childhood: Some theoretical considerations and empirical findings. In P.E. McGhee, & A.J. Chapman (Eds.), *Children's humour* (pp. 27-57). Chichester: Wiley.

Valentine, C.W. (1942). *The psychology of early childhood*. London: Methuen.

Wallon, H. (1949). *Le jeu chez l'enfant*. Extrait des cours de pédiatrie sociale. Paris: Editions Médicales Flammarion.

Wilson, C.O. (1931). *A study of laughter situations among young children*. Unpublished Doctoral Dissertation, University of Nebraska.

Wolfenstein, M. (1954). *Children's humor: A psychological analysis*. Glencoe, Ill.: Free Press.

Zigler, E., Levine, J., & Gould, L. (1966). Cognitive processes in the development of children's humor appreciation. *Child Development, 37*, 505-518.

Zigler, E., Levine, J., & Gould, L. (1967). Cognitive challenge as a factor in children's humor appreciation. *Journal of Personality and Social Psychology, 6*, 332-336.

PART II: COGNITIVE BENEFITS

Introduction

One of the most important practical applications of humor lies in the domain of education. While the humor that we create and appreciate always reflects prior knowledge, it can also be used to support the acquisition of new knowledge. The first chapter in this section by Bryant and Zillmann addresses the question of whether there is a place for humor in the classroom. Special attention is given to humor's capacity to recruit attention and interest and to make learning more enjoyable. Regarding the key question of humor's impact on learning and retention, they are careful to point out that humor appears to have positive effects only under certain conditions. Thus, teachers need to understand these conditions in order to be most effective when combining humor with other instruction techniques.

Williams examines the same question with respect to metaphor. While humor and metaphor enhance learning in different ways, each clearly has an important role to play in the classroom. Metaphor is shown to be an especially effective means of using what one already knows about one object or event to learn about a new one — even when there is initially no apparent meaningful link between the two. Since the use of metaphors should speed up learning, teachers who master instructional metaphors should also become more efficient in the classroom at the same time that they are making learning more enjoyable.

Ziv discusses the link between humor and creativity. Both theory and research indicate that these are positively related, but which causes which? Are children and adolescents who are already (for some undetermined reason) more creative especially attracted to and gifted at humor because humor allows an especially enjoyable outlet for their creative tendencies? Or do children who become especially interested in and competent at humor become more creative as a result? Ziv discusses issues related to these questions, and concludes that increased exposure to humor can actually increase one's level of creativity.

Chapter 2

Using Humor to Promote Learning in the Classroom

Jennings Bryant, PhD
Dolf Zillmann, PhD

SUMMARY. Rationales for using humor in classroom teaching and normative patterns of teachers' humor usage are presented. Several questions are addressed using pertinent research findings as evidence: Does teaching with humor enhance students' attention? Does using humor improve the classroom environment and make learning more enjoyable? Does using humor in the classroom help children learn? Does using classroom humor improve students' creativity? Does using humor in testing lower students' anxiety and promote improved test performance? Should teachers avoid certain types of humor? Guidelines for using humor in classroom teaching are offered.

A curious contradiction emerges when the professional trade literature on the effects of using humor in teaching is compared with the scholarly research literature on that topic. On the one hand, classroom teachers who write in professional journals about their experiences with using humor typically laud its pedagogical benefits and tout it as a highly useful and extremely effective teaching tool for numerous and varied learning tasks and in almost every conceivable classroom context. For example, Cornett (1986, p. 8)

Jennings Bryant is affiliated with the Department of Broadcast and Film Communications, University of Alabama, Tuscaloosa, AL. Dolf Zillmann is with the Department of Communication, Indiana University, Bloomington, IN.

makes these global and unqualified claims for the instructional benefits of humor:

> Humor has something to offer each of us as we work with children of all ages and abilities. Humor can be used to help correct reading problems, control behavioral disorders, build vocabulary, teach foreign languages, and integrate social isolate. Humor can be one of our most powerful instructional resources. . . .[W]e really can learn through laughter.

In contrast, empirical investigations of the effects of using humor in teaching have yielded results which are decidedly mixed, and scholars who have written state of the art reviews on the effects of humor on learning typically have indicated potentially detrimental effects of humor use in addition to delineating the benefits that can be accrued from using humor in teaching. Indeed, their conclusions tend to be replete with caveats and qualifications. For example, Davies and Apter (1980) note that the question of whether humor helps children to learn is highly complex and to be useful must include qualifications of, among other things, "what kind of humour, under what kinds of conditions, with what kinds of subjects and in relation to what kind of learning" (p. 251). Similarly, Zillmann and Bryant (1983) conclude that "any unqualified generalizations, whether they project good or bad consequences of humor use for teaching and learning, are untenable" (p. 188).

Unfortunately, some popularizers who have attempted to reach classroom teachers with summary reports on the use of humor in teaching have adopted questionable strategies for accommodating these mixed findings. One tactic has been to overtly deny the existence of the rather abundant and readily available evidence for negative results of classroom humor use. For example, Krogh (1985, p. 29) reports that "no study has yet found that humor can be detrimental to a classroom." Others have been more covert, citing research evidence which supports their contentions but largely ignoring evidence contrary to their theses (e.g., Cornett, 1986). A third questionable strategy seems to have been derived from good intentions but could have the unfortunate consequence of driving another wedge between scholars of instructional practices and classroom teachers. MacAdam (1985), following a detailed analysis of research evidence which she describes as "contradictory or inconclusive in supporting humor as a facilitatory tool" (p. 332), concludes: "Ultimately, however, the art of the practitioner replaces the intellectual vision of the theoretician in the classroom" (p. 332). It is the latter, divisive quote rather than the former which has been picked up in the trade press by devotees of humor in teaching (e.g., Plotnik, 1985).

In light of these apparent contradictions and the oversimplifications and/or exclusions in some of the previous summary articles on the use of humor in classroom teaching, we have adopted what we hope will be a more integrative and conciliatory strategy for this report. We have posited several specific questions regarding the use of humor in teaching. For each question, we have provided representative claims that teachers have made for the benefits of humor use in that domain as well as synopses of their reported experiences, where appropriate. Then the available research evidence is presented, with limiting or facilitating conditions specified. Finally, we have attempted to provide generalizations, conclusions, and guidelines for using humor in the classroom.

Prior to presenting and addressing our set of questions, it seems prudent to offer some possible explanations as to why the conclusions of classroom teachers frequently differ from the findings of empirical investigations — why the "art" may differ from the "science," as such distinctions are popularly labeled. A number of factors may contribute. First, the style of reporting in trade publications differs substantially from that of peer-refereed scholarly journals. Whereas qualifications or lack of apparent enthusiasm in the former may be interpreted as equivocation or as hedging and thereby result in an editor's decision not to publish the report. In the latter, a reviewer's or editor's perceptions of overgeneralization or lack of objectivity or any other such "excess" or bias may be judged as nonscholarly, leading to a rejection decision. Such stylistic distinctions, as well as differences in the norms for what counts as evidence, may contribute to divergent reporting of "results", thereby, accentuating the observed or experienced differences in the effects of using humor.

Second, most claims for unbridled success with using humor

seem to come from elementary and secondary classroom teachers. Indeed, it has often been noted that teachers of younger children rate the ability to use humor and to have a sense of humor more highly as essential attributes of a good teacher than do do teachers of older students (e.g., Cattell, 1931). In contrast, many if not most of the reports of negative or negligible results from using humor in the classroom come from investigations using college students and college teachers in college classrooms or laboratories. College students purportedly are more intrinsically motivated to learn than are students of compulsory elementary or secondary education; collegians typically have paid good money for their instruction and, therefore, may feel that they have the right to expect "serious" results, and they may have "heard it all" after at least a dozen years of exposure to humorous teachers. Moreover the aesthetic requirements of most college students regarding what is acceptable "jokework" (Freud, 1905) in classroom humor are likely to be more stringent than those of younger students, so elementary and perhaps even secondary school teachers may be able to "get by with" humor that if employed by college professors would result in their getting booed from the classroom. Therefore, college students may not be the most appropriate test population if results are to be generalized to elementary and secondary education.

Third, whereas experimental investigations typically are designed to examine the effects of humor use by so-called average teachers, it appears likely that the highly successful user of pedagogical humor, perhaps the same person who might be inclined to report the results of his or her apparently successful humor practices in a trade journal, is a somewhat atypical teacher. Since his or her teaching style may be more gregarious and outgoing than that of many peers, it seems reasonable that more reserved teachers should not expect the same sort of results from humor use as the so-called "off the wall" teacher for whom humor is a natural outgrowth and expression of an extroverted teaching personality. For these and related reasons, extreme caution should be taken when generalizing about the results of using humor in teaching. When applied to the so-called average teacher, the unbridled claims for success with humor use by teachers who report their experiences in the trade journals may be overly optimistic and liberal; in contrast, the findings from empirical investigations may be too pessimistic and conservative for the teacher who is naturally inclined to employ humor in teaching. Certainly these are sufficient reasons to limit generalizations and to carefully examine claims and research evidence as we ponder our set of questions.

HOW AND WHY DO TEACHERS USE HUMOR IN THEIR CLASSROOMS?

How Humor Is Used

According to Wells (1974), who observed and interviewed elementary school teachers to determine the ways in which they used humor in their classrooms, all of the teachers interviewed considered humor "*a necessary classroom ingredient*" (p. 156, emphasis added). "Superteachers have a sense of humor . . . . Many start each day with a joke . . ." (Miller, 1977, p. 122). Apparently many teachers have come to view humor as something that can only further their educational goals (e.g., Cornett, 1986; Gilliland & Mauritsen, 1971) as something they cannot teach without. Accordingly systematic investigations reveal that teachers use humor extensively in classroom settings as diverse as elementary school (Wells 1974), junior high school (Bryant & Hunter, 1981), and college (Bryant, Comisky, & Zillmann, 1979). These investigations reveal how frequently humor is employed as well as the specific types of humor employed at these different educational levels.

Wells (1974) observed ten elementary school teachers (four male, six female) and approximately 300 fourth to sixth grade students in California public schools. Each teacher was systematically observed for two and one-half hours. Following observation and detailed recording of classroom humor usage, the teachers and sixty randomly selected students were interviewed regarding the teachers' and their students' perceptions of the teachers' humor usage and its impact. Wells found that the elementary school teachers she examined used humor 16.6 times, on the average, per 2 1/2 hour observation period. Male teachers used humor slightly more than 21 times per observation period with their humor usage ranging from a high of 37 to a low of 12 incidents per teacher. Overall female teachers used much less humor than did males. Humor was employed an average of 13.5 times by female teachers with a low of 11 and a high of 22 incidents of recorded humor use per teacher. Male teachers also used a wider range of types of humor than female teachers. The types of humor used most frequently overall by teachers were short, snappy retorts of the "dry wit," "good-natured play," "light-hearted wit," or "unexpected 'off-beat' humor" varieties. Most of the humor used was judged as pleasant and playful, although some sarcastic and hostile humor was employed, primarily by male teachers.

In an investigation of teachers' humor in the college classroom (Bryant, Comisky, & Zillmann, 1979), students at a northeastern university audio-tape-recorded one day's presentation of a random sample of 70 separate classes in which they were enrolled. Following transcription, incidents of teacher humor usage were identified and analyzed. On the average, teachers were found to use humor 3.34 times per 50-minute class. When adjusted for length of teaching session, the elementary school teachers observed by Wells (1974) used substantially more humor ($X = 5.53$ per 50-minute unit) than did the college teachers examined.[1] It should be noted that in Wells' study, all teachers employed at least some humor. In contrast, among the college teachers, nine males (18%) and five females (24%) used no humor whatsoever. If these 14 teachers are removed from the analysis, the revised mean of 4.18 humor usages per session is still well below the approximately 5 1/2 incidents of teacher humor use per 50-minute unit reported by Wells. As in the study of elementary school teachers' humor, male college instructors (n = 49) used substantially more humor ($X = 3.73$ incidents of humor use) than did their female peers (n = 21, $X = 2.43$). The proportional frequency of female-to-male humor use (65%) was highly similar to that found among the elementary school teachers (63.5%).

In general, both male and female college teachers were found to convey their humor primarily through funny stories (39%). The second and third most frequently used formats, funny comments (18%) and jokes (17%), were used differently by male than by female professors. Whereas, funny comments accounted for 42% of female humor use and only 26% of the male humor; male teachers told "jokes" 21% of the time, while female teachers told jokes very infrequently (3% of their total humor usage). In contrast to elementary school teachers' relatively rare use of hostile humor, college teachers used hostile (33%), sexual (8%), and hostile/sexual (5%) humor quite frequently; overall, nearly one-half (46%) of the times that humor was employed, tendentious thema and techniques were utilized.

Bryant and Hunter (1981) employed the methodology and coding schema of Bryant et al. (1979) and assessed the humor use of 80 junior high school (eighth-ninth grade) teachers in Massachusetts public school systems. Overall, humor use was found to be slightly less extensive among these teachers than among elementary school (Wells, 1974) and college (Bryant et al., 1979) teachers, with an average of 2.94 incidents of humor-employed by junior high teachers per 50-minute recording session. The mean humor use is depressed somewhat because 13 male teachers (32.5%) and 17 female teachers (42.5%) used no humor during the assessment period. when these 30 teachers were removed from the sample, the adjusted mean of 3.86 humor uses per teacher per 50-minute recording unit still represents a lower frequency of humor use than that observed for college or elementary school teachers. As in the companion studies, female junior high school teachers used less humor than did their male peers (79% as much humor). For junior high teachers, the most frequently employed humor formats were funny comments (24%), funny stories (18%), and jokes (18%). Substantial gender differences were found in the use of jokes, with male teachers using jokes far more frequently (26% of male humor use) than female teachers (8% of female humor use). The differences are similar to those found by Bryant et al. for college teachers. Gender differences also were found for junior high teachers' use of hostile humor (37% of overall humor usage), sexual humor (4%), and hostile/sexual humor (6%). Combined tendentious humor usage was 47%, almost identical to that found by Bryant eta al. for college teachers. Whereas, male and female teachers were roughly equivalent in the proportion of hostile humor that they employed (males = 40%, female = 35%), the female teachers sampled used no sexual or hostile/sexual humor whatsoever. In contrast, sexual and hostile/ sexual thema accounted for 6.5% and 11%, respectively, of humor usage by male teachers. Among all the teachers examined in these three descriptive studies, male junior high school teachers were the heaviest users of sexual and especially hostile/sexual humor.

In summary, when the findings of Wells (1974), Bryant et al. (1979), and Bryant and Hunter (1981) are considered together, it is apparent that classroom teachers use humor—many quite extensively—in elementary school, junior high school, and college. (There is no reason to doubt that high school teachers use humor as well, and probably somewhat comparably, although empirical evidence to substantiate such appears to be lacking.) Consistently, male teachers were found to use humor more often than female teachers, and males used a far greater number of "jokes" than did females at every level of the educational process examined. The most frequently used humor formats were funny stories (i.e., humorous anecdotes) and funny comments (excluding puns). In the samples of teachers examined, hostile and sexual humor clearly were in use, although not extensively with elementary school children.

Why Humor Is Used

The variety of reasons reported by teachers for using humor is enough to give face validity to the claim that "humor facilitates creativity" (see Ziv, this edition). The ten elementary school teachers observed and interviewed by Wells (1974) included among their reasons for using humor:

> Humor helps reduce tension, enhances student-teacher relationships, helps create warmth, and makes school fun. It eases the burden of daily study and occasionally provides a moment of deep, interpersonal communication between a teacher and a child. (p. 156)

Additionally (cf. Bryant, Comisky, Crane, & Zillmann, 1980), teachers claim that humor stimulates interest in and attention to educational messages (Gilliland & Mauritsen, 1971; Highet, 1963; Middlebrook, cited in Browning, 1977; Welker, 1977); establishes a more "efficient" educational climate (Adams, 1974; Welker, 1977); makes learning more enjoyable (Gilliland & Mauritsen,

1971); aids in teaching sensitive subjects (Adams, 1974); affects children's personalities in positive way (Highet, 1963); improves test performance (Adams, 1972; Horn, 1972; Mechanic, 1962; Monson, 1968); and improves students' perceptions of their teachers (Scott, 1976). Humor has been reported to facilitate learning and appreciation of content in subjects as varied as human sexuality (Adams, 1972), foreign language instruction (deMatos, 1974), and special education (Kauffman & Birnbrauer, 1978); and this list is in no way exhaustive. Obviously, the reasons teachers use humor are as myriad and diverse as the contexts in which humor is used and the purposes toward which its use is applied. In addressing the remainder of our set of questions, we will examine empirical evidence to determine the extent to which it supports several of these claims regarding the use of humor to promote classroom learning.

DOES TEACHING WITH HUMOR ENHANCE STUDENTS' ATTENTION?

Teachers frequently note that humor enhances students' interest in their lessons and focuses attention on the materials to be learned (e.g., Bell, 1978; Hamilton, 1986). Highet (1963) notes that of the many purposes humor serves, "The most obvious one is that it keeps the pupils alive and attentive because they are never quite sure what is coming next" (p. 59). Baughman (1979) finds that many students are bored because they are required to attend classes in which they have no interest; therefore, he advocates using humor to enhance their interest. His underlying rationale is that "Interested pupils learn better than uninterested ones" (p. 26). Davies and Apter (1980) note that humor may play multiple roles in the attention-enhancing process: "It may in the first place help to attract attention to the teacher and to what he is saying. It may then help to maintain that attention over a period of time" (p. 238). Zillmann, Williams, Bryant, Boynton, and Wolf (1980) developed theoretical rationales to support such claims based on physiological concomitants of attention and on a vigilance explanation. They summarize:

In practical terms, this reasoning leads to the prediction that the comparatively inattentive student can be "alerted" through humorous stimuli and that once the student is made more vigilant, his or her alertness will extend into portion of a message that otherwise would be received and processed under inferior conditions of vigilance. (p 172)

Despite these numerous claims and the ready availability of supportive theoretical rationales, a surprisingly meager amount of empirical evidence directly supports the thesis that teachers' humor attracts and maintains students' attention to lessons that they are taught in the classroom. In a study to be discussed more fully in the section on humor's potential enhancement of learning, Vance (1987) included as a secondary measure a report of experimental assistants' assessments of first-grade students' interests in experimental audio cassettes which included various types of humor in addition to educational material in three of the four treatment conditions. Although humor initially failed to elevate students' rated interest in the educational materials presented, relative to interest in stimuli presented as a control, humor maintained initial interest following repeated exposure to the same story, while those children in the no humor control condition exhibited rapidly waning interest in the story. According to Vance (1987, p. 94), "humor may serve to raise flagging levels of arousal, attention, and interest to levels which support optimal information processing." Unfortunately no evidence is provided that the experimental assistants were blind to treatment condition or were naive regarding the purposes of the study; therefore, any conclusions drawn regarding interest and attention must remain suspect because of possible procedural limitations.

Because of the dearth of evidence directly testing the effects of teachers' classroom humor on students' attention and interest, it seems necessary to look to cognate literatures for more convincing support. Markiewicz (1974), in reviewing the effects of humor on persuasion, draws on the findings of four studies to conclude that humor makes serious messages more interesting; and Gruner (1978), after examining the research literature on humor in public speaking and persuasion, notes limited support for the facilitating effects of humor on attention to informative and persuasive speeches. However, the bulk of that research was conducted with adult populations. It is in the literature on children's attention to humorous educational television programs that we find the strongest direct support for the facilitating effects of humor on attention (see the chapter by Zillmann & Bryant in this volume). At the most global level of attention, Wakshlag (1985), in reviewing the evidence for "selective exposure" to educational television programs, concludes that selective exposure to educational television programs is of longer duration when they contain humorous embellishments. Furthermore, Wakshlag, Day, and Zillmann (1981) found that a fast-paced interspersion of humor proved most effective at quickly attracting children to the televised educational material and at maintaining high levels of exposure.

Moving from considerations of selective exposure to attention per se, Zillmann et al. (1980) examined kindergarten and first-grade students' attention to the television screen as a function of variously-paced humorous inserts that were semantically unrelated to the educational messages. They conclude: "The data regarding visual attention leave no doubt about the fact that exposure to humorous stimuli created high levels of attentiveness and these elevated levels of attentiveness extended into the exposure to educational materials" (p. 178). In terms of the most effective pacing of humor, in line with the findings of Wakshlag et al. (1981) on selective exposure, it was found that the presentation of materials at a fast pace produced the highest levels of attention. This is precisely in line with Highet's (1963) advice regarding the ideal use of humor in the classroom:

> The wise teacher will continue to introduce flashes of humor extraneously, because he knows that fifty-five minutes of work plus five minutes' laughter are worth twice as much as sixty minutes of unvaried work. (p. 60)

Although unqualified direct evidence for the effects on attention and interest of using humor in nonmediated classroom instruction is still wanting, a practical note from Zillmann et al. (1980) seems the most appropriate tentative guideline to employ when considering whether to try to use humor to enhance students' attention to their lessons: "In practical terms, the educator who deals with an audience whose attentiveness is below the level necessary for effective communication should indeed benefit from employing humor early on and in frequent short bursts" (p. 178).

DOES USING HUMOR IMPROVE THE CLASSROOM ENVIRONMENT AND MAKE STUDENTS' LEARNING MORE ENJOYABLE?

Effects of Humor Use on Class Environment

Quite obviously the first portion of this question involves a value judgment: What is a good learning environment? What teachers typically mean by a "good classroom environment" or a "good learning environment" can perhaps best be seen by examining various teachers' claims for how humor can facilitate such. "The proper use of humor can promote flexibility, facilitate communication, provide alternative perspectives, and create a feeling of goodwill. All these factors affect . . . school climate" (Ziegler, Boardman, & Thomas, 1985, p. 346). "Laughter binds the classroom in community" (Smith, 1986, p. 19). "By encouraging humor in the classroom, the teacher builds a closer community and allows more freedom between young people and the teacher" (Hamilton, 1986, p. 21). "Teachers who use their sense of humor to maintain a positive classroom atmosphere know how to reverse the direction of negative energy" (Cornett, 1986, p. 15).

> The teacher is the key to laughter and joy in the classroom. If he or she is able to find humor in the moment to moment interactions with pupils and the daily frustrations incurred in a world so closely packed with bodies in search of a behavioral objective, then . . . joy is found in human relationships and learning, and . . . the teacher becomes a model of a happy, caring person. (Wells, 1974, p. 4).

Finally, Davies and Apter (1980), in a summary of the research on learning with humor, note that at the social level a classroom which is characterized by humour is likely to be a happy one, unless the humour is used vindictively by the teacher against the pupils. If humour makes the classroom situation . . . less threatening . . ., then this, in turn, may help to create positive attitudes both to particular subjects and to learning in general. (p. 238)

What most of these teachers seem to mean by a good, positive classroom environment is a setting and situation in which communication is free and open, children are stimulated and do not feel threatened, strong empathetic bonds are established between teacher and students and among students, and feelings of happiness, goodwill, and the joy of learning prevail.

As defined in the previous sentence, a "good classroom environment" could be translated into a testable set of dependent measures, and the effects of various sorts of humor usage by teachers on that operationalization of classroom environment could be examined empirically. However, to the best of our knowledge, only one study has purported to test these relationships directly, and that was conducted with adult subjects. Contrary to the claims of teachers cited previously, Darling and Civikly (1984) and Jacobson (1984) found that college teachers' usage of humor apparently was perceived by their students with "suspicion and hostility, causing students to react defensively and thus damaging the climate for communication" (Jacobson, 1984, p. 25). The type of humor employed apparently was not a key determining independent factor, since usage of either hostile or nonhostile humor increased students' perceptions that the climate was more defensive than supportive. One key to interpreting these results may be seen in gender differences that were reported. Female teachers who used hostile humor and male teachers who employed nonhostile humor were perceived by students as creating the strongest defensive classroom climates. As one possible interpretation, Darling and Civikly suggest that college instructors who employ humor in their classrooms contradict students' perceptions of the way they ought to act, thereby making the students feel defensive. In particular, students may expect female teachers to act more nurturing and male teachers to act more assertive and domineering. Classroom behavior which dramatically contradicts the students' expectations for social structure of the classroom might be expected to create the most defensive and negative classroom environment.

It is difficult to determine just how much credence elementary and secondary school teachers should give to the findings of the study by Darling and Civikly since "classroom climate" is assessed in a limited fashion which may not be entirely appropriate to most elementary and secondary classrooms and since the study was conducted entirely with students in college classes. Nonetheless, until other evidence supports or refutes the present findings and interpretations, at the very least, teachers might be wise to heed this warning: "humor that is not perceived as being open, honest and spontaneous may be more destructive to the communicative climate than an absence of humor" (Darling & Civikly, 1984, p. 804). Certainly it seems unwise to use humor that violates students' expectations for role-appropriate behavior.

Humor Makes Learning More Enjoyable

Highet (1963) writes that the Renaissance teachers, "instead of beating their pupils" (p. 219), used comedies and humor and "made games out of the chores of learning difficult subjects" (p. 219), thereby making "the process of learning perfectly delightful" (p. 219). Bradford (1964) notes, "Of all the things which increase the pleasure taken from study and instruction humor must be among the first" (p. 67).

In a rather indirect test of the premise that humor makes learning more enjoyable, Davies (cited in Davies & Apter, 1980) conducted an experiment in which several difficult topics were taught to elementary school children using a slide-tape presentation with either humorous or nonhumorous embellishments. One of the dependent measures employed assessed whether the inclusion of humor would produce a more favorable attitude toward the educational vehicle. Their findings support the notion that the use of largely entraneous humor would positively influence students' attitudes toward the program.

Even more directly related to the notion that humor makes learning more enjoyable is the study by Zillmann et al. (1980) which was

discussed previously under the question regarding humor and attention. In addition to assessing the effects on visual attention of incorporating unrelated humorous segments into the televised educational messages, the children who served as subjects were asked
how much they *enjoyed* watching the educational material and how
much *interest* they had in the educational material. Children who
watched the educational program in the fast-paced humor condition
reported greater enjoyment in watching than children who watched
the program without humorous accoutrements. The pattern of
results for the measure of interest was the same as that just discussed for enjoyment although the findings only approached statistical significance.

Once again, support for a contention that humor improves yet
another dimension of education (this time, the enjoyment of learning) comes from a research setting slightly different from the typical
classroom learning context. Nonetheless, given consistent supportive evidence and the lack of findings to the contrary, it seems prudent to make the cautious generalization of "it seems like" the
judicious use of humor in the classroom will increase children's
enjoyment of learning as well as their positive disposition toward
the content of their lessons.

DOES USING HUMOR IN THE CLASSROOM HELP CHILDREN LEARN?

In many ways this is the generic question with which this entire
chapter is concerned. This is also the question which probably requires the most stringent qualifications (cf. Davies & Apter, 1980).
Part of the problem is that "learning" has many dimensions. Bradford (1964, p. 70) has said, "Humor's place in teaching is a high
place because it helps us with meanings." Comprehension is indeed
one dimension of learning. According to Scott (1976, p. 18), "Humor can be highly effective in improving the function of our mental
faculties." If we assume that by this statement Scott means information processing, memorization, or the like, then this too is a part
of learning. Scott adds, "Humor is one way . . . which may prove
effective in learning about ourselves" (p. 18). Experiential and affective education also contribute to the larger picture of learning.

However, in spite of all of these ways in which classroom learning might be conceptualized and assessed, most investigations of the effects of humor on learning have involved more traditional dependent measures of learning: acquisition of information, item recognition, recall, and retention. In this section we will present evidence which focuses on these narrow interpretations of learning: acquiring and retaining information from novel sources.

A number of reviews of the effects of humor on learning have been published recently, and those interested in the theoretical underpinnings of what we will discuss will find the following chapters to be useful: Bryant, Zillmann, and Brown (1983), Chapman and Crompton (1978), Davies and Apter (1980), McGhee (1980), and Zillmann and Bryant (1983). Each of these reviews includes considerations of learning outside of the classroom (e.g., educational television) which technically are beyond the scope of this review. However, in this instance, the boundaries between classroom and mediated learning are weakened because many investigations of humor and children's classroom learning have used some form of mediated instruction, primarily, it would seem, in efforts to exert tighter control over manipulated (i.e., humorous versus nonhumorous) instructional messages.

The first experimental study to focus primarily on the effects of humor on classroom learning was conducted by Hauck and Thomas (1972). In this study, the fourth to sixth grade school children who served as subjects contributed the humor rather than the teacher. The children were placed in a task situation in which they developed either humorous or nonhumorous associations between pairs of common objects. The findings of primary relevance to humor were that one day after the association task had been completed, the children recalled objects learned through humorous associations better than those learned via common or ordinary nonhumorous ones, but only under conditions of incidental learning. Intentional learning, which in this instance seems to have been associated with artifically high levels of attention and forced information acquisition, was not affected by the humorous associations.

Another early experimental study on the effects of humor on classroom learning was conducted by Curran (1973). Once again, the subjects (sixth and ninth grade students) were tested under conditions which would appear to force them to be attentive to the instructional materials. In this instance, only intentional learning was tested. The results were similar to those reported by Hauck and Thomas for intentional learning. Humor—in this case, humorous visual aides—was not found to facilitate acquisition of educational information.

Chapman and Crompton (1978) employed slide presentations of educational material designed for five- to six-year-old children. In a humorous version, zoo animals were drawn in a "funny" manner; in a nonhumorous control, the same animals were drawn in a "serious" fashion. Upon presentation of a letter which served as a cue (e.g., "c is for _____"), children were asked to recall as many appropriate zoo animals as possible. In this way, the humor that was used was directly related to the information to be acquired. When tested immediately after exposure to the slide presentations, information acquisition from the humorous version of the presentation was superior to that from the nonhumorous control.

Davies and Apter (1980) report a study employing somewhat older subjects (ages 8-11) which similarly assessed immediate information acquisition from humorous versus nonhumorous versions of slide tape presentations. In contrast to the study by Chapman and Crompton, the humorous stimuli employed were only minimally relevant to the topics being taught. Information acquisition was superior when the slide-tape program contained humor. The use of humor also enhanced children's evaluation of the program. Retention of information was again tested one month after initial treatment and assessment, and remained superior for subjects in the humorous treatment condition.

A recent study by Vance (1987) with first grade children lends further strong support to claims that unrelated humor improves learning. Employing a design with three humor conditions and one nonhumorous control, all children were initially treated so that they achieved states of low interest in and low arousal to an audio-taped reading of a familiar story. The subsequent treatment included a humor experience followed immediately by a serious presentation of novel information (contiguous/immediate), an identical humor treatment followed one week later by presentation of the novel information (contiguous/postponed), or presentation of novel information with humor interspersed within the educational message (integrated). Subjects in the two contiguous humor groups scored higher on immediate information acquisition tests, and those in the contiguous humor/immediate condition scored higher on delayed retention tests than did those in the control group. Those subjects in the integrated humor group did not perform significantly better than those in the control group, possibly because they found the integrated humor to be distracting. The author concludes that "The results of this study support the assertion that the presentation of contiguous humor can lead to improved immediate memory and retention of a subsequently presented message" (p. 94). These findings are supportive of previous research into the effects on information acquisition of using unrelated humor in educational television programs (Zillmann et al., 1980; see the chapter by Zillmann & Bryant in this volume for details).

In summary, increasingly abundant evidence indicates that when children's initial attention and motivation to learn is low, the use of humor in teaching can be expected to help them learn and retain educational information. For teachers of elementary school age children, it seems that humor that is unrelated to the educational message is a particularly safe bet (see section on *Distortion humor*). If students are already motivated and attentive, the use of humor does not seem to produce any beneficial gains on learning.

DOES USING CLASSROOM HUMOR IMPROVE STUDENTS' CREATIVITY?

It is frequently claimed that stimulating divergent thinking effectively promotes creativity. Moreover, many teachers believe that "With the addiiton of humor, even more creativity can emerge" (Krogh, 1985, p. 29). Humor and creativity appear to be highly related conceptually (e.g., Koestler, 1964). And correlational studies typically have reported significant positive correlations between individuals' scores on measures of creativity and indices of their sense of humor (e.g., Singer & Berkowitz, 1972; Treadwell, 1970). In an era in which many schools claim to have instituted curricula that promote divergent as well as convergent thinking and in which teachers and scholars of the gifted and talented are exploring interesting and "painless" new ways to stretch the imaginations of the intellectually able, it seems obvious that scholars would investigate whether or not the use of humor in teaching can facilitate creativity. This research evidence is covered thoroughly in the chapter by Ziv. However, for the sake of completeness, we should note that although the number of investigations in this realm is relatively small, the results rather consistently support the contention that when humor is used appropriately in the classroom, creativity can be enhanced. Ziv specifies guidelines for the ways teachers should use humor to stimulate creativity in their pupils.

DOES USING HUMOR IN TESTING LOWER STUDENTS' ANXIETY AND PROMOTE IMPROVED TEST PERFORMANCE?

Students were creeping into my English class in Room 111 in the Henderson Building. It was the zero hour: the final examination day. Eyes dropped to the floor and hands zigzagged everywhere. Signs of nervous tension were evident.

"Come into your favorite class," I welcomed and the students practically stuck out their tongues. "Sadist," someone said sourly from the back of the room.

Before the tension tightened I asked everyone to spread out, put down their pens, and listen to a Billy Joel song. . . .

As I played Billy Joel's song, "Just the Way You Are," I danced to the lyrics, slung hard candy to outstretched hands, and got the class laughing at me. "Cuckoo," said that same sour voice from the back of the room. At least, I had moved up a notch. . . .

The class laughed.

Humor had diffused the tension, and the tightrope had been loosened. All could breathe freely just the way they were. (Worthington, 1984, pp. 53-54)

Recent years have witnessed a surge in the interest in the role of humor in reducing life stress (e.g., Lefcourt & Martin, 1986; see also the chapter by Martin in this volume). For children, school can be a major source of stress. According to Highet (1963, p. 71), "Wise teachers allow the young a large number of outlets through which this energy can escape. To draw it off into helpless, cheerful laughter is another of the functions of humor in teaching."

Although numerous teachers have advocated the use of humor to reduce tension, thereby creating a more relaxed class atmosphere (Gilliland & Mauritsen, 1971; Scott, 1976; Welker, 1977), evidence to support that general claim appears to be missing. However, probably the principle stress-reducing function for which teachers have advocated using humor in the classroom is in the more narrow domain of reducing test anxiety, thereby potentially improving students' performances on the tests (Adams, 1972; Horn, 1972; Mechanic, 1962; Monson, 1968). For example, Horn (1972, p. 38) claims that "A little humor will often liven up an exercise or even a test. In the case of the latter, a laugh will do wonders toward alleviating the tension many students feel under pressure." Evidence is available to test such claims, but it is quite inconsistent (cf. Chapman & Crompton, 1978; McGhee, 1980).

Smith, Ascough, Ettinger, and Nelson (1971) examined the effects of humor on highly-anxious and moderately-anxious college students' test performance on an actual midterm examination. Humor was found to facilitate recall among student with high anxiety, but the less anxious students, who complained that the humorous material in the test distracted them and impaired their concentration, performed somewhat more poorly when taking the humorous version of the test. From their comments, it would appear that the moderately anxious students were also highly motivated.

Terry and Woods (1975) prepared humorous and nonhumorous versions of test materials comprised of two math problems, a reading comprehension item, and a sequential ordering problem. They administered age-appropriate versions to intact third and fifth grade classes. For third graders, humor embedded in test questions had no impact on verbal performance but resulted in impaired math performance. For fifth grade students, humor had no effect on math performance, facilitated performance on the reading comprehension item, and impeded performance on the sequential ordering problem. It should be noted that prior to testing the students were told that the test would not count toward their class grades, and no indication was given that the students were even minimally anxious; therefore, the confusing pattern of results may or may not provide a valid indication of the effects of humor on test anxiety.

Unfortunately the results of other studies on the effects of humor on test anxiety are no less perplexing. Townsend and Mahoney (1981) employed humorous test items in classroom exams and found, contrary to Smith et al. (1971), that humor was detrimental to the test performance of highly test-anxious college students. A recent study by McMorris, Urbach, and Connor (1985), conducted with eighth-grade students, found that humorous forms of test items had no effect on test performance nor did the inclusion of what were judged by the students to be moderately funny test items affect level of measured anxiety. Taking a different tact in light of the lack of consistency in results of prior studies, McMorris et al. included tests of students' perceptions and evaluations of the humorous test items and their opinions regarding the use of humor in testing. Students tended to judge the humorous items to be less difficult, strongly favored their inclusion on tests, and judged the effects of humor positively. The authors conclude that "If humor helps create positive affect, reduces negative affect, and does not depress scores, its use is warranted" (p. 154).

In light of the lack of any clear pattern to the findings from empirical research, the only advice that we can offer to classroom teachers is to proceed with extreme caution. If students are not apt to be highly anxious over testing, humor does not appear to be useful and can be disturbing. Under conditions of high or mixed test anxiety, it appears likely that the use of humor is likely to hurt the performance of some pupils, help others, and have little or no impact on the test scores of the remainder.

SHOULD TEACHERS AVOID CERTAIN TYPES OF HUMOR? IN PARTICULAR, WHAT ARE THE EFFECTS OF HUMOROUS RIDICULE AND SARCASM? WHAT ARE THE EFFECTS OF USING DISTORTION HUMOR?

Ridicule and Sarcasm

Humorous ridicule and sarcasm are forms of hostile humor. As was noted earlier, many teachers at various levels of the educational process use hostile humor (Bryant et al., 1979; Bryant & Hunter,

1981; Wells, 1974), ridicule and sarcasm included. A benevolent interpretation of why teachers use hostile humor is that they find it to be a potent behavioral corrective, as in the following use of ridicule by a high school teacher.

> A few years ago, Scott was enrolled in my second period English class. Each day, Scott arrived late, at about 9:20, appearing to feel neither contrite nor embarrassed. Although we all felt a degree of annoyance about his rudeness, it didn't seem appropriate to make an issue of the matter each day.
>
> Then one day he didn't arrive at his usual time, nor at all, for that matter. We'd become "programmed" to expect his delayed entrance. However, that day, at the time that we all expected Scott, only a small friendly-looking dog bustled into the room.
>
> Since we were all busy with desk work and quite absorbed in our tasks, there was hardly a stir as the "visitor" sniffed his way up and down the aisles. It was I who broke the silence, asking the class, "Do you suppose that's Scott?" It took them a minute to catch my meaning; but when they did, we all had a good laugh; then nothing more was said.
>
> The next day, when Scott arrived at his usual time, I said to him, "Was that you yesterday?" Naturally, the class burst into gales of laughter; only Scott remained silent. When the laughter subsided, the puzzled boy pleaded with those around him to tell him why they were laughing. When they tried to tell him, I heard him saying, in a perplexed manner, "Dog? Dog?"
>
> From that day on, Scott came to class on time. (Scully, 1984, p. 52)

Other teachers are adamant in decrying the use of hostile humor such as ridicule and sarcasm. Highet (1963, p. 61) warns that "humor [should] not be used to tyrannize a class." Collins (1986) further cautions:

> But sarcasm is brutal. Note the etymology: GK *sarkasmos*, fr. *sarkazein* to tear flesh. Dagger-sharp words, regardless of their wit, puncture self-esteem. Students should be taught what sarcasm is and how to recognize and analyze it, and they

should then be sternly counselled to avoid it. Sarcasm can be as destructive and painful as other forms of humor can be rejuvenating. (p. 20)

The limited research on the effects of using humorous ridicule in teaching is reviewed by Zillmann and Bryant in their chapter in this volume (see section on *Laughter as a Whip*). Their conclusions regarding the efficacy of using ridicule as an educational corrective bear repeating here as they seem to be most appropriate to classroom teaching. They note that ridicule has been shown to be ineffective for preschool children, probably because such indirect and veiled messages may be ambiguous to young children. In contrast, ridicule has proven to be a potent corrective for first-graders. Presumably it would remain an effective educational corrective from there on out.

Zillmann and Bryant also discuss the morality of using ridicule as an educational corrective, suggesting that its use should be embraced only when the ends justify its inherently punitive means and only when no less punitive form of correction is available. In an investigation by Bryant and Parks (1984), conducted with elementary school students in a classroom context, additional, more pragmatic reasons for avoiding ridicule were found. Students watched several videotapes of potential substitute teachers. Those in one condition (ridicule/not justified) saw an otherwise benevolent and personable substitute teacher humorously but viciously ridicule a member of their class. Those students perceived the substitute as someone who would be physically and verbally abusive to her students; they also indicated that the teacher was someone whom they would avoid in selecting classes, and they strongly recommended that the potential substitute teacher not be given work in their school. Students in an experimental condition in which the ridicule was depicted as justified under the circumstances (ridicule/justified), still gave the ridiculing substitute relatively poorer evaluations than were given by peers to the teacher in a control (no ridicule) condition, although the evaluations in the ridicule/justified condition were significantly less negative than evaluations by students in the condition in which the ridicule was not justified.

These results suggest that even though ridicule (and probably sarcasm and other hostile humor used in the service of belittlement) may serve a corrective function, the long-term consequence of diminished esteem in the eyes of students may make the immediate gains in terms of behavioral correction not worth the costs. And when the moral ramifications of demeaning students who have been entrusted into one's care are also considered, ridicule appears to be a costly corrective indeed.

Distortion Humor

Many teachers report having problems teaching with humor because of its inherent ambiguity.

> Today's students don't seem to experience . . . enjoyment with word play. While teaching Steinbeck's *Of Mice and Men*, I mentioned that he refers to "hands" over a hundred times in the work which makes him a real "handyman." Admittedly I was disappointed when no one caught the joke, but I was shocked when I saw some of them recording in their notes, "Steinbeck was a real handyman." I tried to explain the pun to blank faces and raised eyebrows, but it was unsuccessful. (Kaywell, 1984, p. 49)

Many common forms of humor, such as irony, satire, understatement, or exaggeration (e.g., tall tales) depend much more than do puns on distortion for their jokework. Therefore, they have the potential of teaching inaccurate information to young children. Because of the novelty of the images that such distortion humor can convey, it is also possible that such inaccuracies may be particularly easy to remember and especially resistant to memory decay.

All of the research on the effects of distortion humor on learning has been conducted in the context of educational television programs, therefore it is reviewed in this volume in the chapter by Zillmann and Bryant (see *The Irony of Irony*) rather than here. However, because the findings would appear to be equally germane to classroom teachers who might use such humor, Zillmann and Bryant's conclusions and guidelines are excerpted here as well. The evidence does confirm that irony and related distortion humor can create faulty impressions in children. Moreover, this erroneous learning appears to be particularly hard to correct via traditional verbal means of teaching. Therefore, teachers of children, especially young children, should refrain from using such humor unless they are certain that the children have the faculties and knowledge to immediately "get the humor" and make the necessary cognitive corrections. Additionally, when books or audiovisual materials that are a part of the school curriculum contain such humor, the classroom teacher needs to be sensitive to the potential of these resources to misinform. It may even be beneficial for the teacher to explain the humor in the process of making certain that the children have acquired the correct information. Unlike the limited feedback situation that exists in the viewing of educational television programs, distortion humor to which children are exposed in the classroom can, with patience and clear explanations, be "unlearned and learned right." In accomplishing this, the teacher can provide the children with a valuable lesson about the nature of some forms of humor at the same time that subject matter is clarified and learned.

OTHER QUESTIONS FOR ANOTHER TIME

In this chapter we have focused primarily on the principle cognitive elements of learning. The impact of teaching with humor on affective dimensions of the learning process either has not been considered or has been given overly meager attention. However, affective considerations are also important and include major question such as: What are the effects on teacher-student rapport of using various types of humor in the classroom? Does using humor cause students to want to learn more about particular subjects? What are the effects of being the brunt of hostile humor on students' self-esteem? Can humor be used to diffuse hostility and general tension in the classroom? Research evidence is available to enlighten us regarding a few of thes questions; others await systematic inquiry.

Another major set of questions includes considerations of the effects of teachers' use of humor on students' perceptions of their teachers. Does using various kinds of humor alter the teachers' appeal to students? What effect does using humor have on students' perceptions of their teachers' competence? On perceived credibility? On perceived teaching effectiveness? Although such considerations are beyond the scope of the present review, it should be noted that a number of investigations have addressed these issues with quite revealing results (Bryant et al., 1980; Feather, 1972; Field, Simpkins, Brown, & Rick, 1971; Frey, 1973; McKeachie, Lin, & Mann, 1971; Ware & Williams, 1974).

CONCLUSION

Many of the claims by teachers for direct benefits from using humor in the classroom have been evaluated in the crucible of empirical evidence. Clear evidence supporting several of these claims has been discovered. For example, the judicious use of humor has been found to facilitate students' attention to educational messages, to make learning more enjoyable, to promote students; creativity, and, under some conditions, to improve information acquisition and retention. A key word in the previous statement is "judicious." It would appear that success in teaching with humor in even these domains depends on employing the right type of humor, under the proper conditions, at the right time, and with properly motivated and receptive students. As we mentioned earlier, an important facilitating or limiting factor is the teacher. Obviously all sorts of humor use are not for every teacher. But for the teacher who is interested in using humor and who feels comfortable with humor in the classroom, we hope that the evidence we have reviewed, the conclusions we have drawn, and the guidelines we have suggested make teaching with humor more successful and more enjoyable.

NOTE

1. While we make descriptive comparisons between the normative data generated by the studies of Wells (1974), Bryant et al. (1979), and Bryant and Hunter (1981), generalizations should be avoided. The studies feature extreme differences in sample size, sampling procedures, data-gathering protocols, coder-training techniques, and methods of data analysis. To provide just one example of the limits of generality in the study by Wells (1974), which is based on a very small sample size, one of the authors (JB) recently had an opportunity to observe five "master" elementary school teachers for two complete teaching days each. Although the humor profile of four of these teachers fell within the parameters reported by Wells for elementary school teachers, the fifth teacher, although she

was extremely dynamic, warm, and personable, did not use a single bit of humor during the two days of observation. Obviously some very good elementary school teachers use little or no humor.

REFERENCES

Adams, R. C. (1972). Is physics a laughing matter? *Physics Teacher, 10,* 265-266.

Adams, W. J. (1974). The use of sexual humor in teaching human sexuality at the university level. *Family Coordinator, 23,* 365-368.

Baughman, M. D. (1979). Teaching with humor: A performing art. *Contemporary Education, 51,* 26-30.

Bell, T. L. (1978). The geography of humor. *Professional Geographer, 30,* 81-83.

Bradford, A. L. (1964). The place of humor in teaching. *Peabody Journal of Education, 42,* 67-70.

Browning, R. (1977, February). Why not humor? *APA Monitor,* pp. 1, 32.

Bryant, J., Comisky, P. W., Crane, J. S., & Zillmann, D. (1980). Relationship between college teachers' use of humor in the classroom and students' evaluations of their teachers. *Journal of Educational Psychology, 72,* 511-519.

Bryant, J., Comisky, P., & Zillmann, D. (1979). Teachers' humor in the college classroom. *Communication Education, 28,* 110-118.

Bryant, J., & Hunter, M. (1981). [Relationship between junior high school teachers' use of humor in the classroom and students' evaluations of their teachers]. Unpublished raw data.

Bryant, J., & Parks, S. L. (1984). [Effects of teacher on students' evaluations of that teacher]. Unpublished raw data.

Bryant, J., Zillmann, D., & Brown, D. (1983). Entertainment features in children's educational television: Effects on attention and information acquisition. In J. Bryant & D. R. Anderson (Eds.), *Children's understanding of television: Research on attention and comprehension* (pp. 221-240). New York: Academic Press.

Cattell, R. B. (1931). The assessment of teaching ability. *British Journal of Educational Psychology, 1,* 48-71.

Chapman, A. J., & Crompton, P. (1978). Humorous presentations of materials and presentations of humorous materials: A review of the humor and memory literature two experimental studies. In M. M. Gruneberg, P. E. Morris, & R. N. Sykes (Eds.), *Practical aspects of memory* (pp. 84-92). London: Academic Press.

Collins, S. M. (1986). Facets: Humor and sarcasm. *English Journal, 75,* 20.

Cornett, C. E. (1986). *Learning through laughter: Humor in the classroom.* Bloomington, IN: Phi Delta Kappa Educational Foundation.

Curran, F. W. (1973). *A developmental study of cartoon humor appreciation and its use in facilitating learning.* Unpublished doctoral dissertation, Catholic University of America.

Darling, A., & Civikly, J. M. (1984). The effect of teacher humor on classroom climate. *Proceedings of the Tenth International Conference on Improving University Teaching* (pp. 788-806). college Park: University of maryland.

Davies, A. P., & Apter, M. J. (1980). Humour and its effect on learning in children. In p. E. McGhee & A. J. Chapman (Eds.), *Children's humour* (pp. 237-253). New York: Wiley.

deMatos, F. (1974). *Humo(u)r, a neglected feature in foreign language teaching.* Yazingi Institute, Brazil (ERIC Document Reproduction Service No. ED 104150).

Feather, N. T. (1972). Teaching effectiveness and student evaluation. *Australian Psychologist, 7,* 180-187.

Field, T. W., Simkins, W. S., Brown, R. K., & Rich, P. (1971). Identifying patterns of teacher behavior from student evaluation. *Journal of Applied Psychology, 55,* 466-469.

Freud, S. (1905). *Jokes and their relation to the unconscious.* Leipzig: Deuticke.

Frey, P. W. (1973). Student ratings of teaching: Validity of several ratings factors. *Science, 182,* 83-85.

Gilliland, H., & Mauritsen, H. (1971). Humor in the classroom. *The Reading Teacher, 24,* 753-756; 761.

Gruner, C. R. (1978). *Understanding laughter: The workings of wit & humor.* Chicago: Nelson-Hall.

Hamilton, M. G. (1986). Facets: Humor and sarcasm. *English Journal, 75,* 21.

Hauck, W. E., & Thomas, J. W. (1970). The relationship of humor to intelligence, creativity, and intentional and incidental learning. *The Journal of Experimental Education, 40,* 52-55.

Highet, G. (1963). *The art of teaching.* New York: Knopf.

Horn, G. (1972, December). Laughter . . . a saving grace. *Today's Education, 61,* 37-38.

Jacobson, R. L. (1984, July 11). Use of humor by college teachers found to stir suspicion and hostility. *The Chronicle of Higher Education,* p. 25.

Kauffman, J. M., & Birnbrauer, J. S. (1978). *Research to develop effective teaching and management techniques for severely disturbed and retarded children.* (Final Report). Charlottesville, VA: University of Virginia: School of Education. (ERIC Document Production Service No. ED 177 757).

Kaywell, J. F. (1984). Our readers write: Examples of classroom humor. *English Teacher, 73,* 49-50.

Koestler, A. (1964). *The act of creation.* New York: Macmillan.

Krogh, S. (1985). Should school be a laughing matter? *Early Years. K-8, 15,* 29; 75.

Lefcourt, H. M., & Martin, R. A. (1986). *Humor and life stress: Antidote to adversity.* New York: Springer-Verlag.

MacAdam, B. (1985). Humor in the classroom: Implications for the bibliographic instruction librarian. *College & Research Libraries, 46,* 327-333.

Markiewicz, D. (1974). Effects of humor on persuasion. *Sociometry, 37,* 407-422.

McGhee, P. E. (1980). Toward the integration of entertainment and educational functions of television: The role of humor. In P. H. Tannenbaum (Ed.), *The entertainment functions of television* (pp. 183-208). Hillsdale, NJ: Erlbaum.

McKeachie, W. J., Lin, Y. G., & Mann, W. (1971). Student ratings of teacher effectiveness: Validity studies. *American Educational Research Journal, 8,* 435-445.

McMorris, R. F., Urbach, S. L., & Connor, M. C. (1985). Effects of incorporating humor in test items, *Journal of Educational Measurement, 22,* 147-155.

Mechanic, D. (1962). *Students under stress: A study of the social psychology of adaptation.* New York: Free Press of Glencoe.

Miller, M. S. (1977). What makes Superteachers super? *Instructor, 48,* 120; 122.

Monson, D. (1968). Children's test responses to seven humorous stories. *Elementary School Journal, 58,* 334-339.

Plotnik, A. (1985). Bibliolaffic instruction. *American Libraries, 16,* 533.

Scott, T. M. (1976). Humor in teaching. *Journal of Physical Education and Recreation, 7,* 18.

Scully, C. (1984). Our readers write: Examples of classroom humor. *English Journal, 73,* 52.

Singer, D., & Berkowitz, L. (1972). Differing "creativities" in the wit and the clown. *Perceptual and Motor Skills, 35,* 3-6.

Smith, M. R. (1986). Facets: Humor and sarcasm. *English Journal, 75,* 19.

Smith, R. E., Ascough, J. C., Ettinger, R. F., & Nelson, D. A. (1971). Humor, anxiety, and task performance. *Journal of Personality and Social Psychology, 19,* 243-246.

Terry, R. L., & Woods, M. E. (1975). Effects of humor on test performance of elementary school children. *Psychology in the Schools, 12,* 182-185.

Townsend, M. A. R., & Mahoney, P. (1981). Humor and anxiety: Effects on class test performance. *Psychology in the Schools, 18,* 228-234.

Treadwell, Y. (1970). Humor and creativity. *Psychological Reports, 26*(1), 55-58.

Vance, C. M. (1987). A comparative study on the use of humor in the design of instruction. *Instructional Science, 16,* 79-100.

Wakshlag, J. (1985). Selective exposure to educational television. In D. Zillmann & J. Bryant (Eds.), *Selective exposure to communication* (pp. 191-201). Hillsdale, NJ: Lawrence Erlbaum Associates.

Wakshlag, J. J., Day, K. D., & Zillmann, D. (1981). Selective exposure to educational television programs as a function of differently paced humorous inserts. *Journal of Educational Psychology, 73,* 27-32.

Ware, J., & Williams, R. (1974). Studies on the effects of content and manner of lecture presentations. *Behavior Today, 5,* 120.

Welker, W. A. (1977). Humor in education: A foundation for wholesome living. *College Student Journal, 11,* 252-254.

Wells, D. A. (1974). *The relationship between the humor of elementary school teachers and the perception of students.* Unpublished doctoral dissertation, United States International University, San Diego.

Worthington, P. (1984). Our readers write: Examples of classroom humor. *English Journal*, *73*, 53-54.

Ziegler, V., Boardman, G., & Thomas, M. D. (1985). Humor, leadership, and school climate. *Clearing House*, *58*, 346-348.

Zillmann, D., & Bryant, J. (1983). Uses and effects of humor in educational ventures. In P. E. McGhee & J. H. Goldstein (Eds.), *Handbook of humor research: Vol 2. Applied Studies* (pp. 173-193). New York: Springer-Verlag.

Zillmann, D., Williams, B. R., Bryant, J., Boynton, K. R., & Wolf, M. A. (1980). Acquisition of information from educational television programs as a function of differently paced humorous inserts. *Journal of Educational Psychology*, *72*, 170-180.

Chapter 3

Going West to Get East:
Using Metaphors
as Instructional Tools

Patrick S. Williams, PhD

SUMMARY. Theory and research on the dynamics of instructional metaphors, analogies, and models, children's ability to comprehend figurative language, and the effectiveness of figurative devices as instructional tools are reviewed. Conclusions from this theory and research are used to argue that metaphors and other figurative devices can play a uniquely effective role in the acquisition of new knowledge. Recommendations for the design and use of instructional metaphors based on research findings are also presented.

When Columbus headed west across the Atlantic in 1492, he did so for a peculiar reason; he wanted to get to the east. Teaching new concepts to students by using instructional metaphors is a little like what Columbus did—going west to get east.

In his famous dialogue, the *Meno*, Plato (1956) posed another interesting paradox. How, he asked, is it possible to acquire completely new knowledge? If one already knows what he seeks to learn, then what's the point? Yet, if one does not already know what he seeks to learn, then how will he know when he has learned it? It is generally acknowledged today that learning must start with what the student already knows. A great deal of literature in psychology attests to the important role that prior knowledge plays in

Patrick S. Williams is affiliated with the Department of Behavioral Sciences, Wharton County Junior College, Wharton, TX.

79

learning (see Bransford, 1979). Yet, if this is a prerequisite, then learning in areas about which the learner has absolutely no prior knowledge would appear impossible, since there would be no existing cognitive structures to which such "radically new" information could be related. Yet, despite this paradox, learning of radically new information does take place.

In what follows, I will present a case for metaphor as a bridge that effectively carries the learner from that which is already known to that which has yet to be understood. Theory and research on metaphor, the development of metaphoric capabilities, and the effects of metaphor in instruction have increased greatly in the last two decades. Today's educators have available more than enough factual data to significantly enhance the effectiveness of instruction in virtually any area through the deliberate design and application of instructional metaphors.

To begin with, however, a few words on terminology are required. Among theorists, researchers, and practitioners concerned with metaphor, a number of different terms are used in roughly synonymous fashion. Following the lead of Gardner and Winner (1986), I favor the term "metaphor" to refer to any member of a family of figurative devices which includes metaphors, analogies, similes, models (under some definitions), and probably a few others. The major function shared by all types of metaphor is to characterize the attributes of objects, events, situations, or domains of information, and to do so in nonliteral ways.

In the general case of an instructional metaphor, something that the student does not yet know or understand is compared to something else that the student already understands well. For example, when teaching a young child about the earth one might tell him that it's shaped like a ball. The topic of instruction, or that which is being learned about (the earth), may be called the "topic" of the metaphor. The topic is compared to the "vehicle," or that which the student already understands (ball). One may also speak of the "source domain" as the body of knowledge which is already understood, and the "target domain" as the body of knowledge which is to be learned.

Finally, the term "schema" (plural: schemata) refers to the individual's organized mental representation of knowledge about a particular subject matter. In this sense, it means roughly the same thing as "concept" or "conceptualization."

THEORY

It is generally accepted among modern psychologists that learning involves changes in the learner's schemata. Rumelhart and Norman (1981) suggested three ways that existing schemata may be changed by new experience. "Accretion" is the accumulation of new information in existing schemata. "Tuning" is the gradual refinement of a schema due to repeated application in problem solving situations. "Restructuring" occurs when new schemata are created, either to reinterpret old information or to accommodate new information. Each of these processes makes use of already existing knowledge, but it is restructuring, the most radical of the three, which remains mysterious.

According to Vosniadou and Brewer (1987), among the several mechanisms by which knowledge acquisition may occur, only two are likely candidates for the radical restructuring that occurs when learners acquire knowledge in completely new subject areas. The first such mechanism is Socratic dialogue, and the second consists of metaphors, analogies, and physical models.

In explaining "why metaphors are necessary and not just nice" for communication and educational purposes, Ortony (1975) suggested three reasons. His "compactness" thesis suggests that a metaphor efficiently packs a great deal of information into a small linguistic package by transferring large chunks of attributes from a well-understood vehicle to a topic about which little is known. For example, by telling a child that the heart is a pump, a teacher suggests that much of what the child already knows about the purpose, structure, and function of pumps is also true of the heart.

Ortony's "inexpressibility" thesis suggests that metaphors often communicate things that cannot be communicated using literal language. For instance, the language we use to talk about psychological processes is primarily metaphorical. We speak of emotional feelings "coming and going," and of ideas "popping into our heads." Yet, when we attempt to express these same ideas using literal language, we are struck dumb.

The "vividness" thesis suggests that, compared to the mental representations aroused by nonmetaphoric language, the representations aroused by metaphor are more similar to direct perceptual experience. This follows from the metaphor's wholesale transfer of attributes from vehicle to topic. By contrast, when literal language is used to ascribe the attributes of one thing to another, each attribute must be separately transferred in its own linguistic wrapping. The reassembling of each discrete attribute subsequently yields a mental representation that pales in comparison to the original experience. Besides being vivid in a perceptual sense, metaphors are more emotionally vivid, according to Ortony, since they closely resemble actual perceived experience.

Ortony stated that these characteristics of metaphor give it great instructional utility in several ways. For instance, the increased imageability of metaphor contributes to the learnability (Paivio, 1971) of material presented metaphorically. Also, the richness of detail that is transferred from a metaphor's vehicle to its topic provides an effective and efficient way to bridge the gap between known and unknown material. Finally, the perceptual and emotive vividness of metaphor enhances the memorability of material presented metaphorically.

Similarly, Simons (1984) suggested that analogies enhance comprehension of new material in three ways. Through their "concretizing" function, analogies make abstract information more concrete and imaginable. Through the "structurizing" function, the structure of relationships among the key elements in an existing schema serve as the model for the structure of relationships in the new schema. As a result, much information about the new domain does not have to be learned directly; instead the new schema has only to be supplemented with new information. Through the "active assimilation" function, an analogy activates old ideas to which new ones can be anchored, and stimulates the learner to integrate the new information with the previously learned information.

While Vosniadou and Brewer (1987) claimed that metaphor can account for the radical restructuring of schemata, and Ortony (1975) and Simons (1984) suggested reasons why metaphor is a important tool for instruction, Petrie (1979) offered an account of the sequence of cognitive events that takes place when metaphor is used to promote the acquisition of radically new knowledge. The first step in the creation of a new schema by analogy is the learner's subjective feeling that a discrepancy exists between the material to be learned and her current ability to understand that material. The student unsuccessfully tries various methods to make sense of the new material.

In the second step, the teacher provides a metaphor for the learner's consideration. The immediate impact of the metaphor is to suggest to the learner that he deal with the problem situation as if it were similar to a situation he already understands. How would I conceive of the problem situation, the learner might ask himself, if the metaphor were literally true?

In the third step, the student engages in learning behaviors (e.g., asking questions, offering a tentative conceptualization of the problem domain for teacher evaluation, responding to quiz questions) that yield feedback about the adequacy of his latest conceptualization of the problem domain. He then monitors the teacher's feedback and attempts to answer several questions: Has the anomaly between my current mode of understanding and the problem domain lessened? Does the teacher respond to my learning behaviors approvingly? If not, how far off the mark does my current conceptualization seem to be?

The fourth step occurs when the learner corrects his learning behaviors and tries them again. Feedback from these new attempts provides indications about how the ultimately correct conceptualization will differ from initial and intermediate conceptualizations.

This process repeats itself as long as the learner perceives that there remains a discrepancy between the problem domain and his conceptualization of it. In this way, a learner's initial schema for a domain of knowledge undergoes a transformation that results in a totally new schema.

Rumelhart and Norman (1981) stated that acquiring radically new knowledge via analogical processes is absolutely ubiquitous. Like Petrie (1979), these authors offered a theoretical description of the steps in the process. The usual learning sequence proceeds as follows: Upon encountering a new situation, a learner seeks to interpret it in terms of existing schemata. If successful, the learner is said to understand the situation and no new schemata are created.

However, if no existing schemata offer a satisfactory account of the new situation, the next-best schemata are sought out. Since no completely applicable schemata were available, there are mismatches between the one that is used and the new situation. In some cases, essential features of the next-best schema might be absent from the new situation, replaced by different ones.

This set of conditions triggers creation of a new schema. The next-best schema that was applied inappropriately to the new situation serves as the model for the new schema that will be created. Those ways in which the model is found to be inappropriate for the new situation provide an initial set of ways in which the new schema will differ from the old. Characteristics of the old schema that do not contradict the new situation are transferred to the new schema, even though they may not be specifically apparent in the new situation. This transfer process provides for one of the most powerful characteristics of learning by analogy as well as one of the chief reasons why flaws in the new schema may occur. The large scale transfer of attributes from old to new schema allows the learner to make inferences in the new domain without having to have explicit knowledge of the new situation. Thus, a great deal of learning in the new domain takes place very quickly.

RESEARCH

Children's Ability to Comprehend Metaphor

In order for metaphor to be an effective instructional tool, learners must be able to understand metaphors. In the case of normal adults, there is no doubt that they can. For children, however, conflicting research results during the past two decades have clouded the issue. More recently, increasingly sophisticated and insightful research approaches seem to be revealing the reasons for the conflicting results. In short, an accumulation of new evidence indicates that even very young children are capable of understanding some metaphors.

In a review of literature on children's metaphorical abilities, Vosniadou (1987) concluded that the primary constraints on young children's ability to comprehend metaphor are limitations in knowledge and information processing abilities. Since metaphor comprehension involves the transfer of knowledge from one conceptual domain to another, it naturally depends on the knowledge the child already has and on the ability to mentally manipulate that knowledge.

Vosniadou claimed that most researchers of children's metaphorical abilities have failed to consider several relevant, nonmetaphorical shortcomings common to young children. Recent research indicates that when tasks and materials are sensitive to subjects' abilities, even children four years of age or younger can understand metaphorical language. For instance, Vosniadou, Ortony, Reynolds, and Wilson (1984) obtained evidence for metaphor comprehension in 4-year-olds when the children were allowed to enact their metaphor interpretations with toys.

Among the variables that affect metaphor comprehension in young children, but which have been overlooked in much research on children's abilities, Vosniadou (1987) included the following:

1. Linguistic form: Some linguistic forms in which metaphors appear are easier to understand than others. For instance, similes ("An atom is like the solar system") are easier to understand than metaphors ("An atom is a solar system") because the requirement to compare two things is explicit in similes, but implicit in metaphors, and children may not realize that predicative statements are sometimes intended to be comparisons.

Other linguistic factors, such as familiarity with the particular linguistic form used, how explicitly the metaphoric comparison is stated, and how explicitly the metaphorical similarity between topic and vehicle is expressed, can influence ease of metaphor comprehension.

2. Knowledge: To understand a metaphor, a child must understand the words used and the concepts they denote, and be aware of the many relations that can exist between the things being compared. Naturally, metaphors involving familiar terms are the easiest for young children to understand.

3. Concreteness: Young children find metaphors based on physical or perceptual similarity easier to understand than those based on abstract and complex relations, or those that use a physical term to describe a psychological state ("cold" to mean "aloof"). This is

because physical and perceptual properties are usually more salient to a child than relational properties, and they may also represent the only information a child has about an object.

This is not to say that young children are unable to detect similarity between relational properties. Gentner (1977) showed that preschoolers can map relations from the domain of the human body to inanimate objects. Several others (e.g., Brown, Kane, & Echols, 1986; Crisafi & Brown, 1986; Holyoak, Junn, & Billman, 1984) have shown that preschoolers are capable of perceiving the similarity between two stories which are related metaphorically, not only when the similarity is perceptual, but also when the structures of relationships in the stories are similar. Going even further, Verbrugge (1986) concluded that relational similarities between the items in a metaphor might be especially salient for young children.

According to Gardner and Winner (1986), genuine metaphorical thinking involves being able to override one's category boundaries. There is evidence that young children are capable of doing this, and should thus be credited with the capacity for metaphorical thinking. For instance, Hudson and Nelson (1984) showed that children younger than three can spontaneously produce metaphors by using terms outside their ordinary category boundaries, even when they have previously demonstrated that they know what those ordinary category boundaries are. Mendelsohn, Robinson, Gardner, and Winner (1984) obtained similar results.

Effectiveness of Instructional Metaphors

Methodologically sound research testing the effectiveness of metaphors as tools for acquiring new knowledge has been scarce. Following is a sampling of studies that have demonstrated the usefulness of metaphors as teaching and learning tools.

Simons (1984) examined the effect of analogies on comprehension of new material in subjects ranging from 10 years of age to adulthood. Students read or listened to new materials which either did or did not contain analogies. For all age groups, and for a variety of instructional topics, when analogies were used as instructional aids, comprehension improved. Simons cited 10 other studies that demonstrated similar differences in learning with and without analogies. His findings also supported his three hypothetical explanations for the effectiveness of analogy—their concretizing, structurizing, and active assimilation functions.

Vosniadou and Ortony (1983) demonstrated that first- and third-graders recalled and answered questions about texts with metaphors better than texts containing the same factual information without metaphors. Furthermore, children who listened to the texts containing metaphors were no more likely than children in the nonmetaphor group to draw erroneous inferences about the topic domain. This is an important point because a common criticism of instructional metaphors has been that learners may transfer irrelevant facts from the vehicle domain to the topic domain.

Eiser, Eiser, and Hunt (1986) compared the effects of explaining hospitalized children's illnesses to them using metaphorical and nonmetaphorical descriptions. In children aged 7 to 11, they found that some aspects of the children's illnesses were better understood following metaphorical as compared to nonmetaphorical explanations. Other studies using adult subjects have also demonstrated the effectiveness of metaphors as teaching and learning tools (e.g., Evans, 1986; Hayes & Tierney, 1982; Reynolds & Schwartz, 1983).

Finally, two studies suggest that instructional metaphors may be especially useful for those students who have the greatest difficulty learning new material. Gabel and Sherwood (1980) examined the effects of teaching high school chemistry concepts with and without instructional metaphors. Students were also tested for level of logical thinking. Overall, there were no significant differences between the metaphor and nonmetaphor groups on a test of concept comprehension. However, among students who scored lower on the logical thinking test, those who learned using metaphors performed significantly better than those who learned without metaphors. Also, among students in the metaphor group, those who actually understood the metaphors performed better than those who failed to understand them.

Bean, Singer, and Cowan (1985) experimented with analogical study guides designed to help high school biology students comprehend and retrieve basic concepts about cells. Study guides contained three columns, the first listing the structures of the cell, the second listing the functions of each structure, and the third listing the parts of a factory to which the structures of the cell could be compared. Compared to traditional study guides, the analogical study guides were more effective for students with lower grades on previous class tests. For students with average and better-than-average performance on previous tests, the analogical study guides provided no advantage.

APPLICATION

Research on children's metaphoric capabilities and the effectiveness of instructional metaphors suggests several things to consider when designing and using metaphors to improve learning. Some of these are considered in the following.

Concreteness

To effectively foster learning, metaphors need to be concrete in nature. All of the following aspects of concreteness may be expected to contribute to learning: (a) provision of perceptual experience of the metaphoric similarity between topic and vehicle (Dent, 1986; Verbrugge, 1986), (b) provision of metaphors in which the topic and vehicle are related by action and/or perceptual similarities (Vosniadou & Ortony, 1986), (c) provision of pictures of the vehicle, especially for lower ability students (Curtis & Reigeluth, 1984), (d) provision of an abstract model representing the essential elements of the metaphor (Beveridge & Parkins, 1987), and (e) using highly imageable language to explain the metaphor (Marschark & Hunt, 1985).

Topic-Vehicle Similarity

The effectiveness of instructional metaphors appears to be influenced by "goodness of fit" between the things being compared (Vosniadou & Ortony, 1983). This might be accomplished by having the target and source domains of an instructional metaphor differ in the smallest possible number of dimensions (Rumelhart & Norman, 1981), or by having a high degree of connotative similarity (e.g., as measured by semantic differential techniques) between topic and vehicle (Williams, 1987).

Harnessing Children's Tendencies

Young children typically attribute human characteristics to animals and inanimate objects. Vosniadou and Ortony (1983) speculated that one of their metaphors, in which characteristics from a human vehicle were transferred to a nonhuman topic, aided their young subjects' comprehension of the topic especially well because it exploited the natural tendency to anthropomorphize, harnessing it in order to teach something new. Inagaki and Hatano (1987) obtained data that are consistent with this view.

These two studies suggest that instructional metaphors using human or humanlike vehicles may be quite effective, especially for young children, when the attributes to be transferred to the topic are congruent with human characteristics.

Vehicle Well Understood

Curtis and Reigeluth (1984) suggested that the vehicle of an instructional metaphor should be thoroughly explained or described to students before using it to teach new content. Data obtained by Hayes and Tierney (1982) support this point.

Specification of Relevant/Irrelevant Elements

Perkins (1986) pointed out that models of new subject matter are inherently ambiguous. Teachers should, therefore, specifically point out to students those aspects of a metaphor that are applicable in the new domain as well as those that are not. Several other authors have made similar suggestions (e.g., Hayes & Tierney, 1980; Ortony, 1979; Perkins, 1986; Reigeluth & Stein, 1983; Simons, 1984; Verbrugge & McCarrell, 1977).

Placement of Metaphor

Perkins (1986) suggested that instructional metaphors should be presented close to the beginning of a new body of information. Coming early in the learning process, a good metaphor will be useful at each subsequent step along the way.

According to Curtis and Reigeluth (1984), the most effective use of metaphors appears to be as either advance organizers or embedded activators within the material being learned. As an advance organizer, a metaphor may provide information to which the learner can refer later. As an embedded activator, it may be used to explain preceding information and to introduce subsequent information.

Age-Appropriate Difficulty

Nippold, Leonard, and Kail (1984) found that for 7- and 9-year-olds, so-called "proportional" metaphors were more difficult to comprehend than simpler "similarity" metaphors. Proportional metaphors are ones in which four or more elements (rather than the customary two) are compared in a proportional fashion. As an example, Billow (1975) offered "My head is an apple without any core," in which three stated elements (head, apple, and core) must be complemented by an implied fourth (brain) to obtain the proportion: (head:apple), (brain:core). However, there is an easier way to characterize proportional metaphors. They are simply metaphors with elaborated vehicles. In the example just given, the elaborated vehicle, "apple without any core," is a noun phrase rather than a simple noun. In any event, proportional metaphors are understandably more difficult for children to understand than simpler, unelaborated metaphors. The lesson for the teacher using instructional metaphors is that the most effective metaphors are age-appropriate ones.

Besides not being unnecessarily elaborated, instructional metaphors should have clear and unambiguous interpretations. Also, the topics and vehicles of instructional metaphors should be recognizable by learners when they hear their labels. Learners should also be able to identify and understand the semantic features of topic and vehicle that are essential to the metaphor. Finally, tasks on which young children are required to think metaphorically and also *dem-*

onstrate that ability should require a minimum of linguistic skills (Verbrugge, 1986).

Diagnosis of Learner Errors

For any new domain more than one useful instructional metaphor may be available. In fact, metaphors may be useful not only for initially teaching a concept, but also for teaching alternate conceptualizations. According to Rumelhart and Norman (1981), this might be the primary role of metaphor and analogy.

These authors as well as others (e.g., Gentner & Gentner, 1983) state that the difficulties following from thinking based on a particular model are often predictable because among the things transferred from a metaphor's source domain to its target domain are certain operations. Sometimes these operations are applicable in the target domain, and sometimes they are not. Common student problems, therefore, include (a) transferring features of the source domain incorrectly to the target domain, and (b) difficulty learning target domain operations that are not implicit in the source domain. Rumelhart and Norman (1981) suggested using the errors that learners make while learning in a new domain to determine what mental models they are basing their thinking upon. Teacher corrections and subsequent learning activities can then be directed toward modifying or replacing the inadequate models. Another way to help students avoid problems in transferring features from the source domain to the target domain is to provide countermodels that illustrate opposite or contrasting cases. This helps especially when subtle distinctions between domains need to be made (Perkins, 1986).

To make a new domain understandable, students must be provided with metaphorical frameworks that are more appropriate than those they would otherwise use. However, for a new area of knowledge that students know nothing about, any new model that a teacher presents is likely to be incomplete. Perfect instructional metaphors are rare. Rumelhart and Norman (1981), therefore, suggested giving students several different conceptual models based on different metaphors, each one simple, each one making a different point, and each one with its own area of application. Apparently one of the things that happens as a person becomes "expert" in a new domain is that he gets better at choosing the best metaphor for the situation at hand.

Pellegrino (1985) and others have broken down the process of solving the kind of analogy problems contained in many ability tests into distinct component processes. This kind of reasoning may be similar to that required for learners to benefit from instructional metaphors. Teachers who are knowledgeable about the component processes of analogical thinking are in good position to diagnose which processes students are having trouble with as well as to directly train students on each of the component processes.

Direct Instruction in Metaphorical Thinking

Readence, Baldwin, and Head (1986, 1987) developed a method, based on the direct explicit teaching of reading comprehension (e.g., Pearson, 1984), for teaching elementary school children to interpret metaphors. They hypothesized that successfully interpreting a metaphor requires (a) the ability to identify the prominent attributes of the metaphor's topic and vehicle, and (b) vocabulary knowledge of the words contained in the metaphor. These hypotheses were confirmed by Baldwin, Luce, and Readence (1982) and by Readence, Baldwin, and Rickelman (1983) respectively.

The elements of these authors' instructional package included (a) informing students of the purpose of the instruction, (b) explaining how to apply the strategy, (c) modeling the strategy, (d) monitoring students' practice of the strategy, (e) providing feedback as instruction proceeded from simple to complex metaphors, (f) having students try out the strategy while "thinking aloud," (g) helping students develop ways to self-monitor their use of the strategy, and (h) gradually giving students more responsibility for their own learning. The experimental approach to teaching metaphor interpretation proved to be superior to more traditional approaches. In addition, both teachers and students found the program valuable and enjoyable.

Thompson (1986) reported similar results for junior high students involved in a program for learning metaphor interpretation that also focused on component processes. He emphasized using visual aids, such as a chart listing the attributes of a metaphor's topic and vehicle, and indicating those that are shared with the vehicle and those that are not.

Most information processing researchers agree that the processes involved in analogical reasoning include (a) encoding processes, in which the important attributes of the source and target domains are discovered and represented in memory; (b) attribute comparison processes, which include inferring the relationships between the elements in the source domain, and determining the relationship between the source and target domains; and (c) application processes, in which the relationships discovered by the attribute comparison processes are used to determine unspecified information in the target domain (Pellegrino, 1985). Direct instruction on these component processes should lead to more effective analogical reasoning by students and, consequently, a greater likelihood of their benefiting from instructional metaphors.

In fact, two studies found that this kind of training improved analogy problem solving ability in 4th-, 8th-, and 10th-graders (Alexander, Haensley, Crimmins-Jeanes, & White, 1986) and in four-year-olds (Alexander & White, 1986). In the latter case, the effects of training were still evident a month later, and the children's responses indicated that following training they paid greater attention to the higher-order relations within and between pairs of terms in analogy problems.

Pellegrino's (1985) findings suggest that focusing instruction on certain key component skills might yield the greatest dividends in terms of improved analogical reasoning. For instance, the most successful analogical reasoning involves, first of all, understanding and following the "rules of the game," or the steps one must go through when confronting an analogy requiring interpretation.

Furthermore, the best analogical problem solvers spend more time than poorer problem solvers in the encoding phase which means mentally activating and examining what one knows about the source and target domains before going on to subsequent steps in the problem solving sequence. Doing a thorough, precise job at this initial step seems to facilitate the steps that follow. The work of Schustack and Anderson (1979) supports this suggestion.

Conversely, less skilled analogical reasoners typically have trouble with attribute identification processes, such as discovering the relationships that are common to the source and target domains, and ignoring those that are dissimilar.

Student-Produced Metaphors

Perkins (1986) suggested that teachers should not be solely responsible for developing instructional metaphors. Students should also be asked to produce new metaphors and models. Not only will this cause students to become actively and creatively involved in their own learning, but their productions will also provide the teacher with feedback about whether they are understanding the new domain. Students should also be asked to compare and contrast models. This will raise students' level of generality. They will begin thinking in terms of families of metaphors and models rather than just in terms of individual ones.

CONCLUSION

There is a considerable body of theory suggesting that metaphors are useful tools for promoting the acquisition of new knowledge. Examples of these theories were presented.

There has been a great deal of research on the development of metaphoric abilities in children. Until recently, the results of that research have been ambiguous concerning the age at which children are able to understand metaphor. However, recent research indicates that preschool children, and possibly even children younger than three, are capable of understanding metaphor under circumstances that take into consideration the limitations on their knowledge and information processing capabilities.

There is much less sound evidence concerning the effectiveness of instructional metaphors, though research in this area is increasing as interest in thinking skills grows. The available evidence generally supports the view that properly designed instructional metaphors can, indeed, play a uniquely important role in the acquisition of new knowledge.

Finally, there are a number of considerations that teachers wishing to employ instructional metaphors should entertain. These were discussed in the final section.

At the outset, I suggested that using metaphors as instructional tools is a little like what Columbus did — going west to get east. At first glance, it seemed that he was going the wrong way. However, those who maintained faith in his judgment eventually realized that he was on the right track. Not only was his method a valid one for getting where he wanted to go, but in fact, it made considerably more sense than doing things the old way. The fact that he did not end up where he thought he would illustrates two final facts of life about metaphors. First, a metaphor is never perfect. But second, those who are nevertheless willing to follow where a metaphor leads, with a sense of discovery and adventure, may find un-dreamed of riches along the way.

REFERENCES

Alexander, P. A., Haensley, P. A., Crimmins-Jeanes, M., & White, C. S. (1986). Analogy training: A study of the effects on verbal reasoning. *Journal of Educational Research, 80*(2), 77-80.

Baldwin, R. S., Luce, T. S., & Readence, J. E. (1982). The impact of subschemata on metaphorical processing. *Reading Research Quarterly, 17*(4), 528-543.

Bean, T. W., Singer, H., & Cowan, S. (1985). Analogical study guides: Improving comprehension in science. *Journal of Reading, 29,* 246-250.

Beveridge, M., & Parkins, E. (1987). Visual representation in analogical problem solving. *Memory & Cognition, 15*(3), 230-237.

Billow, R. M. (1975). A cognitive developmental study of metaphor comprehension. *Developmental Psychology, 11*(4), 415-423.

Bransford, J. D. (1979). *Human cognition: Learning, understanding and remembering.* Belmont, CA: Wadsworth.

Brown, A. L., Kane, M. J., & Echols, C. H. (1986). Young children's mental models determine analogical transfer across problems with a common goal structure. *Cognitive Development, 1*(2), 103-122.

Crisafi, M. A., & Brown, A. L. (1986). Analogical transfer in very young children: Combining two separately learned solutions to reach a goal. *Child Development, 57,* 953-968.

Curtis, R. V., & Reigeluth, C. M. (1984). The use of analogies in written text. *Instructional Science, 13,* 99-117.

Dent, C. H. (1986). The development of metaphoric competence: A symposium. *Human Development, 29*, 223-244.

Eiser, C., Eiser, J. R., & Hunt, J. (1986). Comprehension of metaphorical explanations of illness. *Early Child Development and Care, 26*, 79-87.

Evans, G. E. (1986). Getting through statistics with the help of metaphors. *Journal of Education for Business, 62*(8), 28-30.

Gabel, D. L., & Sherwood, R. D. (1980). Effect of using analogies on chemistry achievement according to Piagetian level. *Science Education, 64*(5), 709-716.

Gardner, H., & Winner, E. (1986). Attitudes and attributes: Children's understanding of metaphor and sarcasm. In M. Perlmutter (Ed.), *Minnesota symposium on child development: Vol. 19. Perspectives on intellectual development* (pp. 131-158). Hillsdale, NJ: Erlbaum.

Gentner, D. (1977). Children's performance on a spatial analogies task. *Child Development, 48*, 1034-1039.

Gentner, D., & Gentner, D. R. (1983). Flowing waters or teeming crowds: Mental models of electricity. In D. Gentner & A. L. Stevens (Eds.), *Mental models* (pp. 213-226). Hillsdale, NJ: Erlbaum.

Hayes, D. A., & Tierney, R. J. (1982). Developing readers' knowledge through analogy. *Reading Research Quarterly, 17*, 256-280.

Holyoak, K. J., Junn, E. N., & Billman, D. O. (1984). Development of analogical problem-solving skill. *Child Development, 55*, 2042-2055.

Hudson, J., & Nelson, K. (1984). Play with language: Overextensions as analogies. *Journal of Child Language, 11*, 337-346.

Inagaki, K., & Hatano, G. (1987). Young children's spontaneous personification as analogy. *Child Development, 58*, 1013-1020.

Marschark, M., & Hunt, R. R. (1985). On memory for metaphor. *Memory & Cognition, 13*(5), 413-424.

Mendelsohn, E., Robinson, S., Gardner, H., & Winner, E. (1984). Are preschoolers' renamings intentional category violations? *Developmental Psychology, 20*(2), 187-192.

Nippold, M. A., Leonard, L. B., & Kail, R. (1984). Syntactic and conceptual factors in children's understanding of metaphors. *Journal of Speech and Hearing Research, 27*, 197-205.

Ortony, A. (1975). Why metaphors are necessary and not just nice. *Educational Theory, 25*, 43-53.

Ortony, A. (1979). Beyond literal similarity. *Psychological Review, 86*(3), 161-180.

Paivio, A. (1971). *Imagery and verbal processes*. New York: Holt, Rinehart, & Winston.

Pearson, P. D. (1984). Direct explicit teaching of reading comprehension. In G. G. Duffy, L. R. Roehler, & J. Mason (Eds.), *Comprehension instruction: Perspectives and suggestions* (pp. 223-233). New York: Longman.

Pellegrino, J. W. (1985). Inductive reasoning ability. In R. J. Sternberg (Ed.),

Human abilities: An information-processing approach (pp. 195-225). New York: Freeman.

Perkins, D. N. (1986). *Knowledge as design*. Hillsdale, NJ: Erlbaum.

Petrie, H. G. (1979). Metaphor and learning. In A. Ortony (Ed.), *Metaphor and thought* (pp. 438-461). Cambridge: Cambridge University Press.

Plato. (1956). Meno. In E. H. Warmington, P. G. Rouse, & W. H. D. Rouse (Eds. and Trans.), *Great dialogues of Plato* (pp. 28-68). New York: Mentor.

Readence, J. E., Baldwin, R. S., & Head, M. H. (1986). Direct instruction in processing metaphors. *Journal of Reading Behavior, 18*(4), 325-339.

Readence, J. E., Baldwin, R. S., & Head, M. H. (1987). Teaching young readers to interpret metaphors. *The Reading Teacher, 40*(4), 439-443.

Readence, J. E., Baldwin, R. S., & Rickelman, R. J. (1983). Word knowledge and metaphorical interpretation. *Research in the Teaching of English, 17*(4), 349-358.

Reigeluth, C. M., & Stein, F. (1983). The elaboration theory of instruction. In C. M. Reigeluth (Ed.), *Instructional design theories and models: An overview of their current status*. Hillsdale, NJ: Erlbaum.

Reynolds, R. E., & Schwartz, R. M. (1983). Relation of metaphoric processing to comprehension and memory. *Journal of Educational Psychology, 75*(3), 450-459.

Rumelhart, D. E., & Norman, D. A. (1981). Analogical processes in learning. In J. R. Anderson (Ed.), *Cognitive skills and their acquisition* (pp. 335-359). Hillsdale, NJ: Erlbaum.

Schustack, M. W., & Anderson, J. R. (1979). Effects of analogy to prior knowledge on memory for new information. *Journal of Verbal Learning and Verbal Behavior, 18*, 565-583.

Simons, P. R. J. (1984). Instructing with analogies. *Journal of Educational Psychology, 76*, 513-527.

Thompson, S. J. (1986). Teaching metaphoric language: An instructional strategy. *Journal of Reading, 30*(2), 105-109.

Verbrugge, R. R. (1986). Research on metaphoric development: Themes and variations. *Human Development, 29*, 241-244.

Verbrugge, R. R., & McCarrell, N. S. (1977). Metaphoric comprehension: Studies in reminding and resembling. *Cognitive Psychology, 9*, 494-533.

Vosniadou, S. (1987). Children and metaphors. *Child Development, 58*, 870-885.

Vosniadou, S., & Brewer, W. F. (1987). Theories of knowledge restructuring in development. *Review of Educational Research, 57*(1), 51-67.

Vosniadou, S., & Ortony, A. (1983). The influence of analogy in children's acquisition of new information from text: An exploratory study. In J. A. Niles & L. A. Harris (Eds.), *Searches for meaning in reading/language processing and instruction* (pp. 71-79). Thirty-second Yearbook of the National Reading Conference. Rochester, NY: National Reading Conference.

Vosniadou, S., & Ortony, A. (1986). Testing the metaphoric competence of the young child: Paraphrase vs. enactment. *Human Development, 29*, 226-230.

Vosniadou, S., Ortony, A., Reynolds, R. E., & Wilson, P. T. (1984). Sources of difficulty in children's comprehension of metaphorical language. *Child Development, 55*, 1588-1606.

White, C. S., & Alexander, P. A. (1986). Effects of training on four-year-olds' ability to solve geometric analogy problems. *Cognition and Instruction, 3*(3), 261-268.

Williams, P. S. (1987). *Quality in linguistic metaphors*. Unpublished doctoral dissertation, Texas Tech University, Lubbock.

Chapter 4

Using Humor to Develop Creative Thinking

Avner Ziv, PhD

SUMMARY. The chapter presents theoretical as well as empirical evidence relating the concept of divergent thinking or creativity to humor. Humor is viewed as a two dimensional concept involving both appreciation and creativity. Instruments constructed in order to measure these dimensions are briefly described. While most research on humor focused on humor appreciation, a project developed at Tel Aviv University aimed at exploring and enhancing humor creativity among adolescents as well as a project of teaching teachers to use humor are described. Based on experimental studies presented, humor appears to be an efficient aid in developing creative thinking in adolescents.

When the child has grown up and has ceased to play, and after there has been labouring for decades to envisage the realities of life with proper seriousness, he may one day find himself in a mental situation which once more undoes the contrast between play and reality. As an adult he can look back on the intense serious occupation of today with his childhood games, he can throw off the too heavy burden imposed on him by life and win the high yield of pleasure afforded by *humor*. (Freud, 1908, p. 144)

Freud's genius expressed the relation between childhood play

Avner Ziv is affiliated with the School of Education, Tel Aviv University, Tel Aviv, Israel.

99

and humor. He wrote about this relation in an article in which he tried to explain the psychological dynamics involved in creative writing. By relating playful thinking, daydreaming and humor to the act of creation, Freud pioneered ideas which are now in the frontline of modern research on humor. However, we must remember that Freud was writing about "real creativity" in the adult world. In such creativity, there are two aspects: a process and a product. The creative process involves cognitive, internal operations, not directly observable. The product is the observable behavioral result of the cognitive process. In order to be considered creative, these products have to be public (i.e., open to judgment by others). By using such criteria as originality, validity, aptness and "esthetic fit," the products are considered as creative or not. A book, a symphony, a painting or a theory are examples of such creative products. Such products are only very rarely the results of a child's work. In addition to certain ways of thinking and producing, creativity also involves special skills which are in general the result of years of learning.

Since this article focuses on creativity in children and adolescents only, it should be clear that it deals with the cognitive process involved in the creative act alone. The behavioral product open to social evaluation is nonexistent. It is believed that certain cognitive processes are necessary, but not sufficient, conditions to creativity which has to lead to a public product.

Before going into a review of research on the ways in which humor can be used to encourage creativity, it should be made clear that the term "creativity" currently has a different meaning from the one used by Freud. Actually, the new meaning is different from that of almost all psychological writing prior to the '60s. Till then, creativity was conceptualized as a rare talent and creative people where considered those able to produce something valuable in the fields of art and sciences. The first psychological theory of creativity which was widely accepted (Wallas, 1926) described four stages in the creative act: preparation, incubation, illumination and verification. Therefore, creativity was considered to involve long and sometimes tortuous mental operations, a high level of special skills and motivational qualities such as perseverance, need for achievement, and the willingness to do hard work.

Psychological research done in order to investigate relationships between creativity and humor, uses a different meaning of creativity and special tests to measure it. A short description of the "operationalization" of creativity follows.

DIVERGENT THINKING AND CREATIVITY

Guilford published in 1956 his famous theory on the structure of intellect. In his model, he presented five different types of mental operations. Among them, two types of thinking were distinguished: convergent and divergent. Divergent thinking became for some reason synonymous with creativity. As defined by Guilford "the unique feature of divergent production is that a variety of responses is produced. The product is not completely determined by the given information" (Guilford, 1959, p. 472). Very rapidly, divergent thinking was considered as an important element in creativity (as opposed to convergent thinking, which is related to intelligence). The component elements of divergent thinking were measured, and factorial analysis gave results concerning what Guilford (1959) called "primary traits related to creativity." Special tests were constructed to measure these traits. Most creativity tests devised later, following Guilford's impetus, measured the variables he described. These were:

Fluency of thinking. The quantitative aspect of fertility of ideas. Four factors were identified: *word fluency* (the ability to produce words containing a specific letter or a combination of letters), *associational fluency* (the ability to give synonyms for words in a limited time), *expressional fluency* (the production of phrases or sentences expressing given ideas) and *ideational fluency* (the ability to produce ideas to fulfill certain requirements, such as for example "as many as possible uses for a brick").

Flexibility. The ability to avoid old ways of thinking and strike out in new directions. Two kinds of flexibility were found: *spontaneous* (producing a wide variety of ideas) and *adaptive* (as in finding solutions for matchsticks problems).

Originality. Scores are given for *infrequent responses* (in the statistical sense), *remote associations* ("what would happen if"), *cleverness* of responses (such as, for example, in tasks where the subjects are asked to give a title to a short story).

Elaboration. Enrichment of a given stimulus such as a few simple lines, an object or a sketched plan.

Very rapidly, new instruments measuring these and other aspects of divergent thinking were published. These tests were named "creativity tests" and children, adolescents and adults with high scores on these tests were considered "creative." The best known among them are the Torrance Test of Creativity (TTC, Torrance, 1974) and the Wallach & Kogan Creativity Test (Wallach & Kogan, 1965).

It is important to keep in mind that creativity, as measured by tests, relates only to the cognitive aspect and not to the behavioral product. Thus, children and adolescents who are called "highly creative" on the basis of scores on these tests do not necessarily create products generally associated with the work of creative people such as writers, musicians and so on. A different approach is used in humor research. Humor creation is judged by the simple and obvious criteria of creating something judged by others to be humorous. In order to understand the relationship between creativity and humor, a short description of humor measurement in humor research is presented.

HUMOR: CONCEPTUALIZATION AND OPERATIONAL DEFINITIONS

There are many kinds of humor and in this article I shall focus on *intentional humor* (i.e., humor created by people in order to be enjoyed by people). This humor can be conceptualized as a form of communication. The message it transmits is voluntary, and its main objective is to elicit a behavioral response (laughter) reflecting a cognitive-emotional process. A short clarification of terms used in this conceptualization is needed. First, as with any *communication*, it implies three elements: a communicator, a listener and a message. In our case, the communicator is the humorist, (i.e., the originator or the creator of the communication and not someone repeating what he heard (telling jokes proves more about a person's memory than his humor). Second, the humorous message is *voluntary*: the humorist makes it up and transmits it knowingly. Slipping on a banana peel and falling may be perceived as funny, but if the fall is involuntary, no humor (intentional humor, as defined) is involved. The reaction to the humorous communication is on two levels: a *cognitive-emotional* process, and a *behavioral* response. The cognitive-emotional process relates to the feeling of mastery (the cognitive process of understanding) and to the pleasure felt in dealing with emotions in acceptable, nonthreatening ways as well as in the tension release. The behavioral response, smiling and/or laughter, is the expressive and observable element of the internal cognitive-emotional process.

From this conceptualization, two main dimensions of humor can be distinguished: (a) humor creation, and (b) humor appreciation. Most of the published research on humor has measured the appreciation dimension. Goldstein and McGhee (1972) showed that among the 122 studies of humor published since 1900, only nine focused on the creative aspect of humor. In most research projects, subjects were presented with cartoons or jokes and asked to rate them for "funniness" (e.g., see La Fave, Haddad & Maesen, 1976). One well known test, called "sense of humor test" (Cattell & Tollefson, 1963) measured this complex and elusive concept by asking subjects to choose the "funnier" joke in each of 120 pairs of jokes presented. In addition to such measures, observational techniques have also been used, especially with children (McGhee, 1979). These measures can be considered as dealing with the appreciation dimension.

The creative dimension of humor has been investigated using such tasks as asking students to write captions for cartoons. Some studies quantified the production of such captions (Babad, 1974), while others had subjects rate them for "funniness" (Brodzinsky & Rubien, 1977). McGhee (1974) asked children to create humorous answers to double meaning and absurdity riddles, and finally some researchers studied biographies of humorists (Fisher & Fisher, 1981; Fry & Allen, 1975; Janus, 1975; Janus, Bess & Janus, 1978; Wilde, 1973; Ziv, 1984).

In what follows, I will describe results from research projects completed at Tel Aviv University, and a short description of the measurement used. These tests were developed in 1976 when the Tel Aviv Creativity-Humor (TACHUM) project began. Groups of

15-18 adolescents were invited to the University for a discussion session about research on adolescence conducted by adolescents. Before coming to the University sessions, each group completed a *sociometry of humor* test. This was possible since the adolescents knew each other rather well (they were meeting regularly in the scout movement). Their instructor asked them to complete the test. The sociometry of humor test presented to each subject an alphabetical list of all members of the group. Four columns are drawn, each with a title ranging from "has no sense of humor," to "has a very good sense of humor." Each subject places in the appropriate column his evaluation of each of his peers (and also of himself). The scoring is based on allotting one point to a notation on the first column (has no sense of humor), two points in the second column and so on (see Ziv, 1979a, for additional details).

At the University session, adolescents were seated in a circle, and 12 graduate students in psychology specially trained for observation of the different tasks, were sitting around in an external circle. Their task was to observe and note the adolescents' behavior. In addition, a video camera filmed the entire session. Adolescents were given a series of tasks in order to measure the two dimensions of humor:

1. Humor Appreciation

(a) Laughter and smiling. Each student observed two adolescents and noted each occurrence of smiling and laughter. The opportunity for laughter was given by two situations: listening to a recording of a famous comedian and reacting to ideas in a creativity test.

(b) Judgment of funniness. A booklet with 12 captionless cartoons (chosen by a panel of adolescent judges as being highly humorous) was given to each child. They were asked to score each cartoon on a "funniness scale." Previous research (Ziv, 1979b) has shown that people who say they enjoy humor give higher scores to cartoons than those who do not enjoy humor as they are characterized (among other things) by a tendency to consider humorous stimuli as not very funny. The scores on this test were called "humor evaluation."

(c) "Sense of humor" scale. A seven point scale was used to measure individuals' level of humor in their everyday life.

2. Humor Creation

(a) Creativity test. This test was given to the entire group and children answered orally. All those who work on such tasks know that the longer the period allowed for such an exercise, the greater the number of original answers that are given. Many of these original answers are humorous. Each child was given a point on humor creation when he gave an answer that caused three members of the group to smile or laugh.

(b) Cartoon captions. Each child was asked to write captions for the 12 cartoons in the cartoon booklet. These captions were later scored for "funniness" by trained graduate students.

(c) "Sense of humor" scale. Part of this scale also included a seven point scale used to measure the amount of humor produced in the individual's everyday life.

This procedure was replicated with six groups of adolescents. Three main scores were calculated: one for humor appreciation, one for humor creation, and one for "sense of humor" which is the sum of the first two.

In studying the relationship between humor and creativity, we must keep in mind that creativity tests measure only the verbal dimension of the cognitive process supposedly involved in the creative act. Therefore, humorous behavior such as clowning should not be expected to be related to scores on creativity tests. In addition, the investigation of the humor-creativity relation should focus on measures of humor creativity, rather than on humor appreciation.

THE THEORETICAL RELATION BETWEEN HUMOR AND CREATIVITY

Penjon, the French philosopher, was probably the first to note that humor, as well as creativity, uses ways of thinking which are somewhat different to the ones involved in the usual rational thinking based on Aristotelian logic. Although he used different terms, his view is clearly related to our topic. In his article he stated:

"laughter is an expression of freedom, freedom from the strict laws of rational thinking and freedom to play with new ideas" (Penjon, 1891, p. 121). The playfulness involved in humor and laughter is closely related to what is measured by the creativity test. I called this phenomenon *cognitive playfulness* (Ziv, 1981).

Incongruity, one of the main explanations used in cognitive theories of humor, was first introduced by Beattie more than two centuries ago. He wrote:

> Laughter arises from the view of two or more inconsistent, unsuitable, or incongruous parts or circumstances, considered as united in one complex object of assemblage, or as acquiring a sort of mutual relation from the peculiar manner in which the mind takes notice of them. (Beattie, 1776, p. 348)

Many modern theories of humor are based on the incongruity concept (McGhee, 1979; Rothbart, 1976; Schultz, 1972). These theories follow Beattie's approach rather closely and are very helpful in explaining the problem solving process of the person listening to humor. Humor is based on surprise and incongruity, but incongruities can also be interpreted as strange, dangerous or even psychotic. If the listener to the humorous communication is a problem solver, the person creating humor should be considered a "problem constructor." How does he do it? The concept of *bisociation*, proposed by Koestler (1964), is probably the most widely accepted explanation. In his Tryptich model, he suggested humor creation as a model for understanding creativity in the arts and sciences: "The creative act of the humorist consists in bringing about a momentary fusion between two incompatible frames of reference" (Koestler, 1965, p. 94). This fusion is called bisociation, so named "in order to make a distinction between the routine skills of thinking on a single plane" (p. 35). Koestler adds that bisociation is also a main element in scientific creativity.

Although incongruity and bisociation can explain part of the cognitive process involved in humor creation, the explanation is not complete; something which can differentiate between creativity in humor and in other creative acts is still missing. For instance, many symptoms of psychopathology can be viewed as results of bisociation. Claustrophobia is a fusion between two incompatible frames of reference: closed spaces and anxiety. There is nothing in common between claustrophobia and humor. A distinction between science, psychopathology and humor can clarify for us the special clue to humor creation.

Scientific creativity uses general concepts of logic: public and private. Psychopathologic creativity uses paleological or faulty logic described by Arieti (1976). It is a private logic, based on primary processes, which has no meaning but to the individual using it. Finally humor uses a special kind of logic called *"local logic"* (Ziv, 1984). The logic used in humor is "locally" appropriate or appropriate only in a particular sense or context. It is created using divergent thinking but it cannot stand convergent examination. At the same time, it is public and can be understood. An example will best illustrate local logic:

A young woman writes to a matrimonial agency which pairs couple by computer. She is asked to fill in a questionnaire in which she describes the qualities she looks for in a partner. She writes that she would like someone who is not too tall, who likes water sports, who is gregarious and likes formal dressing. The agency sends her a penguin.

There is more than surprise, incongruity and bisociation in this (and most other forms of humor). If the agency would have sent her a horse, it would have been surprising, incongruous and in accordance with the bisociation concept. However, there is more, a certain "fit" exists here. The punch line has local logic: the penguin answers all expressed conditions. Of course, one main condition, not mentioned is not answered. The passage from logic to local logic makes humor possible. The listener has to solve the problem which has some elements of logic, but only within the limited context presented by the joke.

A similar kind of local logic is involved in the creativity tests I described. They ask for divergent thinking but most answers will not stand the examination of convergent thinking. In describing the techniques used by the humorist in his act of creation, Koestler writes about the need for surprise which is attained by an *original* approach to ideas. He also adds the need of "a kind of thinking aside," a shifting of attention to aspects not seen usually. It seems to me that Koestler has described here two elements of divergent thinking as measured in the creativity tests: originality and flexibility.

From all this, it should be expected that humor and creativity (operationally defined as scores on humor and divergent thinking or creativity tests) should be closely related.

HUMOR AND CREATIVITY: EMPIRICAL INVESTIGATIONS

Humor as well as divergent thinking or creativity involves more than cognitive processes. Another common bond between them is a certain attitude towards the environment which I called "*cognitive playfulness*." This attitude implies flexibility in changing frames of references. The flexibility in passing from reality to the imaginary, from seriousness to joking and to an interest in possibilities (in the world "as if") are elements of cognitive playfulness which are important in both creativity and humor.

Cognitive playfulness is readily observable in children. During play, a big box can be an airplane in the morning, a car in the afternoon, and a box to put things in the evening. What a young child does in a concrete, behavioral mode is something done by an older child or an adult in a cognitive mode when answering to a question on the Torrance creativity test concerning "the possible uses of a cardboard box."

Research with elementary school children (Liberman, 1977; Torrance, 1961; Wallach and Kogan, 1965) has shown a significant relationship between playfulness and creativity. Play behavior diminishes with increasing age, as does playfulness with ideas, a victim of growing pressures to be rational and serious. Criticism of "crazy ideas" and nonserious outlooks on life slowly (but very surely) inhibit cognitive playfulness. However, since humor is a trait high on social desirability, it is not discouraged and children and adolescents displaying it enjoy a high social status among their peers (Ganini, 1981). It is possible then that humor keeps alive in certain children and adolescents (probably in adults too) the cognitive playfulness necessary for creative thinking.

Correlational studies have shown significant relations between humor and creativity (Gidynsky, 1972; Hauck and Thomas, 1972; Weisberg and Springer, 1961). However, it should be kept in mind that all these studies measured humor appreciation. Research is rather scarce on humor creation. Getzels and Jackson (1962) found that their high creative adolescents used more humor in their answers to several tests than did low creative ones. McGhee (1980) reports that creativity scores before the age of six did not predict humorous behavior but a significant relation was found after this age. He suggests that creativity is highly unstable during the pre-school and early elementary years. This, and other findings, point out the difference between children's and adult's humor, and it made me focus the TACHUM research project on adolescents and adults who use similar forms of humor.

In order to investigate the relationship between humor and the various aspects of creativity in adolescence, correlational studies were planned. In contrast to the previously mentioned studies, each using a different methodology and each with different instrument measures, four replications using the same tests (with known reliability and validity) were conducted. Humor was measured using both the sociometry of humor test and the humor questionnaire with the two dimensions: humor appreciation and humor creativity. For the divergent thinking measure, the Torrance Creativity Test (TCT) was used. This test measures four aspects of divergent thinking or creativity: flexibility, fluency, originality and elaboration. A score on each aspect is obtained as well as a total score. From four different schools in the Tel Aviv area, one class of 10th graders was randomly chosen. Correlations between the different aspects of humor and creativity tests ranged from .48 to .56, all highly significant relationships. The highest correlations were found between originality and humor creation (Ziv, 1980).

Using a different approach with a different set of subjects, a comparison was made between humorists and nonhumorists. The humorists were chosen in the following way: ninety-eight adolescents (10th and 11th graders) were given sociometry of humor tests in their respective classrooms. Those receiving scores in the upper quartile were called the "humorists" (13 boys and 12 girls). From the remaining adolescents the same number of boys and girls were randomly drawn. The comparison of the two groups on results of the TCT showed significantly higher creativity scores for the humorists. These, as well as the results from the correlational studies, clearly indicate that humor and creativity are closely related. More creative individuals are not only better at creating humor; they also show greater appreciation of humor, say they use humor more in their everyday life, and they are seen by their peers as having a better sense of humor. This relationship was also found in research with adults (Ziv & Diem, 1987).

Another research project (see Ziv, 1976) aimed to study more directly the effects of humor on creativity in an experimental fashion. It was found that adolescents who were given the opportunity to listen to a humorous recording gave significantly more divergent responses on a creativity test than did control groups. One detail of this experiment is worth mentioning for those interested in using humor to enhance creativity. The choice of the humorous recording was important since some humorous stimuli induce laughter while others do not. Very frequently in humor research, the stimuli are chosen by the researcher who uses his own taste and judgment of what is humorous. In this research, the recording was chosen after pretests with eight different humorous recordings played in eight different classrooms of 10th graders. The amplitude and duration of their laughter was recorded, and the record chosen for the experiment was the one eliciting the greatest laughter responses in adolescent groups.

The results of the experiment can be explained by the modeling effects of humor. Listening to humor gives "legitimization" to using incongruities and original ideas and to toying with local logic. Those not having the experience of listening to humor in the classroom chose a more "rational" approach to the test, and their scores on flexibility and originality were lower.

In a second study (Ziv, 1983), the influence of a humorous atmosphere on creativity scores was investigated. Three groups of adolescents participated: two experimental and one control. The first experimental group viewed two humorous video clips (parts of films with Harold Lloyd) that were selected after careful pretesting and found to elicit great laughter responses. After viewing the film, they were asked to write captions for a booklet of 20 cartoons. In the second experimental group, the order was reversed (cartoons first, films later). Children were free to discuss among themselves after the films and cartons were shown. Then, they were asked to complete the TCT test. The control group had only the task of completing the test. Results showed significantly higher scores on the creativity test for the two experimental groups compared to the control one. In a recent article (Isen, Daubman & Nowicki, 1987), a similar study is described in which, for some strange reason, the concept of humor was not once mentioned. In one experiment subjects viewed a five minute comedy video film and then were asked to solve a creative problem. The creative problem was the classic Duncker (1945) demonstration of functional fixedness. The subject's task is to attach a burning candle to the wall in such way that it will burn without dripping on the floor. He is presented with a box of tacks, a book of matches and a candle. Before starting on the task, one group of students viewed a humorous film clip, another a neutral film, and a third group was used as control (no film). Results showed that students viewing the humorous film did significantly better on the problem solving task.

A third study (Ziv, 1983) was aimed at measuring the influence of working on a creativity test following encouragement to give humorous responses. Two groups of adolescents participated, both being given form A of the TCT. Afterwards, the control group continued with form B of the test while the experimental group received special instructions. They were asked to continue the test but "now you are asked to try to give as many humorous answers as you possibly can." Results showed that the experimental group obtained significantly higher scores on part two of the test (scores of the first part were used as covariates for both groups). In addition to the causes of the positive influences of humor on scores of divergent thinking, three additional by-products of the presentation of the humorous stimuli were proposed in order to explain the findings. These were: the introduction of a fun mood, the contagion of laughter appearing in a classroom while watching and listening to humor, and the triggering effect of a humor cue to give original responses. "Fun mood" is a concept introduced by Eastman (1936) who saw it as a main factor explaining humor appreciation. The same stimulus can be considered as humorous under certain conditions and nonhumorous in other conditions. We know for instance that the inability to laugh is one of the main symptoms of depression. The same people, when nondepressed, laugh and can enjoy humor. A person whose wife just left him for the traveling salesman will not appreciate a joke about cuckold and salesmen. In short, the same stimulus may be perceived as serious, even tragic or humorous depending on our mood. In the experiment described, a "fun mood" was introduced in the classroom by showing the films and working with cartoons. This mood probably influenced the children's answers on the creativity test. More "crazy ideas," original bisociations, and greater fluency, improve scores on divergent thinking tests.

One well known characteristic of laughter is its contagious aspect (McGhee, 1979). Laughing together probably augments the fun mood and contributes to the tendency to look for funny, incongruous and original answers to the creativity test. Creating a humorous atmosphere, letting people laugh together not only improves their mood but probably also their willingness to be more free in expressing their original ideas. Of course, the greater readiness to laugh can be induced not only by contagion or fun mood but also by other stimuli such as alcohol (Weaver et al., 1985).

The triggering effect of humor was shown in the experiment in which children received instructions to answer humorously to the creativity test. Such instructions are perceived as a cue for generating unconventional responses. A cognitive playfulness is induced, it's effect being reflected in the answers to the divergent test.

CONCLUSION

Theoretical views as well as the empirical data available point out very clearly the close relationship between humor and creativity. However, it should be clear that what is measured by creativity tests is related to divergent thinking only. Much more is needed from a person to become creative than having a high score on these tests. However, divergent thinking is an important element in the cognitive approach to problems. Many educators have written about the over-emphasis put by schools on convergent thinking. The need to develop divergent approaches, not in place of, but in addition to convergent ones, is accepted by most of those involved in the educational process.

Among the many ways proposed to enhance creativity, humor has been neglected. One possible explanation for this neglect is the belief that humor is a personality trait and that it cannot be learned. Available data (Ziv, in press) suggest the contrary: humorous stimuli are all around us and being open to them can be helpful. Using tasks in which cognitive playfulness is encouraged can improve one's appreciation to humor. Even humor creation can be learned in a certain measure, and various techniques have been developed to teach it. In the framework of the TACHUM project, a one semester course for teachers was conducted. Its objective was to train teachers to understand, create and use humor in their teaching. One example of a semester long exercise is briefly described:

Each week students were instructed to pick 10 cartoons from one weekend newspaper. They were asked to strike out the original captions and create others. At the weekly meeting, all students arranged the cartoons on big cardboard panels. On each panel, the same cartoon with 20 different captions each having a number was presented. Then, all students became "critics." They passed and viewed the panels. On a pre-prepared score sheet, they give a score on "funniness" to all new captions of each cartoon. Then scores were computed, and the highest scores given to each cartoon's caption were announced. A discussion followed: its objective was to understand why these cartoons were considered funny. The functions of humor, the bisociation techniques used, the surprise and incongruity elements as well as originality were discussed. Many new insights on humor creation and appreciation were expressed during these discussions. This procedure went on for an entire semester. A group of judges was given the cartoons from the first and the last two sessions, and was asked to score them on funniness (of course, the judges did not know which captions were from the beginning or the end of the semester). Statistical analysis showed clear differences: the captions from the last two sessions were scored as much more humorous than those from the first ones.

Many such exercises were devised and some are now used in workshop with adolescents. A follow-up of three such courses is now in progress and a description of the techniques used in teaching humor is in press (Ziv, in press).

The tension release aspect of laughter and its contagious effects can influence group cohesiveness. This in turn reduces social anxiety. We know that one of the greatest obstacles to divergent thinking is the fear of criticism from one's social environment. The pressures to be practical, logical and economic in our thinking are trademarks of our cultural values. If social anxiety is somewhat lessened, if judgmental attitudes are not taken as too menacing, "aventurous," novel and original ideas are more easily expressed.

Research on humor has clearly documented a positive relationship with creativity. There is also convincing evidence that increased exposure to humor can enhance the level of one's creativity. Given the growing interest in a balance of emphasis on convergent and divergent thinking among many educators, the importance of improving children's humor skills is evident. What is needed is the dissemination of the accumulated knowledge in humor research to those able to use it. Teachers who would like to develop divergent thinking in their students should try and bring humor into the school. They would also benefit from the positive results showed by research on humor's influence on learning (see Bryant and Zillman chapter in this volume). How this should be done depends mostly on the creative potential of teachers in finding ways to apply academic research to the realities of the educational environment.

REFERENCES

Arieti, S. (1976). *Creativity: The magic synthesis*. New York: Basic Books.

Babad, E. (1974). A multi-method approach to the assessment of humor: A critical look at humor tests. *Journal of Personality, 42*, 618-631.

Beattie, J. (1776). On laughter and ludicrous composition. *Essays*. Edinburgh: Creech.

Brodzinsky, D., & Rubien, J. (1977). Humor production as a function of sex of subject, creativity and cartoon content. *Journal of Consulting and Clinical Psychology, 44*, 597-600.

Cattell, R., & Tollefson, D. (1963). *Handbook for the IPAT humor test of personality*. Champagne, IL: Institute for Personality and Ability Testing.

Duncer, K. (1945). On problem solving. *Psychological Monographs, 58*.

Eastman, M. (1936). *Enjoyment of laughter*. New York: Simon & Schuster.

Fisher, S., & Fisher, R. (1981). *Pretend the world is funny and forever: A psy-*

chological analysis of comedians, clowns, and actors. Hillsdale, NJ: Lawrence Erlbaum Associates.

Freud, S. (1950). Creative writers and day dreaming. In J. Starchey (Ed.), *Standard edition of the complete psychological works of Sigmund Freud* (rev. ed). New York: Hogarth Press.

Fry, W. Jr., & Allen, M. (1975). *Make 'em laugh*. Palo Alto: Science and Behavior books.

Ganini, I. (1981). *Leadership and popularity of humorous adolescents*. Unpublished manuscript. Tel Aviv University, Tel Aviv, Israel.

Getzels, J., & Jackson, P. (1962). *Creativity and Intelligence*. New York: John Wiley & Sons.

Gidinsky, C. G. (1972). *Associative shift, peer rejection and humor response in children: An exploratory study*. Unpublished doctoral dissertation, Columbia University, New York.

Guilford, P. (1956). The structure of intellect. *Psychological Bulletin, 53*, 267-293.

Guilford, P. (1959). Traits of creativity. In H. H. Anderson (Ed.), *Creativity and its cultivation*. New York: Harper.

Hauck, W., & Thomas, J. (1972). The relationship of humor to intelligence, creativity, and intentional and incidental learning. *Journal of Experimental Education, 40*, 52-55.

Isen, A., Daubman, K., & Nowicki. (1987). Positive affect facilitates creative problem solving. *Journal of Personality and Social Psychology, 52*, 1122-1131.

Janus, S. (1975). The great comedians: Personality and other factors. *The American Journal of Psychoanalysis, 35*, 169-174.

Janus, S., Bess, B., & Janus, B. (1978). The great comediennes: Personality and other factors. *The American Journal of Psychoanalysis, 38*, 367-372.

Koestler, A. (1964). *The act of creation*. London: Hutchinson & Co.

LaFave, L., Haddad, J., & Maesen, W. A. (1976). Superiority, enhanced self-esteem, and perceived incongruity humour theory. In A. J. Chapman, & H. C. Foot (Eds.), *Humor and laughter: Theory, research and applications*. London: Wiley.

Liberman, J. (1977). *Playfulness: Its relation to imagination and creativity*. New York: Academic Press.

McGhee, P. (1974). Development of children's ability to create the joking relationship. *Child Development, 45*, 552-556.

McGhee, P. (1979). *Humor: Its origin and development*. San Francisco: W. H. Freeman & Co.

McGhee, P. (1980). Development of the creative aspects of humor. In P. McGhee, & A. Chapman (Eds.), *Children's humor*. New York: John Wiley & Sons.

Penjon, R. (1891). Le rire et la liberte. *Revue Phylosophique, 2*, 113-125.

Rothbart, M. K. (1976). Incongruity, problem-solving and laughter. In A. J.

Chapman, & H. C. Foot (Eds.), *Humor and laughter: Theory, research and applications*. New York: John Wiley & Sons.

Schultz, T. R. (1972). The role of incongruity and resolution in children's appreciation of cartoon humor. *Journal of Experimental Child Psychology, 13*, 456-477.

Torrance, E. P. (1961). Priming creative thinking in the primary grades. *Elementary School Journal, 62*, 139-145.

Torrance, E. P. (1974). *The Torrance test of creative thinking*. Lexington, MA: Ginn & Co.

Wallach, M., & Kogan, N. (1965). *Modes of thinking in young children: A study of the creativity-intelligence distinction*. New York: Holt Reinhart & Winston.

Wallas, B. (1926). *The art of thought*. New York: Harcourt & Brace.

Weaver, J., Masland, J., Kharzimie, S., & Zillman, D. (1985). Effects of alcoholic intoxication on the appreciation of different types of humor. *Journal of Personality and Social Psychology, 49*, 781-787.

Weisberg, P., & Springer, K. (1961). Environmental factors in creative functioning. *Archives of General Psychiatry, 5*, 64-74.

Wilde, L. (1973). *The great comedians*. Secaucus, NJ: Citadel Press.

Ziv, A. (1976). Facilitating effects of humor on creativity. *Journal of Educational Psychology, 68*, 318-432.

Ziv, A. (1979a). Sociometry of humor: Objectifying the subjective. *Perceptual and Motor Skills, 38*, 431-432.

Ziv, A. (1979b). *L'humour en education: Approche psychologigue*. Paris: Editions Sociales Francaises.

Ziv, A. (1980). Humor and creativity. *The Creative Child and Adult Quarterly, 5*, 159-170.

Ziv, A. (1981). *The psychology of humor*. Tel Aviv: Yahdav.

Ziv, A. (1983). The influence of humorous atmosphere on divergent thinking. *Contemporary Educational Psychology, 8*, 68-75.

Ziv, A. (1984). *Personality and Sense of Humor*. New York: Springer.

Ziv, A., & Diem, J. M. (1987). *Le sens de l'humor*. Paris: Dunod.

Ziv, A. (in press). *Studying humor seriously; Uses of humor in education* (Hebrew).

PART III:
SOCIAL AND
EMOTIONAL BENEFITS

Introduction

This section examines the ways in which humor can contribute to children's social and emotional functioning and development. McGhee suggests that the ability to use humor effectively in ongoing social interaction can be viewed as a social skill, and that the possession of such skills makes an important contribution to one's overall level of social competence. The social functions of humor, both for the humor initiator and the social group, are also discussed. What motivates the humorous child's early interest in humor? McGhee suggests that many children learn that initiating humor in social contexts allows them to maintain an already developed assertive and dominating style of social interaction, and to do so in a way that also allows them to gain attention and affection from others.

Martin begins with the basic assumption that the path toward growing up is inevitably pebbled with varying amounts of stress. He develops the view that the ability to use humor in the midst of stress plays an important role in daily coping effectiveness. This coping skill should help promote healthy emotional adjustment in both children and adults, but acquiring the skill as a child may be especially important for using it as a adult. Accordingly, Martin

117

underscores the importance of parents supporting the development of their child's sense of humor in this respect as well as serving as models of how to use humor to help cope with stress in their own lives.

Chapter 5

The Contribution of Humor to Children's Social Development

Paul E. McGhee, PhD

SUMMARY. Humor's ability to contribute to children's social development is examined in this chapter. It is suggested that humor be viewed as a component of social competence. General social functions of humor are discussed, including the facilitation of social interaction, development of friendships and popularity, provision of a socially acceptable means of expressing hostility, and softening of an assertive/dominating style of interaction with others. Humor's usefulness in helping the humor initiator search for or communicate information (such as like or dislike for another) or to save face is also discussed. It is concluded that the development of heightened early humor helps to optimize children's social development.

Apte (1987) recently noted that "having a sense of humor has become a core value in American society." We look very favorably upon those who have a good sense of humor and generally take pride in having one ourselves. It has long been known that humor and laughter are most likely to occur in social contexts, but although numerous studies have been completed on social aspects of children's humor and laughter (see Chapman, 1983; and Chapman, Smith & Foot, 1980, for a review), little attention has been given to the ways in which the early enhancement of a child's humor skills contributes to social development in a broader sense. The present

Paul E. McGhee is affiliated with Laboratoire de Psychologie Différentielle, Université de Paris, V, Paris, France, and the Department of Human Development and Family Studies, Texas Tech University, Lubbock, TX.

119

article conceptualizes humor as a valuable component of effective social functioning, and suggests that the child or adolescent who becomes especially adept at inserting humor into ongoing social interaction may be expected to demonstrate higher levels of inter-personal competence in other respects as well. That is, a child (or adult) considered to be a socially competent person may be ex-pected to have developed a broad range of interpersonal skills. The timely and effective use of humor is merely one — albeit an impor-tant one — of these skills.

HUMOR AS A COMPONENT
OF SOCIAL COMPETENCE

Research on social/interpersonal competence among both chil-dren and adults has increased sharply in the past decade. The most consistently agreed-upon definition of interpersonal competence fo-cuses on the achievement of interpersonal goals (e.g., see Ford, 1982; Krasnor & Rubin, 1983). Individuals may vary in the particu-lar goals they pursue, but we can consider the child or adult to be more competent to the extent that s/he is successful in reaching the goal being pursued. Presumably, the socially competent child has a relatively broad range of social skills to draw from and is able to exercise some degree of flexibility in tailoring his or her behavior so as to be most appropriate and most effective in the present social context. As noted above, humor is viewed here as simply one form of behavior that the individual may call upon in the process. Kane, Suls and Tedeschi (1977), Foot (1986) and others have emphasized the effectiveness of humor in achieving interpersonal goals. Foot noted that "functionally, there are few more useful social skills than humour."

Anderson and Messick (1974) considered the enjoyment of hu-mor, play and fantasy to be one of 29 different aspects of social competence that might be displayed by young children. Consistent with this view, Connolly and Doyle (1984) found that preschoolers who engaged in more frequent and more complex fantasy play scored higher on several different measures of social competence. No data were obtained on humor, but preschool children who engage in frequent fantasy play may also be expected to be frequent initiators of humor (see McGhee, 1979a).

Measures of interpersonal competence (with some exceptions) have generally not included items on humor initiation. This being the case, a strong argument for the contribution of humor initiation skills to social competence might be made if measures of interpersonal competence can be shown to be significantly positively related to measures of humor initiation.

Empirical Support for the Link Between Humor Initiation and Interpersonal Competence

Both Turner (1980) and Bell, McGhee and Duffey (1986) argued that the extent to which one monitors one's verbal and nonverbal behavior, as a function of situational cues present, might be considered an index of one's interpersonal competence. High self-monitors have been found to demonstrate greater social sensitivity (Geizer, Rarick & Soldow, 1977) and greater control over their display of emotions (Snyder, 1974). It would seem, then, that high self-monitors should be better able to judge when humor might be appropriate in a given situation and to effectively produce it when it seems called for. Consistent with this view, Turner (1980) found that among college students high self-monitors were more likely than lows to generate humorous remarks both in spontaneous discussion groups and, when specifically asked to do so, in a humorous monologue. They also rated themselves as being more witty than did low self-monitors and produced captions to cartoons that were judged to be funnier than those produced by lows. Similarly, Bell, McGhee and Duffey (1986) found that college students who rated themselves as more frequent initiators of humor had higher self-monitor scores. Even among a sample of elderly women, high self-monitors reported that they did more joking.

I know of no published data which specifically link humor production among children to measures of social competence. However, I have obtained (unpublished) data for four- to six-year-olds demonstrating a significant positive relationship between frequency of humor initiated during spontaneous social play and numerous items on the California Preschool Social Competence Scale (Levine, Elzey & Lewis, 1969).

While little research has been completed along these lines, then, the data that do exist support the view that the initiation of humor in social interaction is positively related to one's overall level of social competence. The fact that this link appears to be present as early as the preschool years suggests that the early development of skills at producing humor may contribute to social development throughout childhood.

Humor's contribution to social competence may be, at least in part, achieved through its impact on communication skills. That is, an effective communicator frequently uses humor to attract or maintain attention, to express views otherwise difficult to communicate, etc. Surprisingly, Carson, Skarpness, Shultz and McGhee (1986) found that even among four- to five-year-olds communicative competence (as measured by the Communication Developmental Age Scale of the Developmental Profile II; Alpern, Ball & Shearer, 1980) was significantly positively related to frequency of both verbal and behavioral initiation of humor. Children who were more advanced in their communicative development not only initiated humor more often; they also laughed more at the humor of other children and at other events around them than did children delayed in their development of communicative competence. Sherman (1984) conceptualized shyness among eight- to thirteen-year-olds as a form of inadequate communication skills. Consistent with the above findings, he found that children who see themselves as shy also see themselves as not being very funny.

GENERAL FUNCTIONS OF HUMOR INITIATION

If we accept the view that humor plays an important role in the development of children's social skills, what kinds of positive functions can it be expected to perform both for the initiator of the humor and for the group in which the humor occurs? Humor researchers have pointed to several important functions of humor in social interaction. Some of these are of a very general nature and operate in a broad range of social situations while others are very specific to the social context in question. The former are discussed in the next section and the latter are discussed in the section following.

Facilitation of Social Interaction

From the group's point of view, the most commonly referred to positive function of humor is that it serves as a "social lubricant" (e.g., see Martineau, 1972). It makes social interaction easier and more enjoyable. The individual who knows when and how to use humor puts others at ease and creates an environment in which all forms of communication are easier. Along these lines, Kane, Suls and Tedeschi (1977) noted that "a cheerful demeanor is an invitation to interaction. Ready humor indicates a spontaneity and joy in relating to others . . ." (p. 16). While the "need" for humor to make communication easier in certain situations is undoubtedly greater for adolescents and adults than for children, the acquisition of this social skill during childhood paves the way for its eventual effective use.

The most important research finding along these lines is that those who initiate humor more often have been found to actually show more social participation or to be judged by their peers as being more sociable at both the preschool (McGhee & Lloyd, 1982) and junior high school levels (Masten, 1986) as well as among adults (Duncan, 1984; Goodchilds & Smith, 1964). Thus, children who become more interested in and skilled at humor may be expected to play important roles in most forms of social interaction throughout childhood.

Popularity and Friendship: The Receipt of Positive Forms of Attention from Others

It is difficult not to like someone who makes you laugh. Thus, children who become more skilled at producing humor (and this should result from doing it more often) in social contexts should be more popular among their peers and find it easier to develop new friendships. Research findings have supported this view for children (Sherman, 1985), adolescents (Fabrizi & Pollio, 1987; Masten, 1986; Ziv, 1984) and adults (Goodchilds, 1972; O'Connel, 1969). Sherman found that children who were rated by their peers as being less humorous were specifically singled out as children they liked the least. It was the children that were given higher humor ratings who were most often picked as someone they would like to do things with (e.g., eat lunch, study, or go to a movie). Sherman described these children with lower peer humor ratings as "socially distant." Consistent with this finding, Masten found that limited humor production was associated with being withdrawn, quiet, shy or unhappy. By college age, "entertainingness has been found to be one of three basic dimensions of friendship" (Murstein & Burst, 1985). Since humor undoubtedly plays a major role in determining one's entertainingness, the role of humor in friendship development and popularity is not surprising.

Masten (1986) notes that the connection between humor and popularity among peers may be partly a result of heightened social-cognitive abilities. Citing Pellegrini's (1985) finding that "social problem-solving abilities and interpersonal awareness are related to peer reputation in middle childhood," she argues that:

> The appreciation and creation of most humor requires social "know-how," in terms of either getting or creating the joke or of sharing the humor with others appropriately. Hence the level of social awareness, knowledge, and sensitivity would be expected to mediate humor behaviors as well as other social activities that contribute to peer reputation. (p. 471)

This suggested heightened social sensitivity among humor initiators is consistent with McGhee's (1980) finding in a longitudinal study that for both boys and girls, early attempts to seek attention, recognition, affection and emotional support were all positively related to frequency of initiation of some form of humor. He concluded that young humorists already had a history of being especially sensitive to adult reactions and appeared to gear much of their behavior toward getting some kind of positive reaction from adults. It is likely that these efforts are extended to peers as well once the child enters school. Consistent with this view, Damico and Purkey (1978) found that class clowns were rated by their teachers as being higher in attention-seeking than other children. The fact that these children are more popular among their peers suggests that they are generally very successful in achieving the attention and affection they are seeking.

Chapman and his associates proposed over a decade ago that when humor and laughter occur in a social context there is generally a strong sense of "sharing the social situation" (Chapman, 1976, 1983; Chapman, Smith & Foot, 1980). This sets the stage for friendships, as noted previously, but also opens the door to more intimate forms of interaction. Thus, Foot (1986) noted that humor is often used as a means of self-disclosure of information that might otherwise be difficult to communicate. Especially during adolescence, joking about something may be used to express fears or anxieties on the one hand and sexual interest on the other. Sanford and Eder (1984), for example, found that young adolescents often used humor to deal with sensitive issues (e.g., sexuality and embarrassing experiences). Greater feelings of intimacy should be produced as a result of these kinds of difficult self-disclosures.

Provision of a Socially Acceptable Means of Expressing Aggression or Hostility

Direct expressions of aggression or hostility are not received positively by either children or adults. Several studies have shown that aggressive children are less popular (e.g., Moore & Updegraff, 1964; Rubin & Daniels-Beirness, 1983). Freud (1960) noted long ago that humor provides a means of expressing aggressive (or sexual) feelings in a way that is not only socially acceptable, but even valued — if done cleverly. Thus, perhaps one of the most important social functions of humor stems from its inherent ambiguity. We can use humor to say either exactly what we mean or just the opposite. If a hostile joke or remark backfires, we can always take it back by claiming that we were "only joking." Wolfenstein (1954) noted that children first begin to use a "joke facade" (i.e., to distance themselves from more direct expressions of aggression by couching it in a joke) at 6-7 years of age. This is also the age at which children start to become capable of understanding double meanings in jokes (McGhee, 1979a), an accomplishment which is a necessary prerequisite for using humor to indirectly accomplish some social purpose. Finally, this age is a major period of transition in the acquisition of a broad range of social-cognitive skills (Shantz, 1983). These findings make a strong case for the view that it is during the elementary school years that children first begin to use humor to achieve social goals.

Several studies now support the view that children with an early predisposition toward aggressive behavior tend to become especially interested in humor and become more frequent initiators of it than their less aggressive peers. In a longitudinal study, McGhee (1980) found that elementary school children had a history of heightened aggression from the preschool years until their present age. Positive relationships between measures of humor initiation and aggression have also been found in college students and in a group of elderly women (Bell, McGhee & Duffey, 1986) and among both amateur (Fisher & Fisher, 1981) and professional (Janus, 1975) comedians. McGhee (1980) argued that these findings are consistent with the Freudian view that children learn to rechannel their hostile feelings and aggressive behavior into a form (jokes, clowning behavior, etc.) that is better received by others.

It is important to note that these data are correlational in nature and that while the correlations are significantly positive they are generally moderate in strength. That is, many children with early patterns of aggressive behavior do not become budding humorists. While no data have been collected along these lines, it seems likely that (at least many of) these children continue to express their aggression in a more direct form as they enter adolescence. The work of Singer and his associates (Singer & Singer, 1979) suggests that it is children with high fantasy skills in a general sense who are least likely to overtly express aggression (e.g., after watching television programs high in violence). These children express their aggressiveness in their fantasy play instead of in overt behavior. Singer has successfully developed fantasy training programs with the specific goal of providing children an indirect means of expressing aggression.

Since humor can be viewed as a form of fantasy activity (see McGhee, 1979a), the same kind of approach might be adopted to teach humor skills to school-aged children. That is, humor training programs might be established either for children in general or for those children classified as "behavior problems" because of their aggressive behavior. No systematic studies of such an approach have yet been completed, although Goodman (1983) has frequently provided humor-skills-training workshops for children in recent years. Since children seem to respond very favorably to such experiences, this may provide an effective tool for helping parents, teachers and others working with children to help manage their aggressive behavior.

Softening of an Assertive/Dominating Style of Interacting with Others

I suggested some years ago (McGhee, 1979b) that children learn very early to use humor as a means of exercising control and power over others (see Ziv, 1984, for a related view). This view was based on findings (McGhee, 1976, 1980) which showed that elementary school children who were more frequent initiators of humor had a history not only of prior aggression (as described previously, but of a general pattern of assertive behaviors toward their peers as early as age three. For example, they talked more, showed more precocious language development, tended to have higher energy levels and were rated as more dominant. Both physically and verbally, then, they had prior histories of being in control of social interaction.

Subsequent studies have supported this view. Thus, McGhee, Bell and Duffey (1986) found that both college students and elderly women who rated themselves as being frequent initiators of humor also rated themselves as being more socially assertive. Among children and adolescents, both teachers (Damico & Purkey, 1978) and peers (Masten, 1986; Ziv, 1984) are more likely to view frequent rather than infrequent humor initiators as being leaders. Studies of adults have also shown humor initiators (especially "wits") to have more power and influence in group interaction (Goodchilds, 1959; O'Connel, 1969; O'Quinn & Aronoff, 1981). The fact that being a humorist tends to make one more likeable undoubtedly contributes to the enhanced social power of humorists. That is, it is much easier to influence people when they like you.

Taken together, the findings discussed in the two preceding sections suggest that children who are physically and verbally dominant over other children tend to become especially interested in humor and try more often to be funny. Since young children tend to be very direct in their interaction style, it is likely that many of these children learn that direct domination is not well received by other children. The adoption of a more humorous style of relating to peers allows a child to maintain dominating patterns of behavior with others while at the same time bringing some enjoyment to them. The child who is often joking or clowning around is likely to retain control of the "strings of social interaction" by continually producing events to which others (are obliged to) respond. By being entertaining and making others laugh, the child learns how to continue dominating others without triggering a negative reaction—and probably without producing any sense of being socially dominated.

SPECIFIC FUNCTIONS OF HUMOR INITIATION

In addition to the mentioned general social functions of humor, a number of specific social goals might also be served by telling jokes or otherwise initiating humor. No attempt has yet been made to determine when children begin to use humor in these ways. While they may begin to appear during the elementary school years, these functions of humor seem to be most typical of adolescents and adults. (See Foot, 1986, for a more extended discussion of these points.)

Search for information. Telling a joke or making a playful/joking comment focusing on a particular theme (e.g., abortion, drugs, etc.) or group (e.g., parents, teachers, another racial-ethnic group, etc.) allows one to discover something about the other person's attitudes, motives and values as a function of their reaction. Hearty laughter, indignation and indifference by the recipient give the initiator very different messages about the extent to which views associated with the joke theme are shared. In this sense, humor can serve as a kind of "social probing." The nature of others' reactions to our jokes also provides a means of judging how well we are accepted by them.

Communication of information. One of the most interesting social properties of humor is that it allows a person to say something "without really saying it." This allows us to take more of a risk in discussing embarrassing topics or in self-disclosing anxieties, fears or other intimate feelings which are difficult to communicate (see Sanford & Eder, 1984). Humor may also be used to indirectly communicate sexual interest in someone (Davis & Farina, 1970). Some adolescents may even use humor to "unmask hypocrisy." They may "use ridicule or sarcasm to show that we do not believe the ostensible motivation for someone's behavior" (Foot, 1986). All of these more sophisticated uses of humor are made possible by the inherent ambiguity of humor.

Communication of liking or disliking. In addition to communicating ideas, humor can be used to express our feelings toward someone. Sharing humor communicates that one likes the other person. The opposite message can also be given, however, by telling jokes which ridicule the ideas or values known to be held by the other. The nature and extent of one's reaction to another's humor can similarly be used to express positive or negative feelings toward the other.

Saving face. A skilled humorist can use a joke or playful remark to replace embarrassment (e.g., due to spilling food on oneself, getting caught in a lie, or committing some other "faux pas") with laughter. Similarly, if tension or hostility between two individuals threatens to provoke a confrontation, a humorous remark can defuse the tension and hostile atmosphere and open the way to a more constructive form of interaction. Each party, in the context of the joke, can back off from the confrontation without losing face.

CONCLUSION

The main purpose of this article was to establish support for the view that heightened skills at producing humor in social interaction contribute positively to social development. Data obtained with both children and adults indicate that skills at introducing humor into ongoing social interaction are closely associated with measures of general social competence. Moreover, both theory and research (see Masten 1986; McGhee, 1979a) suggest that enhanced humor development should be associated with higher levels of cognitive and emotional (e.g., as a result of better coping skills) competence as well as social competence. The fact that the humorist is also generally able to make interaction easier in awkward situations and tends to be more popular combine with this image of interpersonal competence to create a very positive picture of the child (or adult) humorist.

But there appears to be a negative side of humor as well. In spite of their intellectual ability to use a "joke facade" to curb or hide hostile intent or attitudes, elementary school-aged children are often cruel and direct in their humor at someone else's expense. While this quality appears to gradually diminish for most children as they enter adolescence, there are clearly many who retain a more hostile style of joking with and about others. The strong positive relationships found between aggressive and humor initiation among children adds further to a generally negative picture of the young humorist. Moreover, McGhee (1980) found that the amount of prior aggressive behavior was predictive of the amount of hostile humor shown by children as well as overall amount of humor initiated.

It is important to note that there may be certain points in childhood during which frequent humor initiation is most likely to be associated with generally negative patterns of behavior. Thus, Fabrizi and Pollio (1987) found that among 7th graders, humor initiation in a school setting was associated with:

> the so-called "disruptive" behaviors of calling out, being out of one's seat, as well as the tendency to interact regularly with other children in the class and to be talked to about it by the teacher . . . being funny seems to be part of a constellation of acting-out behaviors . . . in need of the control—which the teacher regularly does . . . . (p. 125)

By the 11th grade, however, being funny was associated only with positive forms of behavior in the classroom. Consistent with this change, Ganini (1981; cited by Ziv, this volume) found that adolescents who were humor initiators—especially the more creative ones—were most likely to be seen as leaders by their peers.

During the difficult period of transition into adolescence, then, children may use their humor skills in ways that adults consider very negative. But is this incompatible with the proposed link between humor and social competence? If the socially competent child is one who is effective in achieving social goals, then the nature of the social goals of 7th graders need to be considered. To the extent that their goals are defying authority, asserting independence, gaining approval of peers, etc., then disruptive forms of humor in fact reflect competent social behavior. The problem is that the child's goals in social interaction do not necessarily correspond to those that parents and teachers might prefer the child to have.

Clearly, then, humor may be used by children in either socially constructive or destructive ways. At this point, we have no data on the long-term stability of hostile or disruptive forms of humor, so it is impossible to say whether the child who uses humor in negative ways eventually becomes an adult who does so. While an aggressive quality may remain in the humor of some individuals, it appears to be the assertive, dominating features of behavior that are most likely to be maintained by humor initiators into adulthood.

In conclusion, although all children develop some level of skill at initiating humor, it is children who develop early aggressive and otherwise assertive styles of interaction who subsequently become the most frequent initiators of humor. The development of heightened skill at using humor enables these children to maintain an assertive and socially dominant style of interaction in a way that gains them attention and even popularity and friendships. Given the numerous positive social functions associated with the effective initiation of humor, and the positive relationship with measures of social competence, the development of heightened skills at initiating humor clearly makes a significant contribution to children's social development.

REFERENCES

Anderson, S., & Messick, S. (1974). Social competence in young children. *Developmental Psychology, 10*, 282-293.

Apte, M. (1987). Ethnic humor versus "sense of humor": An American sociocultural dilemma. *American Behavioral Scientist, 30*, 27-41.

Bell, N.J., McGhee, P.E., & Duffey, N.S. (1986). Interpersonal competence, social assertiveness and the development of humor. *British Journal of Developmental Psychology, 4*, 51-55.

Carson, D.K., Skarpness, L.R., Schultz, N.W., & McGhee, P.E. (1986). Temperamental and communicative competence as predictors of young children's humor. *Merrill-Palmer Quarterly, 32*, 415-426.

Chapman, A.J. (1976). Social aspects of humorous laughter. In A.J. Chapman & H.C. Foot (Eds.), *Humour and laughter: Theory, research and applications* (pp. 155-185). Chichester, England: Wiley.

Chapman, A.J. (1983). Humor and laughter in social interaction and some implications for humor research. In P.E. McGhee & J.H. Goldstein (Eds.), *Handbook of humor research. Vol. 1. Basic Issues* (pp. 135-157). Nw York: Springer-Verlag.

Chapman, A.J., Smith, J.R., & Foot, H.C. (1980). Humour, laughter, and social interaction. In P.E. McGhee & A.J. Chapman (Eds.), *Children's humour* (pp. 141-179). Chichester, England: Wiley.

Connolly, J.A., & Doyle, A. (1984). Relation of social fantasy to social competence in preschoolers. *Developmental Psychology, 20*, 797-806.

Damico, S.B., & Purkey, W.W. (1978). Class clowns: A study of middle school students. *American Educational Research Journal, 15*, 391-398.

Davis, J.M., & Farina, A. (1970). Humor appreciation as social communication. *Journal of Personality and Social Psychology, 15*, 175-178.

Duncan, J. (1984). Perceived humor and social network patterns in a sample of task-oriented groups: A reexamination of prior research. *Human Relations, 37*, 895-907.

Fabrizi, M.S., & Pollio, H.R. (1987). A naturalistic study of humorous activity in a third, seventh, and eleventh grade classroom. *Merrill-Palmer Quarterly, 33*, 107-128.

Fisher, S., & Fisher, R.L. (1981). *Pretend the world is funny and forever: A psychological analysis of comedians, clowns, and actors.* Hillsdale, N.J.: Erlbaum.

Foot, H.C. (1986). Humour and laughter. In O. Hargie (Ed.), *A handbook of communication skills* (pp. 355-381). London: Croom Helm.

Ford, M.E. (1982). Social cognition and social competence in adolescence. *Developmental Psychology, 18*, 323-340.

Freud, S. (1960). *Jokes and their relation to the unconscious.* New York: Norton. (Originally *Der witz und seine Beziehung zum unbewussten.* Leipzig: Deuticke, 1905.)

Geizer, R.S., Rarick, D.L., & Soldow, G.F. (1977). Deception and judgment accuracy: A study in person perception. *Personality and Social Psychology Bulletin, 3*, 446-449.

Goodchilds, J.D. (1959). Effects of being witty on position in the social structure of a small group. *Sociometry, 22*, 261-272.

Goodchilds, J.D. (1972). On being witty: Causes, correlates and consequences. In J.H. Goldstein & P.E. McGhee (Eds.), *The Psychology of Humor* (pp. 173-193). New York: Academic.

Goodchilds, J.D., & Smith, E.E. (1964). The wit and his group. *Human Relations, 17*, 23-31.

Goodman, J. (1983). How to get more smileage out of your life: Making sense of humor and then serving it. In P.E. McGhee & J.H. Goldstein (Eds.), *Handbook of humor research*. Vol. 2. *Applied Studies* (pp. 1-21). New York: Springer-Verlag.

Janus, S.S. (1975). The great comedians: Personality and other factors. *American Journal of Psychoanalysis, 35*, 169-174.

Kane, T.R., Suls, J.M., & Tedeschi, J. (1977). Humour as a tool of social interaction. In A.J. Chapman & H.C. Foot (Eds.), *It's a funny thing, humour* (pp. 13-16). Oxford: Pergamon.

Krasnor, L.S., & Rubin, K.H. (1983). Preschool social problem solving: Attempts and outcomes in naturalistic interaction. *Child Development, 54*, 1545-1558.

Levine, J.L., & Zigler, E. (1976). Humor responses of high and low premorbid competence alcoholic and nonalcoholic patients. *Addictive Behaviors, 1*, 139-149.

Martineau, W.H. (1972). A model of the social functions of humor. In J.H. Goldstein & P.E. McGhee (Eds.), *The psychology of humor* (pp. 101-125). New York: Academic.

Masten, A.S. (1986). Humor and competence in school-aged children. *Child Development, 57*, 461-473.

McGhee, P.E. (1976). Sex differences in children's humor. *Journal of Communication, 26*, 176-189.

McGhee, P.E. (1979a). *Humor: Its origin and development*. San Francisco: Freeman.

McGhee, P.E. (1979b). Humor as a means of controlling social interaction. Paper presented at meeting of the Second International Conference on Humor, Los Angeles.

McGhee, P.E. (1980). Development of the sense of humour in childhood: A longitudinal study. In P.E. McGhee & A.J. Chapman (Eds.), *Children's humour* (pp. 213-236). Chichester, England: Wiley.

McGhee, P.E., Bell, N.J., & Duffey, N.S. (1986). Generational differences in humor and correlates of humor development. In L. Nahemow, K. McCluskey-Fawcett, & P.E. McGhee (Eds.), *Humor and aging* (pp. 253-263). New York: Academic.

McGhee, P.E., & Lloyd, S.A. (1982). Behavioral characteristics associated with the development of humor in young children. *Journal of Genetic Psychology, 141*, 253-259.

Moore, S.G., & Updegraff, R. (1964). Sociometric status of pre-school children related to age, sex, nurturance-giving and dependency. *Child Development, 35*, 519-524.

Murstein, B.L., & Brust, R.G. (1985). Humor and interpersonal attraction. *Journal of Personality Assessment, 49*, 637-640.

O'Connell, W.E. (1969). The social aspect of wit and humor. *Journal of Social Psychology, 79*, 183-187.

O'Quinn, K., & Aronoff, J. (1981). Humor as a technique of social influence. *Social Psychology Quarterly, 44*, 349-357.

Pellegrini, D.S. (1985). Social cognition and competence in middle childhood. *Child Development, 56*, 253-264.

Rubin, K.H., & Daniels-Beirness, T. (1983). Concurrent and predictive correlates of sociometric status in kindergarten and grade 1 children. *Merrill-Palmer Quarterly, 29*, 337-351.

Sanford, S., & Eder, D. (1984). Adolescent humor during peer interaction. *Social Psychology Quarterly, 47*, 235-243.

Shantz, C. (1983). Social cognition. In J.H. Flavel & E.M. Markman (Eds.), *Handbook of child psychology*. Vol. 3. *Cognitive Development* (4th ed.). New York: Wiley.

Sherman, L.W. (1984). Intrapersonal perceptions of shyness and humor as related to intrapersonal perceptions of social distance and humorousness. Paper presented at meeting of the Fourth International Conference on Humor, Tel Aviv.

Sherman, L.W. (1985). Humor and social distance. *Perceptual and Motor Skills, 61*, 1274.

Singer, J., & Singer, D. (1979). The values of the imagination. In B. Sutton-Smith (Ed.), *Play and learning* (pp. 195-218). New York: Gardner Press.

Snyder, M. (1974). The self-monitoring of expressive behavior. *Journal of Personality and Social Psychology, 30*, 526-537.

Turner, R.G. (1980). Self-monitoring and humor production. *Journal of Personality, 48*, 163-172.

Wolfenstein, M. (1954). *Children's humor*. Glencoe, Ill.: Free Press.

Ziv, A. (1984). *Personality and sense of humor*. New York: Springer.

Chapter 6

Humor and the Mastery of Living: Using Humor to Cope with the Daily Stresses of Growing Up

Rod A. Martin, PhD

SUMMARY. This chapter suggests that parents, teachers and other caretakers who actively nurture a child's sense of humor may be equipping him or her with an important coping skill. A theoretical model of stress and coping is presented, and a discussion is made of the ways in which nonhostile, self-accepting, realistic humor, and laughter may represent a healthy, broad-spectrum coping strategy. A review of the extant research literature reveals that, although results have been generally promising, research in this area remains rather limited. Finally, some practical suggestions are given for encouraging the development of a healthy sense of humor in children.

During the course of growing up, children are faced with a changing and sometimes threatening environment that presents progressively greater demands for adaptation and growth. For some children, these demands are harsh, unpredictable and almost intolerable while others are fortunate to live in a relatively benign and supportive environment. Whatever the severity, however, the demands of growing up are often stressful, and the child who possesses a broad repertoire of coping strategies and resources will be most successful in adjusting to and surmounting these stresses. The central argument of this chapter is that the ability to respond with

Rod A. Martin is affiliated with the Department of Psychology, University of Western Ontario, London, Canada.

135

humor and laughter in the face of adversity represents an important skill in the child's coping repertoire.

STRESS AND COPING

In recent years, the concept of stress has received a great deal of attention in the research and clinical literatures as well as in the popular media. Stress has been conceptualized by researchers in several different ways, each approach contributing useful information about the phenomenon. One approach to stress attempts to elucidate the characteristics of stressful environmental events or situations. This approach is represented by the life events measures pioneered by Holmes and Rahe (1967) who hypothesized that the essential characteristic of stress is change in one's life situation requiring adaptation and adjustment. Subsequently, other researchers have noted that stress may also result from situations that are unpredictable and uncontrollable, and from conflict, frustration, or pressure to perform or conform. For children, stressors may include changes in place of residence or school, loss of a parent through death or divorce, conflict and tension in family interactions, child abuse, ostracism or teasing by peers, academic pressures and frustrations, and peer pressure to conform and engage in unacceptable behavior.

A second approach to stress emphasizes the responses of the individual under stress. This approach was pioneered by Walter B. Cannon (e.g., 1932) and Hans Selye (e.g., 1976) who investigated the physiological changes occurring in animals exposed to a variety of noxious stimuli. Research along these lines on humans as well as lower animals has highlighted the fact that, as a species, we have inherited finely tuned neurological and endocrinological mechanisms for mobilizing energy very quickly in response to environmental threats to our well-being. However, it has often been noted that many of the threats that we encounter in the everyday interpersonal relationships of our modern society are ones that cannot be appropriately dealt with by either fighting or running, so that the physiological fight/flight response becomes redundant and potentially injurious to bodily systems, particularly when it remains chronically aroused (Frankenhauser, 1984).

Other researchers taking a response-based approach have examined the emotional effects of stress, noting that feelings of anxiety, anger and depression often accompany stressful experiences. Still others have focused on cognitive effects such as difficulty concentrating, obsessive and inflexible thinking, and impaired problem-solving abilities as well as behavioral disturbances such as withdrawal, lethargy, hyperactivity, and aggression (cf. Cohen, 1980). Thus, children under stress are likely to exhibit a variety of somatic complaints, emotional disturbances, and cognitive impairments.

Finally, the transactional model championed by Richard Lazarus and his colleagues (e.g., Lazarus & Folkman, 1984) emphasizes that the experience of stress is personal and subjective, depending on how individuals appraise events in their lives. As a result of different learning histories, personality styles, coping abilities, and so on, different individuals may encounter the same unpleasant event and appraise it quite differently as either a threat to be avoided or tolerated or as a challenge to be overcome. The degree to which an individual appraises an event as a threat will determine the degree to which the stress reactions mentioned are likely to occur.

Combining the contributions of each of these approaches, stress may be defined as a set of adverse physiological, emotional, cognitive and behavioral reactions to events or situations that are perceived by the individual as threatening to his/her well-being and taxing his/her coping abilities. From a developmental perspective, the types of environmental situations and events that are perceived as stressful are likely to change over time as a function of the child's changing cognitive sophistication, emotional maturity, interpersonal skills, and behavioral competence.

A second concept that needs clarification is that of coping. Coping may be defined as any efforts to reduce, tolerate, or transcend the demands that are created by stressful transactions (cf. Coyne & Holroyd, 1982). Thus, coping involves active efforts rather than simply passive responses to stress; although an individual's coping strategies are not necessarily always well conceptualized or even consciously chosen. Coping strategies may take several different approaches to dealing with stressors (cf. Lazarus & Folkman, 1984). First, appraisal-focused coping is aimed at changing one's perceptions and cognitions so that a situation originally appraised as threatening and intolerable is reappraised as challenging and controllable, or even as benign (cf. Ellis, 1977). Second, emotion-focused coping strategies attempt to reduce the physiological arousal and tension accompanying emotional reactions to stress. Examples of such techniques include relaxation, meditation, and catharsis. Third, problem-focused coping involves efforts to actively change the external situation in order to render it less stressful. Included in this category would be such strategies as systematic problem solving, assertiveness, and behavioral self-management.

HUMOR AND LAUGHTER IN COPING

Humor and laughter may be seen as representing a broad-spectrum coping strategy that may have beneficial effects in each of the coping domains outlined in the preceding section. As an *appraisal-focused* coping strategy, a humorous response to a stressful situation may enable the individual to view the situation from an alternate perspective and reappraise it as less threatening and, therefore, less stressful (Dixon, 1980). Many theorists and researchers, taking a cognitive approach to humor, have contended that the essence of humor is the perception of incongruity in two disparate trains of thought that are brought together in a novel and surprising way (e.g., Koestler, 1964; Suls, 1983). In order to perceive the incongruity and "get the joke," the individual needs to make a rapid shift in information processing from one line of thought to another that changes the significance of the original perspective. As O'Connell (1976) points out, a person with a good sense of humor, who tends readily to notice the ludicrous aspects of his/her life situation, is one who "is skilled in rapid perceptual-cognitive switches in frame of reference" (p. 327).

One might speculate that the ability to readily shift perspective in order to perceive the humorousness of life would also serve the person well in times of stress in reappraising the situation from different vantage points and thereby reducing its threatening qualities. This view of the role of humor is echoed in Rollo May's (1953) suggestion that humor has the function of "preserving the sense of self. . . . It is the healthy way of feeling a 'distance' between one's self and the problem, a way of standing off and looking at one's problem with perspective" (p. 54). Thus, people with a sense of humor are ones who are not locked into one way of looking at things. They can alter their perspective and, while remaining realistic about life, can laugh at its ludicrous aspects and thus diminish its threats. A more objective and flexible perspective on a problem situation, coupled with a reduction in anxiety and threat, is likely in turn to facilitate more effective problem-solving efforts.

Humor and laughter may also be seen as having *emotion-focused* coping effects. As Dixon (1980) suggests, laughter and mirth may have a cathartic effect, serving to discharge pent-up emotions. It is important to recognize that humor may be used in a maladaptive way as a means of defending against reality through denial or repression of emotion. However, a humorous outlook that recognizes the reality and pain of adversity yet refuses to succumb to it, can attenuate the feelings of fear, anger and depression and perhaps mitigate the potentially noxious physiological effects of chronic emotional arousal.

This view of the emotionally liberating effects of humor is perhaps best elaborated by Freud (1928). Freud distinguished between jokes or wit on the one hand and humor on the other. He viewed jokes and wit as means of briefly expressing repressed aggressive and sexual id impulses, whereas humor in his view is a positive, life-affirming approach to the world and to oneself. Freud (1928) stated that, by means of humor, "one refuses to undergo suffering, asseverates the invincibility of one's ego against the real world, and victoriously upholds the pleasure principle, yet all without quitting the ground of mental sanity" (p. 217). To Freud, a sense of humor was "a rare and precious gift." Interestingly, Freud viewed this healthy form of humor as a function of the superego reassuring the anxious ego, and asserting in the face of hardship, "Look here! This is all that this seemingly dangerous world amounts to. Child's play—the very thing to jest about!" (p. 220). Since the superego is seen as an introjection of socializing agents, particularly parents, the Freudian view would suggest that children who develop a healthy sense of humor are those whose parents provide a model of positive acceptance and security rather than a harsh and overly demanding set of proscriptions.

In addition to the beneficial effects of humor on mood, the physiological processes accompanying laughter may counteract the effects of stress-related emotional arousal in the body. Although the research to date has been rather limited, there is some evidence that hearty laughter may serve to reduce muscle tension, autonomic arousal, and blood pressure, and increase blood oxygen levels (cf. Goldstein, 1987). Thus, frequent laughter may have effects similar to those of relaxation or meditation in attenuating the physiological effects of emotional tension and arousal (Robinson, 1983).

Besides the effects on appraisal and emotion, humor may also be seen as a potentially useful *problem-focused* coping strategy. In particular, humor is often an effective way of reducing interpersonal tensions and conflicts and thus directly changing the situations that often cause stress (Chapman, 1983). Numerous anecdotes could be told of how a judicious use of humor has defused tense and hostile confrontations in situations ranging from international summit meetings to school playgrounds. On a day-to-day basis, individuals with a healthy sense of humor seem to be adept at greasing the wheels of interpersonal reactions, reducing friction and stress in others' lives as well as their own.

The sort of humor that is effective in this regard is nonhostile and affirmative, communicating a sense of the commonality of human experience. In addition, it is a type of humor that involves not taking oneself too seriously, and being able to recognize and laugh at one's own foibles in a self-accepting way. As Allport (1950, p. 280) has stated, "the neurotic who learns to laugh at himself may be on the way to self-management, perhaps to cure." Again, it is important to recognize that humor is a two-edged sword, and that it is often also used to express aggression and thus aggravate interpersonal tension, as in derision, sarcasm, and racist jokes. As will be further amplified, the potentially beneficial and liberating effects of humor, coupled with its potential for destructiveness, underscore the importance of teaching children to distinguish between the two ways of using humor and to develop a healthy and appropriate sense of humor.

RESEARCH EVIDENCE

The present author, in collaboration with Herbert Lefcourt, has conducted a series of investigations designed to examine the moderating effect of the sense of humor on the relationship between stressors and moods (Lefcourt & Martin, 1986; Martin & Lefcourt, 1983, 1984). Although these studies focused on university students, the results may also have implications for the stress-buffering role of humor in children as well. The approach taken in this research was derived from earlier work using life events measures (e.g., Holmes & Rahe, 1967) that demonstrated a small but robust correlation between the number and severity of recent stressful life experiences reported by subjects and subsequent ill health, accidents, depressed moods, anxiety, and other forms of psychological distress (cf. Holmes & Masuda, 1974; Paykel, 1974; Rabkin & Struening, 1976). Noting the small magnitude of these correlations, several researchers have suggested that differences in personality may serve to render some individuals more vulnerable to the adverse effects of stressful events while protecting others. For example, Kobasa (1979) has investigated a personality variable called hardiness, comprising an amalgamation of internal locus of control, commitment to goals, and a sense of challenge in response to stressors. Kobasa has demonstrated that individuals characterized by high levels of this personality variable are less likely to become ill subsequent to stressful events than are those who are low on this variable. Our strategy was therefore to examine whether the sense of humor might play a similar stress-buffering role.

The first step in this research involved the development of methods for measuring individual differences in sense of humor. It was assumed that individuals differ in fairly stable and predictable ways in the degree to which they sense, enjoy, and create humor in their lives. A search of the literature revealed that most of the self-report humor tests that had been developed assessed differences in the degree to which individuals appreciate various *types* of humor, such as sexual, aggressive, or nonsensical humor. Thus, typical measures presented subjects with a series of jokes and cartoons of various types and asked them to rate the degree to which they found each one to be funny. However, we were more interested in the degree to which individuals enjoy and produce humor regardless of type. Ultimately, four self-report measures assessing different aspects of the sense of humor were employed. The first two of these were subscales from Svebak's (1974) Sense of Humor Questionnaire. One of these, the Metamessage Sensitivity Scale, assesses the degree to which respondents report that they are able to notice humorous aspects of their environment; while the other, the Liking of Humor Scale, measures the degree to which they report enjoyment of humor and the humorous role. The remaining two measures were developed by us. The first of these, the Situational Humor Response Questionnaire (Martin & Lefcourt, 1984), is composed of a series of descriptions of common life situations varying in stressfulness, and subjects are asked to report the degree to which they would be likely to respond with mirth (smiling and laughter) in each situation. Thus, this measure was designed to assess subjects' sense of humor in terms of the frequency with which they display mirth in a wide variety of life situations. The final test, the Coping Humor Scale (Martin & Lefcourt, 1983), was designed specifically to assess the degree to which subjects report using humor as a means of coping with stressful experiences.

Initial psychometric investigations with each of these humor measures revealed acceptable levels of internal consistency and test-retest reliability. In addition, validational support was provided by significant correlations between these scales and such criteria as: the frequency and duration of subjects' laughter during an interview; peer ratings of subjects' sense of humor and their tendency not to take themselves too seriously; the number of witty remarks and rated humorousness of an impromptu comedy routine in the laboratory; the rated humorousness of a narrative produced while watching a stressful film; and the number of witty comments produced spontaneously in response to a test of creativity.

In addition to these self-report measures of sense of humor, we also employed a behavioral assessment technique, adapted from Turner (1980). This method involves asking subjects to make up a humorous monologue in the laboratory by describing a group of miscellaneous objects on a table in as funny a way as they can. The tape recorded monologues are then scored by trained judges for number of witty comments and overall wittiness. We assumed that subjects who are more successful at creating humor in such an impromptu situation are likely to be ones who tend to be humorous in their everyday lives. This assumption was borne out by correlations with the self-report measures and the subjects' friends' ratings of their sense of humor. In another variation of this technique, we had subjects make up a humorous narrative while watching a stressful silent film entitled *Subincision*. This film, employed by Lazarus and colleagues (1962) in their early research on stress, depicts the initiation rites of a group of adolescent males in an aborigine tribe of Australia in which a painful operation is performed on the penis and scrotum using sharpened pieces of flint. Ratings of the humorousness of the subjects' narratives were taken to provide an index of their ability to produce humor under stress.

Each of these measures of the sense of humor (both self-report and behavioral) were employed in a series of studies on the stress-moderating effects of humor. Besides the humor measures, the subjects in these studies were also administered two other tests: (a) a measure assessing the number of stressful life events that they had experienced during the preceding year, and (b) a mood adjective checklist assessing their predominant moods such as anxiety, depression, anger and fatigue. Significant interactions were obtained with three of the four self-report measures and each of the behavioral measures of humor. Further analyses revealed that, as predicted, these interactions were due to stronger correlations between stressful events and disturbed moods for subjects with lower scores on the humor measures as compared to those with higher humor scores. Thus, individuals with a weak sense of humor, as measured by our assessment instruments, tended to show a marked increase in disturbed moods with increases in prior stressful events, whereas those with a stronger sense of humor revealed little or no increase in mood disturbance even under high levels of stress. These results were interpreted as supportive of our hypothesis that a sense of humor serves to protect individuals from the adverse effects of stress. A recent study by Porterfield (1987) failed to replicate this interactive finding using two of the self-report humor scales and a measure of depression as the outcome variable, although a significant negative correlation between sense of humor and depression was obtained.

In another study (Lefcourt & Martin, 1986), we employed an experimental methodology in which we had subjects view the *Subincision* film and randomly assigned them to groups in which they were instructed to create either a humorous narrative, or an intellectual narrative, or to watch the film in silence. The results of this study revealed that subjects with a low sense of humor, as measured on the Coping Humor Scale, revealed significantly less disturbances of affect on self-report measures and nonverbal behavior indices when they were in the humorous narrative condition as compared to the intellectual narrative and no-narrative conditions. In contrast, subjects with a high sense of humor revealed low levels of mood disturbance in all three conditions, suggesting that they may have employed a humorous coping strategy regardless of the instructions that they were given.

More recently, in several as-yet-unpublished studies, we have begun to extend these findings to physiological measures of immune system functioning, namely salivary immunoglobulin A (S-IgA). S-IgA is one of a number of immunoglobulins produced by the immune system that defends the individual against upper respiratory tract infections. Using a small sample size ($n = 9$), Dillon, Minchoff, and Baker (1985) found a strong correlation ($r = .75$) between subjects' IgA levels and their scores on our Coping Humor Scale. These researchers also found that subjects listening to comedy tapes, but not to nonhumorous tapes, showed significant increases in S-IgA production, a finding that we have replicated in recent research. In addition, we have recently found that self-report measures of the sense of humor exert a moderating effect on the relationship between stressful life events and S-IgA in a manner similar to that obtained previously with mood disturbance. Thus, some preliminary evidence suggests that the stress-buffering effects of humor may extend also to reduced susceptibility to physical illnesses.

The preceding research made use of university students as subjects, and some caution should, therefore, be taken in extending the results to children. However, some support for the generalizability of these findings to a younger population is provided by a study by Masten (reported by Garmezy & Tellegen, 1984). This study, involving 93 children in grades 5 to 8, was part of a larger project investigating academic, behavioral, and social competence as characteristics of stress-resistant children. Using a set of cartoons as stimulus materials, Masten developed measures for rating her subjects' ability to comprehend, appreciate, and generate humor. These measures were then correlated with several indicators of competence. Among other findings, the results revealed a positive relationship between the children's ability to generate humor and their overall competence and stress resistance. In action, among children who were judged as coming from families experiencing particularly high levels of stress, those who were more competent had higher humor generation scores than did those with low social/behavioral competence.

In summary, although the research to date has been rather sparse, evidence is beginning to accumulate in support of the notion that a humorous outlook on life may be an important asset in effective coping. Further research is needed to elaborate the mechanisms involved in humorous coping. There is reason to believe that a sense of humor in adults has developmental roots in childhood (McGhee, 1986). Thus, helping children to develop an active sense of humor may be an important means of improving their ability to cope with stress during childhood as well as preparing them to deal with the stressors of adult life.

CHILDREN'S HUMOR AND COPING

Adults who are interested in helping children to develop a healthy sense of humor need to be aware of the developmental aspects of humor in children, so as to accommodate their humor to the cognitive level and emotional needs of the child. Although a thorough review of the developmental humor literature is beyond the scope of this chapter (for reviews see McGhee, 1979; 1983; McGhee & Chapman, 1980; Nahemow, McCluskey-Fawcett, & McGhee,

1986; and Chapter 1, this volume), several themes drawn from various theoretical approaches will be noted.

Researchers taking a cognitive approach to humor development (e.g., McGhee, 1979) have noted that children's humor productions follow a developmental sequence that parallels Piagetian stages of cognitive development. From this perspective, children need to develop particular cognitive capacities in order to understand specific forms of humor. For example, in order to find humor in acting on one object as if it were another object, a child must have attained the preoperational stage and have an image-based representational capacity. Similarly, some degree of concrete-operational thought is required for a child to enjoy the double meanings of words occurring in puns and many types of jokes (McGhee, 1983). The cognitive perspective has also emphasized the importance of a "mastery-play cycle" in humor development. As McGhee (1983, p. 115) notes, "once a child becomes confident of the normal relationship between stimulus elements or achieves a new level of understanding through acquisition of new cognitive skills, he/she enjoys distorting that knowledge or understanding in the guise of a joke." Thus, a child's joking about an idea or concept may indicate a sense of mastery over it while, at the same time, providing a means for checking the accuracy and limits of that mastery (Horgan, 1981).

Levine (1977) has extended this "pleasure-in-mastery" notion of humor by suggesting that humor and laughter are associated not only with the mastery of cognitive concepts, but also with mastery in emotional and interpersonal domains. In this regard, several studies have shown that individuals who have a sense of mastery over events in their own lives (i.e., internal locus of control) display more mirth and humor production ability in a variety of situations than do those who conceive of themselves as having less control and mastery (Lefcourt, Sordoni, & Sordoni, 1974; Lefcourt, Antrobus, & Hogg, 1974; Lefcourt & Martin, 1986, ch. 6). Levine suggested that since early experiences of mirth in children are often associated with pleasurable feelings of control and competence, later expressions of humor and laughter may at times occur as a means of attempting to recapture those feelings of mastery and to dispel feelings of anxiety in threatening situations.

Psychodynamically oriented researchers have focused on similar themes in emphasizing the emotional or "tendentious" aspects of humor. Freud (1905) theorized that jokes and witticisms are methods of expressing sexual and aggressive impulses in a socially acceptable manner. Drawing from this Freudian view and from her own investigations, Wolfenstein (1954) suggested that children's humor productions serve an important developmental function in helping the child to cope with the stress, anxiety, guilt, and other emotions associated with the successive stages of psychosexual development. Similarly, Loeb and Wood (1986) have outlined a developmental model of humor based on Erikson's eight stages of psychosocial development, suggesting that humor may be one method of dealing with conflicts arising from developmental crises of trust versus mistrust, autonomy versus shame, and so on. Thus, humor may reflect an attempt not only to gain mastery over cognitive concepts, but also to exert emotional dominance over the things that represent a threat or conflict to the individual. An analysis of a child's spontaneous jokes may be a method of identifying the emotional issues that are most salient to him or her at a given time.

The social-learning approach to humor focuses on the effects of the environment on the individual's humorous behavior. Children who are provided with positive models of humor and are reinforced for their attempts at humor are likely to acquire a broader repertoire of humorous behaviors such as laughter and joketelling (cf. Brown, Wheeler, & Cash, 1980). In this regard, McGhee, Bell, and Duffey (1986) found that both college students and elderly women who rated themselves as being frequent initiators of humor also tended to rate their same-sex parents as having done frequent joking, clowning, and playful teasing when they were growing up. Thus, early parental modeling of humor may have an impact that endures throughout life. Further information regarding parental influences on children's humor comes from longitudinal research by McGhee (1980). Children aged 3 to 5 who showed heightened humor development had mothers who were generally warm, approving and protective. In 6- to 11-year-olds, however, the opposite was the case, with high sense of humor children having mothers who were not protective or babying, but who encouraged their children to solve problems on their own. Thus, humor development in children may be facilitated by a warm, protective environment during preschool years, and encouragement of autonomy in later childhood.

NURTURING A SENSE OF HUMOR IN CHILDREN

In view of the evidence that a healthy sense of humor is an important asset in coping with the adversities of life, it seems important for parents and caretakers to seek to encourage a humorous outlook in their children. In many respects, though, it appears that humor and laughter do not need to be taught to children — they are as natural to children as breathing. Watching newsreel footage of war-torn countries such as Lebanon in recent years, one is struck by the images of children playing and laughing amid the bombed-out ruins. In situations that are seen as serious and devastating by adults, children often seem more apt to recover their sense of optimism and playfulness. Thus, it is perhaps adults that need to learn from children how to recapture a humorous and playful approach to life, rather than the other way around.

Nonetheless, adults may play an important role in encouraging and nurturing humor in children and avoiding squelching it with unnecessary seriousness. Parents can demonstrate to their children the value that they place on humor by participating with them in times of play and laughter. This involves not only physical play with children, but also engaging in playing with words, concepts and ideas. This sort of playful thinking teaches children to think flexibly and creatively (see Ziv, this volume), to notice double meanings and analogies, and to shift perspective easily, all of which are skills that enter into the production of humor. Enjoying with children the telling of favorite jokes and, more importantly, the creation of new jokes, further stimulates their humor abilities. Adults need to be aware of the developmental aspects of humor noted earlier, and accommodate themselves to the type of humor that can be most appreciated by their own children at their particular stage of development.

It is important also to avoid inhibiting laughter and attempts at humor in children by making fun of them. People who are teased or ridiculed for an unusual style of laughing may become excessively self-conscious about laughing and may, therefore, have difficulty enjoying hearty, uninhibited laughter. Similarly, children need to be aware that even the funniest people make attempts at humor that fall flat at times. As with learning to ride a bicycle, developing ability in humor requires falling on one's face numerous times, but then having the courage to pick oneself up and try again. All of this underscores the importance of healthy self-esteem for the development of a sense of humor. Lefcourt and Martin (1986) found significant positive correlations between a measure of self-esteem and scores on the sense of humor measures. Individuals with low self-esteem are likely to be anxious, constricted, and serious, all of which interfere with humor development. Thus, part of encouraging a sense of humor in a child involves nurturing a sense of self-worth, competence, and self-confidence.

Besides nurturing and encouraging the innate sense of humor and play in children, it is important for parents to serve as models of a healthy use of humor. Children are notorious for using humor and laughter as instruments of cruel ridicule and coercion. Children who suffer from some physical deformity, or in other ways stand out as being different from the norm, are well aware of the power of jokes and laughter for inflicting pain. In their own use of humor in their interactions with others, adults can provide a model of the kind of healthy, nonhostile humor that we are discussing here. The distinction between "laughing at" versus "laughing with" another person is one that is not always easy to draw, and discussions of this issue with children in the context of real interactions may be helpful. Another useful approach, when children are heard making derogatory humorous statements or telling racist jokes, is to ask them in a nonthreatening manner to explain what is funny about that joke or statement. In thinking through the meaning of the joke and discovering the latent hostility in it, the child may be able to recognize the inappropriateness of it.

In addition to modelling a nonhostile sense of humor, parents can provide their children with a model of the use of humor in the presence of adversity, problems and pain. In demonstrating humor as a coping response, one needs to be careful to avoid minimizing the reality of the painfulness and unpleasantness of stressful situations. Laughter should not be used as a way of denying unpleasant emotions, either in oneself or in others. A healthy use of humor in adverse circumstances will be accompanied by increased, rather than decreased, self-awareness, and will enhance reality-based coping. Thus, attempts to cajole a child into laughing at times when he or she is upset about something are generally inappropriate.

The most effective approach is for parents to demonstrate the use of humor when they themselves are experiencing stress. Thus, the parent who is able to produce a wry comment concerning the ludicrousness of the situation when he or she is in the midst of an argument, experiencing physical pain, or feeling frustrated, is likely to stimulate a humorous approach to adversity in the child. This sort of modelling helps the child to realize that pain and difficulties are an inevitable part of life, and that it is unrealistic to wait until life is free of problems before finding humor in it. Even in the midst of serious and difficult life situations, glimpses of the ludicrous or whimsical may often be obtained and enjoyed, without ignoring or distorting reality.

A particularly interesting use of humor in parenting is exemplified by a friend of the author. This woman has an especially well developed sense of humor and is adept at employing it with her 10-year-old foster child. Besides modelling a humorous outlook on life, she has found that humor may be effectively used as a means of enforcing rules without crushing the child's self-esteem. For example, one of the rules of the house stipulates that winter boots must be removed before walking on the carpets. This rule has been formulated in a humorous manner by saying that anyone who walks on the carpet with boots on will immediately explode. If the child forgets and breaks the rule, this woman and her husband respond by making loud exploding noises. The child is thus reminded of the rule and quickly complies, without feeling put down.

As another example, this woman, in seeking to modify inappropriate behaviors in her foster child, has drawn on the "word of the week" idea in the popular children's television program hosted by

Pee Wee Herman. In the program, children play a game in which they throw up their hands and scream whenever a particular "word of the week" is heard in conversations. In applying this game to behavior modification, this friend of the author targets a particular problem behavior in her foster child that needs to be reduced or eliminated, and labels it the "behavior of the week." Whenever the child engages in this behavior, she responds by throwing up her hands and screaming in true Pee Wee Herman fashion. She has found that this technique is more effective (and more fun for both child and parent) than methods based on punishment or elaborate token economy schemes. Again, the important point is that a serious message is conveyed in a humorous and playful manner that avoids eroding the child's self-esteem. In contrast, reprimands that are given without humor often not only signal that an inappropriate behaviour has occurred, but also convey to a child the message that he or she is inferior or should feel very guilty for "blowing it again."

CONCLUSION

Childhood is often portrayed as a carefree time of blissful play and freedom from responsibility. However, a more accurate view would recognize that, much like adults, children experience considerable pain, both emotional and physical, intermixed with the pleasures and joys. A healthy sense of humor may be an important element in the child's coping repertoire for dealing effectively with the stresses of childhood. The experience of mastery through humor learned in the crucible of childhood will also serve the individual well in later adult years.

Humorous responses in times of adversity may be effective in mitigating the aversive consequences of stress in several ways. By providing alternative perspectives on the situation, humor allows for a reappraisal of the threatening nature of the problem, permitting one to view it more objectively and potentially engage in more effective problem solving. In addition to the cognitive benefits, humor and laughter in times of stress may reduce disturbances of mood and mitigate adverse physiological effects of painful emotions. Finally, a sense of humor may be effective in bringing about actual change in the environmental situation by reducing interpersonal conflicts. A healthy sense of humor is one that is nonhostile and that does not deny or distort reality.

Parents and other caretakers can nurture such a salutary sense of humor in children, first, by encouraging the child's spontaneous attempts at humor production and laughter and bolstering self-esteem, and, second, by modelling a nonhostile, reality-based sense of humor that takes perspective and recognizes the ludicrous aspects even of difficult situations, defeats and failures. A growing body of theoretical and empirical evidence indicates that parents who thus inspire a humorous approach to life in their children may be equipping them with an important method for coping with the adversities that they will encounter throughout their lives.

REFERENCES

Allport, G. W. (1950). *The individual and his religion*. New York: Macmillan.

Brown, G. E., Wheeler, K. J., & Cash, M. (1980). The effects of a laughing versus a nonlaughing model on humor responses in preschool children. *Journal of Experimental Child Psychology, 29*, 334-339.

Cannon, W. B. (1932). *Bodily changes in pain, hunger, fear, and rage*. New York: Appleton.

Chapman, A. J. (1983). Humor and laughter in social interaction and some implications for humor research. In P. E. McGhee & J. H. Goldstein (Eds.), *Handbook of humor research* (Vol. I, pp. 135-157). New York: Springer/Verlag.

Cohen, S. (1980). Aftereffects of stress on human performance and social behavior: A review of research and theory. *Psychological Bulletin, 88*, 82-108.

Coyne, J., & Holroyd, K. (1982). Stress, coping and illness: A transactional perspective. In T. Millon, C. Green, & R. Meagher (Eds.), *Handbook of clinical health psychology* (pp. 103-127). New York: Plenum.

Dillon, K. M., Minchoff, B., & Baker, K. H. (1985). Positive emotional states and enhancement of the immune system. *International Journal of Psychiatry in Medicine, 15*, 13-18.

Dixon, N. F. (1980). Humor: A cognitive alternative to stress? In I. G. Sarason & C. D. Spielberger (Eds.), *Stress and anxiety* (Vol. 7, pp. 281-289). Washington, DC: Hemisphere.

Ellis, A. (1977). *Reason and emotion in psychotherapy*. Secaucus, NJ: Lyle Stuart.

Frankenhauser, M. (1984). Psychology as a means of reducing stress and promoting health. In K. M. J. Lagerspetz & P. Niemi (Eds.), *Psychology in the 1990's* (pp. 315-327). Holland: Elsevier.

Freud, S. (1905). *Jokes and their relation to the unconscious*. Leipzig: Deuticke.

Freud, S. (1928). Humour. Reprinted in J. Strachey (Ed.), *Collected papers of Sigmund Freud (Vol. 5)*. New York: Basic Books, 1959.

Garmezy, N., & Tellegen, A. (1984). Studies of stress-resistant children: Methods, variables, and preliminary findings. In F. J. Morrison, C. Lord, & D. P. Keating (Eds.), *Applied developmental psychology* (Vol. I, pp. 231-287). Orlando, FL: Academic Press.

Goldstein, J. H. (1987). Therapeutic effects of laughter. In W. F. Fry & W. A. Salameh (Eds.), *Handbook of humor and psychotherapy: Advances in the clinical use of humor* (pp. 1-19). Sarasota, FL: Professional Resource Exchange.

Holmes, T. H., & Masuda, M. (1974). Life changes and illness susceptibility. In B. S. Dohrenwend & B. P. Dohrenwend (Eds.), *Stressful life events: Their nature and effects* (pp. 45-72). New York: Wiley.

Holmes, T. H., & Rahe, R. H. (1967). The social readjustment rating scale. *Journal of Psychosomatic Research, 11*, 213-218.

Horgan, D. (1981). Learning to tell jokes: A case study of metalinguistic abilities. *Journal of Child Language, 8*, 217-224.

Kobasa, S. C. (1979). Stressful life events, personality and health: An inquiry into hardiness. *Journal of Personality and Social Psychology, 37*, 1-11.

Koestler, A. (1964). *The act of creation*. London: Hutchinson.

Lazarus, R. S., & Folkman, S. (1984). *Stress, appraisal and coping*. New York: Springer.

Lazarus, R. S., Speisman, J. C., Mordkoff, A. M., & Davison, L. A. (1962). A laboratory study of psychological stress produced by a motion picture film. *Psychological Monographs, 76* (Whole No. 553).

Lefcourt, H. M., Antrobus, P., & Hogg, E. (1974). Humor response and humor production as a function of locus of control, field dependence and type of reinforcements. *Journal of Personality, 42*, 632-651.

Lefcourt, H. M., & Martin, R. A. (1986). *Humor and life stress: Antidote to adversity*. New York: Springer-Verlag.

Lefcourt, H. M., Sordoni, C., & Sordoni, C. (1974). Locus of control: Field dependence and the expression of humor. *Journal of Personality, 42*, 130-143.

Levine, J. (1977). Humour as a form of therapy: Introduction to symposium. In A. J. Chapman & H. C. Foot (Eds.), *It's a funny thing, humour* (pp. 127-137). Oxford: Pergamon Press.

Loeb, M., & Wood, V. (1986). Epilogue: A nascent idea for an Eriksonian model of humor. In L. Nahemow, K.A. McCluskey-Fawcett, & P.E. McGhee (Eds.), *Humor and aging* (pp. 279-284). New York: Academic Press.

Martin, R. A., & Lefcourt, H. M. (1983). Sense of humor as a moderator of the relation between stressors and moods. *Journal of Personality and Social Psychology, 45*, 1313-1324.

Martin, R. A., & Lefcourt, H. M. (1984). The Situational Humor Response Questionnaire: A quantitative measure of the sense of humor. *Journal of Personality and Social Psychology, 47*, 145-155.

May, R. (1953). *Man's search for himself*. New York: Random House.

McGhee, P. E. (1979). *Humor: Its origin and development*. San Francisco: Freeman.

McGhee, P. E. (1980). Development of the sense of humor in childhood: A longitudinal study. In P.E. McGhee & A.J. Chapman, A.J. (Eds.), *Children's humor* (pp. 213-236). Chichester, England: Wiley.

McGhee, P. E. (1983). Humor development: Toward a lifespan approach. In P.E. McGhee & J.H. Goldstein (Eds.), *Handbook of humor research, Vol. 1* (pp. 109-134). New York: Springer-Verlag.

McGhee, P. E. (1986). Humor across the life span: Sources of developmental change and individual differences. In L. Nahemow, K.A. McCluskey-Fawcett, & P.E. McGhee (Eds.), *Humor and aging* (pp. 27-51). New York: Academic Press.

McGhee, P. E., Bell, N. J., & Duffey, N. S. (1986). Generational differences in humor and correlates of humor development. In L. Nahemow, K.A. McCluskey-Fawcett, & P.E. McGhee (Eds.), *Humor and aging* (pp. 253-263). New York: Academic Press.

McGhee, P. E., & Chapman, A. J. (1980). *Children's humor*. Chichester, England: Wiley.

Nahemow, L., McCluskey-Fawcett, K. A., & McGhee, P. E. (1986). *Humor and aging*. New York: Academic Press.

O'Connell, W. E. (1976). Freudian humour: The eupsychia of everyday life. In A. J. Chapman & H. C. Foot (Eds.), *Humor and laughter: Theory, research, and applications*. (pp. 313-330). London: Wiley.

Paykel, E. S. (1974). Life stress and psychiatric disorder: Applications of the clinical approach. In B. S. Dohrenwend & B. P. Dohrenwend (Eds.), *Stressful life events: Their nature and effects* (pp. 135-149). New York: Wiley.

Porterfield, A. L. (1987). Does sense of humor moderate the impact of life stress on psychological and physical well-being? *Journal of Research in Personality, 21*, 306-317.

Rabkin, J. G., & Struening, E. L. (1976). Life events, stress, and illness. *Science, 194*, 1013-1020.

Robinson, V. M. (1983). Humor and health. In P. E. McGhee & J. H. Goldstein (Eds.), *Handbook of humor research* (Vol. II, pp. 109-128). New York: Springer/Verlag.

Selye, H. (1976). *The stress of life* (Rev. ed.). New York: McGraw-HIll.

Suls, J. M. (1983). Cognitive processes in humor appreciation. In P. E. McGhee & J. H. Goldstein (Eds.), *Handbook of humor research* (Vol. 1, pp. 39-57). New York: Springer/Verlag.

Svebak, S. (1974). Revised questionnaire on the sense of humor. *Scandinavian Journal of Psychology, 15*, 328-331.

Turner, R. G. (1980). Self-monitoring and humor production. *Journal of Personality, 48*, 163-172.

Wolfenstein, M. (1954). *Children's humor: A psychological analysis*. Glencoe, IL: The Free Press.

PART IV:
USING HUMOR
AS AN INTERVENTION TECHNIQUE

Introduction

Given that humor helps children cope with stress, it follows that adults might be able to help children cope with certain high stress situations by skillfully adding humor to the environment in which the stress occurs. Two stressful situations shared by many children are short-term stays in hospitals and visits to the dentist's office.

The first article in this section, by D'Antonio, discusses the potential value of humor—initiated by either the child or by hospital staff—in helping children deal with their fears and anxieties related to hospital procedures, assaults on their body, isolation from their family, etc. D'Antonio suggests that humor may be most effective in facilitating coping when combined with other forms of play behavior. Nevo then provides guidelines for how dentists can use spontaneous humor to minimize anxiety related to the dentist's office. While no research on this topic has yet been completed, prior work on the use of humor in "systematic desensitization" suggests that humor should help provide a mood or frame of mind that is incompatible with anxiety.

Dental and hospital-related stress may be intense, but they are generally of a short-term nature. If a child has major life stresses with which he is unable to cope, can humor help? Ventis and Ventis address this question by examining humor's usefulness in therapy with children. Its use within different therapeutic approaches is discussed, along with the question of the function of child-initiated humor as opposed to therapist-initiated humor.

Chapter 7

The Use of Humor with Children in Hospital Settings

Irma J. D'Antonio, RN, PhD

SUMMARY. The emotional impact of illness and hospitalization on children can elicit overwhelmingly traumatic and fear-producing stresses. The child's usual ways of coping may not reduce these stresses. Humor which involves aspects of the child's understanding of illness and hospitalization can reduce stress to a manageable level. Humor integrated with play is advocated to enable the child to understand the intentions of humor in a less threatening manner. The particular age of the child to include the child's ways of thinking and expressing self are considerations in planning for the use of humor. Changes in behavior of children with whom humor has been introduced resulted in decreased fears related to the strangeness of the environment inside and outside the body.

The effect of hospitalization on the child can be viewed as similar to the effect of visiting a newly-discovered planet to the adult. Everything is different from previous experiences. The ambience of the hospital and how a hospital functions is different from home. Interactions with hospital personnel are different than with family and friends. The illness or injury that necessitates being in a hospital can be life-threatening. The child is asked to cope with strangeness of the environment outside and inside the body.

The focus of this chapter will include the emotional impact of illness and hospitalization on children and the usefulness of humor,

Irma J. D'Antonio is Professor and Chairperson, Nursing Department, Mount St. Mary's College, Los Angeles, CA.

157

with play, to enable coping with hospital-related stresses. The integration of humor with play is advocated because of the possible misinterpretations of the intentions of humor. To ponder the advantages of humor for coping with stress is not a consideration of this chapter (see chapter by Martin, in this volume). In this paper, it is assumed that humor has benefits to the human spirit that are beyond measurement. It can be one of the most valuable tools for healthcare providers working with children.

EMOTIONAL IMPACT OF ILLNESS AND HOSPITALIZATION

Illness affects the psychological, sociological, spiritual, and physical aspects of a child's life. Emotional awareness during illness and hospitalization is increased because of "those things" done to and for the body. There is also an increased arousal state in children who encounter stressful situations on a daily basis because of hospital routines. For example, certain treatments and drugs administered may produce a feeling of depersonalization. Treatments involving immobilization result in a decrease in body awareness and changes in body sensations. A 15-year-old in a complete body cast, which weighed almost as much as she did, talked about a summer job for herself, "rolling down cement" (Wessel, 1975).

Another phenomenon that occurs during hospitalization includes the incorporation of equipment, used for treatment, into a child's body space. There are many examples of a child crying when a healthcare provider approaches within a certain distance of a casted limb. This should produce no pain, but the child cries as though in pain. An 8-year-old, Bobby, cried when anyone touched his intravenous tubing to inject medication into the tubing. This should produce no pain. But Bobby had incorporated, over time, the tubing as being a part of his body space. Drawings and stories he told of his drawings indicated to the nurse that Bobby saw the tubing as an essential part of himself, especially related to pain. When a child perceives a part of the body as producing pain, the reaction is to get rid of it—or keep people away from it—similar to an adult wanting the dentist to just extract the pain-producing tooth. Children fear pain.

Fears and Fantasies Related to Illness and Hospitalization

The age of the child and the fears associated with an illness and hospitalization are related. Some studies have found that there are differences in fears between hospitalized and non-hospitalized children. In a study by Astin (1977), hospitalized children were found to have more intense fears than non-hospitalized children. The most intense fears for this group of hospitalized children were ranked as drugs, safety, and loss of home. The fear of drugs included feelings of having no control over the medications received, a feeling of loss of control from the effects of certain medications, and a threat to self-preservation. Fears of safety included being in a strange setting where the "rules" are unknown. The loss of home included separation anxiety. Children did not know how to interact with healthcare providers.

Children in hospitals are trying to cope with fears that include abandonment, death (annihilation from procedures or treatments), losses (of body part or function), intrusions on body space and boundaries (body image issues), injury or mutilation (pending surgery), and a new environment (usually seen as hostile). Children may also perceive treatments as retribution for past misdeeds and respond as though they were being attacked. Because these are fears and concerns of most hospitalized children, an added dimension must be considered for the child who has been attacked in the home.

Abused children pose special problems because of their particular development. They are fearful and suspicious of physical contact which is a necessary part of examinations or treatments. They are particularly alert for environmental dangers. The following characteristics of abused children have been identified.

1. orientation to danger, exhibited as distrust, tension, and guardedness
2. visual and auditory hyperalertness
3. avoidance and denial in unpleasant and anxiety-provoking situations
4. impaired ability for enjoyment

5. inability to play freely, laugh or enjoy play in an uninhibited fashion
6. poor peer relationships related to aggression and avoidance
7. socially inappropriate behavior
8. low self-esteem, reflected by verbal and nonverbal indications of self-depreciation and lack of confidence
9. inability to accept limitations
10. hypervigilance to the external environment which resulted in decreasing abilities to concentrate
11. compulsivity (Malone, 1966)

The conclusions of the author are that these characteristics contribute to immediate survival in the abusive home. The impact of the illness and hospital may be seen as another dimension of abuse to these children.

Interactions of healthcare providers may be viewed by the child as abusive or depriving. Because food or fluids may be limited or withheld completely from the child who is undergoing surgery, anesthesia, or particular treatments, the child may experience feelings of deprivation or fears about impending deprivation. Michael was a 3-year-old immobilized boy with a right arm cast in a sling who told his mother a dream about the doctor putting a cast on his mouth (Haver, 1974). The fear was that he would be treated post-casting the way he was treated pre-casting (i.e., withholding of fluids and food). It was characteristic of his way of thinking which included his fantasies.

Children often use fantasies to explain illness and hospitalization when the impact is intense and there are limitations imposed by restrictions. Often everything that happens to the child or that is seen or heard to happen to another child is reflected in a dramatic way. Children have a tendency to:

— put things together because of superficial resemblances (a cast to "roll down cement").
— impute human motives to inanimate objects ("that machine wants to take all my blood").
— have one object stand for another ("bring that spaceship [gurney cart] over so I can cut out into space").
— use inconsistencies for their own purposes.

Susan, an adolescent girl immobilized in a body cast, was told to "be good" by her mother. She fantasized to the nurse about all the ways she could be "bad" in a body cast (i.e., "really hammer people on the head"). One child who would never walk again told stories of being a ballerina.

Children in the hospital rely on the use of fantasy and humor to reduce tension and resolve conflict. The use of a professional clown to help children cope psychologically with illness has also demonstrated benefits to the physical condition of the child (Long, 1987). The fantasies evoked by the clown may be beneficial. Children recognize a clown in costume and realize that the intentions of the clown are to "make me laugh." A clown can "poke fun" at doctors, routines, and treatments, and things and events that are fearful to the child. A clown can say and do things to elicit humorous responses more rapidly than a healthcare provider who must take time to get to know the child and vice versa.

The use of humor is a hospital setting necessitates an understanding on the part of the adult of the difference between the child's sense of humor and the adult's (see Bariaud, this volume). A clown would not be effective for the young child who is afraid of those dressed in costumes, including Santa Claus. Children's ways of thinking are important considerations.

Children's Thinking About Illness and Hospitalization

The age and the thinking characteristics of the child are important to consider. Because preschoolers accept their own point of view or perception, they may not clarify or verify it with the adult. Information "taken in" through the senses regarding events in the hospital (especially via sight, sound, and touch) evoke personal meanings in the child that may necessitate an adult explanation.

It is not uncommon for a preschooler to view the treatment of another child as something that is done to all children. Cindy, age 4 years, often asked, "Gonna do dat to me?" as she nodded her head in affirmation when her roommate was given an injection. Reassurance did not change her viewpoint. Linda, age 5 years, feared sounds she did not hear in her home. Even hospitalized adults are disturbed by the paging system, "Code Blue to 511," or a con-

stantly ringing phone in the nurses' station, or the opening and clos-
ing of elevator doors. Preschoolers may recall some past events and
experiences to which the adult can compare and alleviate the fears,
but this age child lives in the "here and now." One event may take
on an all-important meaning (centration) such as the amount of
blood drawn into a small tubing being perceived by the child as
"taking all my blood." Even visual demonstrations of the amount
of fluid in containers will not change the viewpoint.

It appears to be difficult for hospitalized preschoolers to adjust to
contextual changes. The reasoning from particular to particular
(transducive reasoning) often results in the child explaining and as-
sociating an illness with a particular prior behavior. Mary Ann
stated to her dolls (all five lined up during a play session), "I have
to take all your blood cause you're bad." Another child's explanation of illness was described as, "little worms in apples are germs.
Some are in my head" (Pidgeon, 1977). There is a lack of differen-
tiation between concept and perceptual content resulting from preoperational thinking.

Thoughts of school age children are related to perceptions and
concrete reality. They can understand a series of events such as
blood tests and x-rays that are used to solve a health problem and
the relationship of these to the cause. They often see that one event
is the result of a preceding event and the cause of another. They also
may be inaccurate. A 10-year-old with diabetes gave the explanation of causation of illness as,

> When I was about four, I went to visit my grandfather. He
> usually gave me candy. The shock of his dying and my grand-
> mother dying is partly the cause, I think. Sometimes my dad
> would have candy on the table. Sometimes I'll take a piece.
> (Pidgeon, 1977)

Characteristic thinking includes the addition and combination of
successive actions. Rick, a 12-year-old, said, "If I do my exercise
and eat all my food my muscles will stay good."

The thinking of the adolescent includes an exhaustion of all possibilities in arriving at the solution of the cause of illness. Dee, an
adolescent with scoliosis reviewed all the history of family members, and all the past events in her life that would or could lead to

the present problem. Some adolescents express the amount of knowledge they have based on the remembrance of past experiences, unavailable to the younger child. Kim, a 16-year-old, stated that she could "take the test to be a doctor cause I've been examined so much I know every part of me."

These selected examples give a brief overview of the ways children think about their experiences. When they do not find explanations, they experience fear and fantasies which usually are "played out."

PLAY IN HOSPITAL SETTINGS

An increase in fears and stress may result in the child being unable or unwilling to play. A child who does not play in the hospital should arouse as much concern as a child who does not eat or sleep. Play in hospital settings may be discussed in terms of factors that influence play (Bolig, 1984) and interpretations of play behavior (D'Antonio, 1984). Information about the child's play should be elicited when the child is admitted to the hospital with other historical data, such as the number of admissions to the hospital. A play history may prove to be valuable.

Play History

A verbal history can elicit information from the child such as "I never played," or "I used to watch other kids play." These comments give insights into those children who have experienced a feeling of emptiness, or perhaps boredom often related to chronic illness such as a congenital heart defect. They will provide insight into where to begin with play and humor activities (e.g., "I wanted to play but didn't know how," or "my sister NeNe used to play, but not me"). If play is viewed as a form of work, for example, the child will feel as though the completed task is the all-important aspect. This child would not find it humorous if someone knocked down blocks that had been built into a house or tower or bridge.

A record of the play history and running notes on the child's verbal and behavioral activities during play provides information for the adult which can be used to determine when to use humor and the type of humor to be used. Each child establishes particular patterns of play which are most characteristic of that child's personality organization. The play of some children is repetitious, avoids combinations, and involves limited use of materials in the hospital. This may indicate the amount of trust or understanding by the child of the environment. Play, for Piaget (1947), is an activity which is dominated by the child's assimilation of the external world. This external world of the hospital is "played out" by the child in many ways. For example, fears children have of what others will do to them, such as injections of medications, are re-enacted or practiced on toys. This type of play appears to decrease the stress related to the situation.

Play Observations

Observation of play and the way in which toys are used, as well as the activity level, can help adults understand stresses for the child. One schoolager continuously "filled in" plastic containers with plaster of paris in a playroom because he had been told by the doctor that he was to have a skin graft to "fill in" the hole in his leg wound which was not healing (D'Antonio, 1986).

Play observations may include the amount of play, type of play, toys used during play, content of play, purpose of play, and affect or mood of the child during particular aspects of play. The past history and experiences of the child and the present experiences in the hospital provide a broader base for planning the use of humor.

USEFULNESS OF HUMOR IN COPING WITH HOSPITAL-RELATED STRESS

Children appear to feel the benefits of humor. The use of humor by children in hospitals reveals their fears as well as many other themes. An 8-year-old immobilized male who had been struck by a car was asked by a nurse, "You ran in front of a car, huh?" The child replied, "No, it ran in front of me" (Ebmeier, 1982). A 12-year-old male when asked by a nurse, for teaching purposes, the type of medication he was receiving via intravenous therapy replied, "rat poison" (Edison, 1976). This use of humor appeared to be designed to elicit responses from nurses that indicated to the child that it was a safer environment (i.e., children thought the nurses would treat them in a less threatening way). Sandra said to the nurse, "I'll bet you won't be able to give me that shot now that I made you laugh."

Kikuchi (1977) related the story of a male patient who, "in jest," told the nurses that they were the "Gestapo," and he was their "prisoner." He saved all the cotton fluffs which were used during his venipunctures and glued them to his hospital room wall by his bed for everyone to see the "evidence" of this treatment. His play themes involved fighting a war. He said "next Christmas" he was going to "give" his "leukemia away." Children who have had abdominal surgery refer to their stitches has having a "zipper up the front." One child who was the recipient of an organ transplant said, "Just like a used car lot, I got used parts" (Neff, 1973).

These findings suggest that school-age children do use humor to reduce hospital-related stress. Preliminary findings of a study of 52 abused 3- and 4-year-olds (D'Antonio, 1986), however, indicate that humor was expressed by only half of the children and joking was nonexistent. Therefore, the spontaneous initiation of humor by these children may not be an effective means of reducing stress. Older abused children, however, may prove to be more efficient in using humor to cope. Humor involves a venturing forth into the environment which may not have been possible in the home environment of the abused child. Often times, this venturing forth is prohibitive in the hospital environment. Information about how humor is used by the child in the home and examples of humor may be elicited with the play history when the child is admitted to the hospital.

Incorporating Humor into the Hospital Setting

Since many children seem to cope better with hospital stress by creating humor in connection with it, coping might also be facilitated by the use of humor by hospital staff. However, prior to considering adult use of humor in stressful situations, a discharge of the intensity of emotions and energy through physical play should be considered. For example, the difference between laughing and crying when being tickled appears to be related to the level of intensity of the tickling and the child's perception of the intentions of the tickler. Alexandra was a 3-year-old who responded with laughter when tickled by the nurse during a physical examination. With the same nurse, when she saw a stethoscope, she perceived the continuation of the examination as an intrusion on her person and tickling did not produce the same response. When the tickling was of low-level intensity, she laughed. With an increase in intensity and perceived threat, she cried.

To plan an effective positive use of humor, it is important to assess several other areas in the child's life experiences. Past experience with hospitalization, illness, with nurses and with other healthcare providers can give clues to possible humorous content.

Methods of using humor must be planned according to the age of the child and to the observed effects of illness or hospitalization. For example, the feelings of a "defective body" will be very different for a young child beginning to develop a concept of the physical self and body image, and a schoolage child who uses the body for "work." An adolescent female who stated developmental concerns related to illness as "most girls my age start a hope chest, but I'd just like to have a chest" (Neff, 1973). Such expressions are also found in connection with fears and are often age-specific. Thus, characteristics of thinking and play of particular age groups should be incorporated into the plan for the use of humor.

Integration of Play and Humor

The use of humor with other aspects of play is an important consideration with children. Humor related to the source of illness may be too threatening unless used with play, especially if the context is the hospital environment. For example, the use of projective techniques may be considered such as drawing a person, tree, and house and adding humor after the child has told the story, or the adult telling a humorous bit about the drawings in a way that maintains the child's integrity. The use of three wishes (asking the child if the child could be anyone or be anything, what three things would be chosen) can elicit three persons or things about which one could look for humorous aspects.

An example occurred with 8-year-old Mark who was hospitalized for open-heart surgery. His first choice of someone he could be was a fireman, "to put out fires." The nurse's response that firemen are called upon to act quickly so that he "might get caught with his pants down" elicited two minutes of laughter in this child who was so fearful of surgery. Jokes about aggressors or changes in his body after surgery were also effective.

With older children, especially females, writing "funny" stories was successful in reducing stress and enabled joking about illness and hospitalization. These stories often dealt with sharing power with a caregiver such as a nurse or laboratory technician, or changes in body appearance and function. Stories involved exaggerations and double entendres and dealt with themes of danger and rescue. Stories give an opportunity for the control of persons and objects which can be manipulated however the child desires. Nine-year-old Nikki loved to tell stories about a yo-yo. This child was immobilized when she was connected to a dialysis machine. She gave the yo-yo human characteristics and herself characteristics of the yo-yo that were humorous and creative.

The role of the adult in these situations involves being emotionally available, sensitive, understanding, and accepting, so that it is safe for humor to be spontaneously expressed by the child. The adult provides opportunities for the child to play out feelings through humor, and bring fears to the surface where they can be identified and mastery can be attempted. Humor, through play, reinforces the child's feelings of security. The before-hand giving of cues that humor is to be used in nonhumorous situations enhances that security and appears to be satisfying to children.

Humorous communications given by the adult, such as verbal play on words, jokes, witticisms, cartoons, clowning, and practical jokes, elicit statements or behaviors from the child that reflect feelings of amusement: they smile, giggle, chuckle, and laugh. These responses are ways to measure the effective use of humor.

Robinson (1977) states that we send messages through humor so that the other person "gets the message." The humor must "fit" to be amusing. To "get the message," the person using humor must make it clear that humor is the intent. The joke-frame should be stated age appropriately. The cue that humor is being initiated, verbally or nonverbally, can include statements like, "Let me tell you a story," or "Let's play doctor and nurse." This immediately grabs the attention of the child and sets the stage. The other aspect of initiating humor relates to the child being able to respond to the humor. The child may "get it" but be unable to physically respond because of immobilization. Or the child may not "get it" and will not respond by laughing or smiling or other identifying characteristics of humor. To reduce the level of stress in the hospitalized child, the humor should involve aspects of the child's illness, level of understanding, and hospital environment.

The use of humor should lead to less panic and tension related to treatments and procedures. This may be revealed in their story-telling, description of events, or other behavior. There is usually more subsequent cooperation with necessary treatments and routines. There may also be less after-shock and less retention of fear after leaving the hospital. The effect of humor on the physical, psychological, sociological, and spiritual life of the hospitalized child is important to caregivers who must deal with the pain and trauma that they inflict on children because of necessary treatments.

In summary, the use of humor by healthcare providers with children in the hospital setting has not yet been systematically studied. There is some evidence, however, which suggests that children themselves often use humor to decrease stress regarding illness and hospitalization. When carefully and appropriately introduced by adults, humor should similarly help the child reduce this stress.

The impact of illness and hospitalization must be considered in relation to the particular age of the child and that particular child's way of thinking. Because communication and play involve the child's way of expressing self, it should be used prior to and in conjunction with humor. Changes in behavior of the child with whom humor has been introduced have been evidenced particularly in relation to coping with stress.

Humor requires an atmosphere where there is mutual respect and trust. To bring humor into another's life is gratifying. To reduce stress for children through the use of humor is an act of love.

REFERENCES

Astin, E. W. (1977). Self-reported fears of hospitalized and non-hospitalized children aged ten to twelve. *Maternal-Child Nursing Journal, 6,* 17-24.

Bolig, E. (1984). Play in hospital settings. In T. D. Yawkey & A. D. Pellegrini (Eds.) *Child's Play: Development and Applied* (pp. 323-343). Hillsdale, N.J.: Erlbaum.

D'Antonio, I. J. (1986). Playfulness in abused children, Research Presentation. Pittsburgh: University of Pittsburgh, May, 1986.

D'Antonio, I. J. (1984). Therapeutic use of play in hospitals. *Nursing Clinics of North America, 19(2),* 359.

Ebmeier, J. (1982). Manifestations of guilt in an immobilized child. *Maternal-Child Nursing Journal, 4,* 109-115.

Edison, C. C. (1976). Reintegration of ego functioning during recovery from a cerebral insult. *Maternal-Child Nursing Journal, 7,* 87-98.

Haver, K. (1974). Reactions of a three-year-old boy to partial immobilization. *Maternal-Child Nursing Journal, 3(2),* 133-138.

Kikuchi, J. (1977). An adolescent boy's adjustment to leukemia. *Maternal-Child Nursing Journal, 6,* 36-42.

Long, P. (1987). Laugh and be well? *Psychology Today, 10,* 28-29.

Malone, C. A. (1966). Safety first: Comments on the influence of external danger in the lives of disorganized families. *American Journal of Orthopsychiatry, 34,* 3-12.

Neff, J. A. (1973). Psychological adaptation to renal transplant. *Maternal-Child Nursing Journal, 2,* 111-119.

Piaget, J. (1947). *The Psychology of Intelligence*. London: Routledge & Kegan.

Pidgeon, V. A. (1977). Characteristics of children's thinking and implications for health teaching. *Maternal-Child Nursing Journal, 6,* 1-8.

Robinson, V. M. (1977). *Humor and the Health Profession.* Thorofare, N.J.: Charles Slack Co.

Wessel, M. L. (1975). Use of humor by an immobilized adolescent girl during hospitalization. *Maternal-Child Nursing Journal, 4,* 35-48.

Chapter 8

The Use of Humor by Pediatric Dentists

Ofra Nevo, PhD
Joseph Shapira, MD

SUMMARY. Pediatric dentists have suggested several behavioral techniques for alleviating anxiety of children in their clinic. Until now there has been no report of the use of humor in dental settings, even though it has been found effective in reducing anxiety.

A sample of pediatric dentists was interviewed and observed in order to study their use of humor. It was found that dentists use humor in a consistent way in accordance with the systematic desensitization model. Dentists create a playful-humorous atmosphere using verbal and nonverbal cues. They produce humorous bisociations, incongruities, rhymes, absurdities, exaggerations and puns. Their humor serves several functions: social, emotional, cognitive, informational, and motivational.

It has been estimated that 35 million potential patients in the U.S.A. are too frightened to arrange for their own dental care, and an estimated additional 20 to 30 percent fear visits to the dentist enough to make them only occasional users of dental services. These facts should be sufficient motivation for studying the problem of alleviating anxiety in the dental clinic.

Dentists usually cope with this anxiety by administering drugs

Ofra Nevo is affiliated with the Department of Psychology, University of Haifa, Haifa, Israel. Joseph Shapira is affiliated with the Hadassa School of Dental Medicine, The Hebrew University, Jerusalem, Israel.

This article is based partially on data published in the *Journal of Dentistry for Children*, April 1986, 97-100. The authors would like to thank the editor for the permission to use these data.

producing sedation, analgesia or anaesthesia. These drugs pose two major problems: the uncertainty of the patients' reaction to them and the danger of drug dependency to cope with anxiety. It is safer and of much greater benefit to the patient, particularly when the patient is a child, to enjoy psychological techniques to train him to be rational about the treatment. The patient should be seen as a person entitled to a meaningful therapeutic experience that is not only pain-free but that also leads to an increase in self-confidence.

Since dental visits can indeed be stressful events for many children and the anxiety associated with dental visits may influence the child's willingness to accept dental care or to follow certain courses of treatment, dentists have tried to use several behavioral modification techniques to alleviate the child's anxiety. Among the techniques mentioned are modeling (Adelson & Goldfried, 1970), behavior shaping (Rosenberg, 1974), and systematic desensitization (Melamed, 1975; Wright, 1975).

To the best of our knowledge, the use of humor to reduce anxiety has not been reported in the dental-care literature. Yet, we believe humor to be an important behavior that can be systematically used in the child dental clinic. Ventis (1973) was the first to point out the potential of humor as a counter-conditional response to anxiety. He based his idea on the systematic desensitization technique (Wolpe, 1969). Systematic desensitization consists of introducing the patient to a response that is incompatible with the anxiety. The anxiety-producing stimuli are presented *gradually* in conjunction with contradictory responses. This usually results in diminishing the anxiety through the principle of counter-conditioning. Traditionally, deep muscle relaxation has been used to lessen the anxiety, but recently emotive-cognitive imagery was effectively employed (Lazarus & Abramovitz, 1962). In emotive-cognitive imagery, the patient is encouraged to experience imaginatively relaxing situations, instead of, or coupled with muscle relaxation. Ayer (1973) has demonstrated the effectiveness of emotive imagery in dental settings.

Ventis (1973), Smith (1973), and Phillips and Judd (1978) have shown that humor can be successfully employed within a systematic desensitization model. They were able to show that the use of humor resulted in diminishing anxiety (Ventis, 1973), anger (Smith,

1973) and even "pains of broken heart" (Phillips & Judd, 1978). (See Ventis in this volume, for a more detailed discussion along these lines.)

A detailed analysis of the examples provided in these studies reveals the methods used to produce humor. Therapists as well as patients create incongruities through exaggeration, absurdities, representation by opposite, reversals, puns and play on words. They create humor by inventing bisociations (a term coined by Koestler, 1966, see chapter by Ziv, this volume) where humor is a result of perception of a situation in two habitually incompatible frames of reference. By using these methods, anxiety-producing stimuli are cognitively changed into humorous stimuli. In our opinion, such an approach seems highly relevant and can be adapted to the fearful child in the dental clinic.

The idea of the present study took shape when the first author took her two sons to a new dentist. One visit to this new dentist reduced their long-held anxiety connected with dentists. They now go willingly to their treatment (not to mention the alleviation of their mother's anxiety!). One of the characteristics of this dentist was his use of humorous statements, play, and imagination. This formed the basis for cooperation between a pediatric dentist and a psychologist of humor.

Ten specialists in pediatric dentistry (eight men and two women), on the faculty of the Hadassah School of Dental Medicine, Jerusalem, were interviewed. This group of dentists is highly professional and combined the use of modern dentistry with sensitivity to behavior management of children. Each dentist was interviewed individually and asked to recall his exact conversation during a typical visit—including the admission of the patient, seating him in a chair, explaining the equipment and the course of treatment. At the end of the interview, specific questions concerning the functions of humor were asked. Three dentists were observed in actual work, to verify the interviews. When the dentists were asked an open-ended question about their use of humor, they were generally not aware of their frequent and systematic use of it. Later analysis of their behavior and verbalizations revealed the following picture.

THE USE OF HUMOR BY WELL-TRAINED DENTISTS

The usual procedure mentioned by most of the dentists was as follows: When a child walks into the clinic, he is usually met by a smiling receptionist who takes him to the waiting room, where he can amuse himself with books, cartoons, games and toys. When his turn comes, he is greeted cheerfully by the dentist who smiles at him and tries to make small talk with some humorous remarks, usually about the last holiday, hair-style or a current TV hero. By these three simple acts, the dentist and his staff give the child non-verbal and verbal cues to perceive the situation as playful and non-threatening. The child needs cues precluding seriousness and needs to be put in a "humor set" in order to be able to perceive the situation as humorous (Berlyne, 1972; McGhee, 1972; Rothbart, 1976).

All the dentists interviewed used the same technique (Tell, Show and Do) as developed by Addelston (1959). The dentist first tells the child what he is going to do (Tell) and then shows the equipment (Show) and only thereafter proceeds to perform (Do). The object of the technique is to desensitize the child gradually to the anxiety-provoking stimuli in the dental clinic. Dentists using it are encouraged to use language and concepts which are easy for the child to understand. This led to the development of a special language of euphemisms based on bisociations of concepts from the child's world to the anxiety-provoking medical terms. The use of special language resulted in the production of a *special humorous dictionary* which is presented in Table 1.

TABLE 1. Standard Humor Dictionary

Dental Terminology	Humorous Terminology
The dental chair	Airplane, spaceship, elevator, see-saw. (Fly with the chair "up" and "down")
Opening the mouth	"Open your mouth like a lion!" "Let's see if you still have teeth (or a tongue)"
Light	"We use a light because your mouth does not have windows."
Topical anesthetics	"Orange juice or jam to numb your cheek or gums." "I have pudding in three flavors: Orange, Banana or Strawberry. You can choose which."

Local Anesthetic	"The teeth go to sleep. You stay awake to help." (Personification of the teeth) "The teeth drink from a bottle. Don't drink so fast!"
When a few drops leak into the mouth, the taste is awful	The dentist makes all sorts of sympathetic sounds like "ich . . ., fichs . . ." Making noises to district attention. Never mention the word "injection."
Big mirror	"Take the mirror and see if you still look pretty (or handsome)." "It feels funny but you look O.K.!" "Can you see brown-black staining with a big hole? This is the place where Carious and Bactus live."
Rubber dam	Rain coat
Rubber dam clamp	"It's a tooth ring; put it on your finger and see if it fits!"
Suction	Vacuum cleaner
Air syringe	Nice poof poof!
Slow-speed turbine (drill)	Tractor, bulldozer.
High-speed turbine (drill)	Fireman's hose
Saliva ejector	A duck drinking; a pump.
Cavities	Cariouses and Bactuses.
Filling matrix	Baking pan.
Filling	Making a cake. "Do you have silver-colored play-dough in your kindergarten?"
Forceps	"Like a parrot with two wings, the screw is the eye of the parrot. The parrot is looking for food." "These are metal fingers! Can you pull out your teeth with your fingers?"
X-Ray Equipment	Tooth camera "I'm going to take pictures of your teeth and see how pretty they are." "The camera looks big and funny. It's got a big head that goes up and down like a steam-shovel. It has a big nose that takes pictures."

The basic assumption is that the child of this age is ready to play, to "assimilate in fantasy" (McGhee, 1972), to make believe "as if" the chair is an airplane. The child knows it is not true but he or she is ready for a game, ready for fun. (For discussion of application of fantasy in the dental clinic see Jinks, 1955.) In addition to the common humorous terminology, some dentists reported individual variations:

1. Rhymes. Some use rhymes specifically for the younger patients. (Rhymes are in Hebrew!) For example: "Halashon Telech Lishon" — The tongue will go to sleep. "Notzi et Hashahor Mitoch Hachor" — Let's take the black out of the hole.

2. Riddles and questions (for older patients). "When do you eat matza?" "Passover!" "When do you eat turkey?" "Thanksgiving." "And when do you eat sweets?" "All the year!" "No Never!"

3. Absurdities and exaggerations and representation through the opposite. "It's going to hurt a lot!" (When in fact it does not hurt at all). "Next time I will try harder!" If the patient asks, "How do you put my mouth to sleep?" Some answer with exaggerations: "I have a five-kilo hammer and I pound hard with it."

4. Allusions to popular media heroes. Some make bisociations with popular TV programs and books, the most popular being "Carius and Bactus," a humorous cartoon book describing two heroes representing the bacteria involved in caries. It seems that dentists are sensitive to the age of their patients. When working with pre-schoolers (aged 3-6), they rely on rhymes and fantasy while with other children (11-13), they are apt to use riddles with exaggerations. This corresponds with findings on developmental changes in humor preference (McGhee, 1979; Chapter 1, this volume). Some dentists pointed out that "one should laugh with the patient not at him." Some instances of humor that did not work are when the patient was disparaged. Therefore, it is safer to direct humor at the equipment, the mother, or the dentist himself, but not at the patient.

Dentists referred in their interviews to several functions of humor:

- Diversion of attention
- Reducing anxiety of mother, dentist and child
- Creating and maintaining rapport
- Transmission of information through enjoyable means
- Increasing interest and involvement of both child and the dentist

As for the last function of humor, dentists have one of the highest rates of professional burnout (Pines, Aronson & Kafry, 1981). Creating humor and communication may combat such burnout by promoting more relaxing relationships.

CONCLUSIONS

It has been demonstrated that some dentists use humor consistently within the systematic desensitization model. They supply cues to create humor sets. They present anxiety producing stimuli gradually following the Tell-Show-Do model in conjunction with humorous incongruities and bisociation. Humor, trivial as it seems, when used with regard to patient's needs can serve as a useful and inexpensive method for controlling anxiety and achieving better cooperation with the patients. It might help the dentists to cope with conflicts and burnout in their profession.

In the future, more rigorous research is needed to show the specific contribution of humor to managing anxiety by comparing patients' reactions to treatment with and without humor. From our observations of dentists at work, we are impressed that once dentists acquire some skill in using it, humor can provide a very effective tool in helping to minimize and control anxiety associated with the dental treatment.

REFERENCES

Addelston, R., & Goldfried, M. R. (1970). Modeling and the fearful child patient. *Journal of Dentistry for Children, 27*, 476-478.

Adelson, H. K. (1959). Child patient training. *Fortnightly Review of the Chicago Dental Society, 38*(7-9), 27-29.

Ayer, W. (1973). Use of visual imagery in needle phobic children. *Journal of Dentistry for Children, 40*, 125-127.

Berlyne, D. E. (1972). Humor and its kin. In J. H. Goldstein & P. E. McGhee (Eds.), *The psychology of humor*. New York: Academic Press.

Jinks, G. M. (1955). The application of fantasy to paedodontics. *The Journal of the Canadian Dental Association*, July, 3-7.

Koestler, A. (1966). *The act of creation*. London: Hutchinson.

Lazarus, A., & Abramowitz, A. (1962). The use of "Emotive Imagery" in the treatment of children's phobias. *Journal of Medical Science, 108*, 191-195.

McGhee, P. E. (1972). On the cognitive origins of incongruity humor: In J. H.

Goldstein & P. E. McGhee (Eds.), *The psychology of humor*. New York: Academic Press.

McGhee, P. E. (1979). *Humor: Its origin and development*. San Francisco: Freeman.

Melamed, B. G. (1975). Behavioral approaches to fear in dental settings. In M. E. Hensen, M. Eixler & D. Miller (Eds.), *Progress in behavioral modification* (Vol. 7).

Phillips, D., & Judd, R. (1978). *How to fall out of love*. New York: Popular Library.

Pines, A. M., Aronson, E., & Kafry, D. (1981). *Burnout: From tedium to personal growth*. New York: The Free Press.

Rosenberg, H. M. (1974). Behavior modification for the child dental patient. *Journal of Dentistry for Children, 41*, 111-114.

Rothbart, M. (1976). Incongruity problem-solving and laughter. In T. Chapman & H. Foot (Eds.), *Humor and laughter: Theory, research and applications*. London: Wiley.

Smith, R. E. (1973). The use of humor in counter-conditioning of anger responses: A case study. *Behavior Therapy, 4*, 576-580.

Ventis, W. L. (1973). A case history: The use of laughter as an alternative response in systematic desensitization. *Behavior Therapy, 4*, 120-122.

Wolpe, J. (1969). *The practice of behavior therapy*. Oxford: Pergamon Press.

Wright, G. Z. (1975). *Behavior management in dentistry for children*. Philadelphia: W. B. Saunders Co.

Chapter 9

Guidelines for Using Humor in Therapy with Children and Young Adolescents

W. Larry Ventis, PhD
Deborah G. Ventis, PhD

SUMMARY. This chapter begins with a discussion of prominent characteristics of therapy with children and issues relevant to the use of humor in children's therapy. Applications of therapeutic humor are presented and discussed in the contexts of: (a) psychodynamic psychotherapy, (b) the use of humor in behavioral treatments, predominantly of child phobias, (c) humor in family therapy, and (d) purposeful use of games and stories. Finally, possibly directions for future applications are discussed.

Recent publications (e.g., Fry & Salameh, 1987; Kuhlman, 1984) reflect an increasing interest in potential applications of humor across a broad range of psychotherapeutic approaches. These examples, however, deal predominantly with humor in adult psychotherapy. Levine (1980) reviewed therapy applications with children, but he focused exclusively on psychodynamic therapy. To begin our consideration of therapeutic uses of humor with children, we will discuss some general points that differentiate child therapy from work with adults. As contrasted with the adult who voluntarily seeks treatment, the child is more typically brought to therapy by the parents, or required to attend by an outside agency. In this cir-

---

W. Larry Ventis and Deborah G. Ventis are with the Department of Psychology, College of William and Mary, Williamsburg, VA.

179

cumstance, the child is likely to begin therapy in a state of bewilderment, fear, or as an adversary to the therapist whom he or she feels forced to see. When this is the case, it can be a relief and a source of reassurance if the therapist shows a playful or humorous perspective early on. Whatever else is to come, the relationship begins with a shared interest in playful fun.

Another prominent difference between child and adult treatment consists of the fact that children lack adult verbal skills and cognitive abilities. The major accommodation to this fact in traditional psychotherapy methods has been the use of play therapy, in which the child's play behavior is encouraged by a therapist and then used like a response to a projective technique to make sense of the child's experience. Although the title, play therapy, might lead one to expect the playful inclusion of humor, in fact it is relatively rare to see any references to humor in the play therapy literature, and journal accounts of cases typically seem rather grimly analytical.

A final general difference between child and adult therapy is the fact that usually the therapist has far greater potential control over significant aspects of the child's environment than exists in the typical adult case. The parents are often motivated or can be encouraged to make significant changes for the child's sake. This potential for control, combined with the fact that environmental changes in childhood can prevent more serious pathology later, has resulted in agreement between theoretical perspectives otherwise at odds over the importance of environmental manipulations, changing the environment can be highly beneficial for children (e.g., Freud, 1936).

Other general issues to consider in using humor in therapy with children are implicit in the developmental literature on children's emerging abilities. In some ways, humor may be more easily integrated into child psychotherapy than into adult treatment. Kuhlman (1984) has noted possible advantages in attempting to use humor therapeutically with children: namely, the child's normal mode of experiencing tends to be a playful perspective in which there is considerable vacillation between fantasy and reality, and the younger the child the more this tends to be the case. Thus, techniques using humor in therapy with children use a mode of experience that the child is accustomed to and may well prefer, a fact that prompts

Kuhlman (1984) to refer to the therapist's use of humor as "a form of global empathy" (p. 98).

Simons, McClusky-Fawcett, and Papini (1986) in an overview of developmental theories of humor, describe the psychoanalytic, cognitive developmental, and social-learning perspectives. The respective theories stress different functions of children's humor as well as different influences affecting it. Psychoanalytic theory, exemplified in Wolfenstein's (1954) work stresses two themes in children's humor: (a) humor content is derived from the child's psychosexual motivational conflicts; and (b) humor serves as a constructive defense mechanism enabling the child to express and cope with the conflicts experienced. These themes will be apparent in the section that follows on traditional psychodynamic treatment.

Cognitive developmental theory emphasizes the changes in content and form of humor material that is appreciated and generated by children of differing ages due to their differing cognitive abilities. Piaget, in trying to clarify the differences between his invariant functions of assimilation and accommodation, presents fantasy play as the purest example he can find of the process of assimilation, and the young child is highly invested in fantasy (Flavell, 1963). For the preoperational child, fantasy play is a pleasurable means of spontaneously practicing and expanding his or her cognitive abilities without the frustrations of the limits inherent in the real environment. The children's therapist who initiates humor should benefit from a general awareness of normative expectations for humor of children of differing ages, regardless of the therapist's theoretical perspective. The reader is referred to McGhee (1979) and Chapter 1 of this volume for an overview of developmental differences in children's humor.

In both of the preceding perspectives, humor is assumed to reflect one's sense of mastery of affective conflicts in the psychoanalytic view, and of cognitive abilities in the cognitive developmental. Social learning theory, in contrast, emphasizes the effects of environmental processes such as modeling, reinforcement, and punishment, on the child's behavioral expression of humor and the forms such expression may take. Therapists are one source of these processes influencing humorous behaviors, whether purposeful or not.

Developmentally, humor, laughter, and smiling may serve different functions for children of differing ages. Functions summarized by Simons, McClusky-Fawcett, and Papini (1986), which seem to be of particular relevance to therapy, include the facilitation of peer attachments in early childhood via such behaviors as smiling at peers and sharing humor with others. They also discuss general communication and socialization functions in later childhood including such things as using humor for personal satisfaction, relating with others via humor, and as an expression of cognitive and social mastery (see Chapter 10 of this volume for a discussion of social aspects of humor). As will become apparent, the applications of some of these functions in therapy are often independent of the theoretical orientation from which they are derived.

There are, of course, potential dangers in using humor with children in therapy. First, the therapist must keep in mind that because children do not have the same cognitive abilities as adults, there is more potential for the child to misinterpret the therapist's humor or experience it as representative of ridicule or a lack of seriousness about the child's problems. In accommodation to this, the therapist would do well to avoid humor directed at the client. More generally, it seems critical to keep in mind that humor is a means to therapeutic ends and not an end in itself in therapy.

With this brief background as an orientation, examples of therapeutic applications within specific theoretical frameworks are presented in the following sections.

THERAPEUTIC APPLICATIONS

Traditional Psychodynamic Psychotherapy

Consistent with the general orientation of psychodynamic therapists of imposing meaning on patient productions, most of the examples of use of humor with children within this perspective focus on child initiated humor. Orfanidis (1972) reported on the production of humor in therapy of 10 children, between the ages of 7 and 10. Methodologically, the study is limited because it consists of the subjective categorization and interpretation of spontaneous humor productions after they were observed. Nonetheless, her findings are informative. She concluded that the functions of humor for these children included deriving pleasure, sharing aggressive and fearful feelings, breaking down social barriers, and attempting to master anxiety. The most common humor techniques reported in Orfanidis' sample were incongruity and disparagement of others.

The following example is of spontaneous humor generated in a session shortly after the child had been told he would be switched to another school the following year, a fact that was quite distressing, partially because he was fearful of rejection due to intellectual inadequacy.

> JOHNNY: You're retarded! You're goin' in the retarded room . . . You aren't retarded, but you sure talk retarded . . . Ask anybody else. What do you think they'll say? Guess what they'll say! (mimicking) Retarded!
> THERAPIST: I'm retarded?
> JOHNNY: Yes . . . I'm not retarded (giggle) . . .
> (Then Johnny expressed concern that his therapist might discontinue treatment with him.)
> THERAPIST: You'll still see me.
> JOHNNY: That's good because I might get a *real* dumb guy. (p. 152)

The therapist interpreted this sequence to mean that the child was using ridicule of the therapist to conquer his own fear of eliciting rejection due to intellectual inadequacy. Simultaneously, he was sharing this fear with the therapist, and deriving some sense of pleasure from the interaction.

This child was unique in this sample in his ability to spontaneously produce fairly complex humor from anxiety arousing situations; such humor production should not be expected routinely. The following instance is less distinctly an attempt at humor, but is more representative of children in the sample with less serious disorders.

> Jerry, an eight-year-old boy who had become the scapegoat for family problems since his brother had been run over by a car five years before, frequently made comments when he heard ambulance sirens. At one time the therapist asked him if he had ever been in an ambulance and he replied, laughing,

"No! And I intend not to! But if I do, it won't be to get hurt (giggle). I'll be the driver (giggle) because if I were ever to get hurt, it wouldn't be fun." (p. 153)

Thus, the basis for the humor here is that of the child placing himself in the mastery role of being the driver, but the humor is not particularly funny to an adult. The giggling would appear to be associated with both anxiety and increased feelings of mastery at the reversal of roles.

Tolor (1966), who briefly summarized his experience of joke-telling by child clients 7 to 13 years of age, drew similar conclusions. He viewed the jokes as reflecting a positive motivation of wanting to share an enjoyable experience with another, and further, he construed the child's joking to be an assertion of mastery over emotionally charged content.

In contrast to merely reporting on humor volunteered by children in psychodynamic therapy, Yorukoglu (1974) advocated the technique of encouraging the child client to tell his or her favorite joke. His report is based on 150 jokes collected from approximately 650 children ranging in age from 7 to 16 years. Yorukoglu notes several cases where the favorite joke provided remarkable insight regarding the child's basic conflict, and claims that for 75% of his clients the relationship between the favorite joke and the core conflict was clearly established. Yorukoglu also told the favorite joke to the parents with the child's permission. He found that using the joke to illustrate the child's core conflict often greatly facilitated the parents' understanding of their child's feelings.

Domash (1975) reported a case study of a 9 1/2-year-old borderline psychotic boy who used humor in psychotherapy as one means of relating to the therapist and to gain a sense of mastery over his fears. The following example shows an ability, early in therapy, to keep the interaction at a level he could handle.

When the therapist, in the early part of treatment, at times overzealously interpreted behavior in an effort to make contact with Danny, he would turn to her, saying with a toss of his hand, "Keep it low. Keep it low." (Domash, 1975, p. 266)

Noting that, in this case, humor served functions from permitting gratifying contact with others to permitting the expression of feelings and gaining some sense of mastery over his fantasies. The author's recommendation to other therapists for such children is to reinforce their humor by letting them know it is enjoyable.

Shaw (1961), in addition to encouraging humor for some of the functions described in the preceding, also used it to explore family dynamics, posing humorous situations and noting how the child reacts in the humorous context to different family members. He also says that humor can set the tone of an institution just by its presence even if not used in more targeted ways. Thus, in the psychodynamic approach, those using humor tend to analyze the humor as revealing significant conflicts, or foster it as an aid to the therapeutic relationship or the child's sense of mastery.

Behavior Therapy

In contrast with the preceding section, behavior therapists who have used humor in child treatment tend to introduce the humor themselves, to try to accomplish specific goals, and frequently give minimal rationale for its inclusion. Predominantly, it has been used in fear reduction techniques. An early example is that of Lazarus and Abramowitz (1962) who used emotive imagery in systematic desensitization to successfully treat 7 to 9 phobic children, ranging in age from 7 to 14 years. The procedure is conducted in game-like fashion. The children imagine themselves in story scenes with favorite TV heroes, comic book characters, etc., in situations designed to elicit anxiety inhibiting feelings such as self-assertion and mirth. Phobias specifically mentioned as being successfully treated include fear of dogs, the dark, and school, and the average treatment interval was 3.3 sessions. Subsequent case studies have involved stories focused on Batman (Jackson & King, 1981), Paul Bunyan (Kravetz & Forness, 1971), Christmas and a visit to Disneyland (Lazarus, Davison & Polefka, 1965). For guidelines in the use of emotive imagery with children, Rosentiel and Scott (1977) suggest: (a) adapting the imagery to the age and ability of the child, (b) using some of the child's own thoughts and fantasies, (c) the inclusion of nonverbal cues to facilitate treatment, and (d) using the child's self-report of images during treatment.

Some fear reduction techniques have combined *in vivo* approach to the feared stimuli with a game-like atmosphere to accomplish the desired goal. Croghan and Musante (1975) treated a 7-year-old boy who was phobic of high buildings by initiating an approach to tall buildings in the company of the therapist, and if the child became fearful, games such as skipping the cracks in the sidewalk, counting the number of times they could glance at the building, and kicking the building a specific number of times, were initiated. During a snowstorm the child and the therapist also threw snowballs at the buildings.

Humor was also employed in the context of modeling with guided participation to modify a 6-year-old boy's extreme social withdrawal from peers (Ross, Ross & Evans, 1971). In this instance, humor was used to present a coping model (i.e., the model showed fear similar to that of the client, but modeled overcoming it) to elicit interest, and to inhibit anxiety, as in the preceding cases cited. The following fearful questions by the model were in response to the therapist's suggestion that the model interact with a child:

> "What if he says, 'here's an elephant?' when all I want is a red crayon?" "What if he calls me a slippery banana?" "What if he says, 'Go away funny bunny'?" . . . S was interested, very attentive, and often amused . . . At no time during these exchanges did S exhibit signs of fear arousal. (Ross, Ross & Evans, 1971, p. 278)

Another study involving *in vivo* desensitization was done with a 4-year-old boy who was so phobic of loud sudden noises that he would become extremely frightened at even the sight of an inflated balloon (Tasto, 1969). In this case, a mildly humorous response induction aid was employed by having the father place a dime inside a balloon. The child could have the dime if he popped the balloon. At first, the balloon was only slightly inflated. Subsequent balloons were inflated more completely until eventually the child could comfortably pop a fully inflated one. As was true in the previous cases cited, the humorous interaction was only a single ingredient in a sequence of therapeutic procedures that included gradually encountering a hierarchy of loud noises in the company of the therapist or his father.

Oddly, it seems that humorous books and cartoons have rarely been used in therapeutic procedures with children. The first author successfully treated an 8-year-old boy and his 12-year-old sister, both of whom were dog phobic. The approach combined training in relaxation with modeling and guided participation. An early homework assignment consisted of giving the children a book of dog jokes (Friedman, 1986) and a book of dog cartoons (Gross, 1985). Their assignment was to pick their favorite jokes and favorite cartoons during the week before the next session so they could show them to the therapist. The intent was to model and encourage a perspective toward dogs other than fear, to facilitate the formation of a pleasant and comfortable relationship, and to set the tone that the process of mastering fear could be pleasant. The children did seem to enjoy the task, showed some enthusiasm for presenting their choices, and the eventual outcome was successful.

The only other use of commercially available humor material that the authors encountered was a treatment for thumbsucking in children between 3 1/2 and 5-years-old (Bishop & Stumphauser, 1973). In this study, each child was placed before a TV set on Saturday morning when cartoons were on. The children were informed that if they sucked their thumb the TV would be turned off. It would be turned back on only if they stopped sucking their thumb. The procedure was regarded as time-out from positive reinforcement, namely the cartoons. The thumbsucking was eliminated in four treatment sessions, and a generalization measure of thumbsucking one month later during a story time showed a complete absence of the treated response for 2 of the 3 children treated and a very low rate for the third.

Family Therapy

In contrast to the dominant psychodynamic practice of tolerating and encouraging children's humor productions when they occur and using them to clarify dynamics, and the behavior therapists' primary use of humor within established techniques to promote feelings of mastery and to counter anxiety and fear, family therapy with

children as the identified patients sometimes takes a new and different tack. First, consider the case of children who themselves are
witty and comical to an extreme. Fisher and Fisher (1987) have
written about the dynamics of the comic child, the child whose
trademark attribute is attention-eliciting, sometimes exhibiting bizarre humorous statements and behaviors. In their work with children, they have found that about 10% of their clients fall into this
category. Their writings in this area focused on both a humorous
pattern of behavior as a reflection of family problems and the importance of humor in treatment. They tried to convey to the parents
that their child's absurd behavior is a reaction to an absurd family
situation. Thus, the child's response to the situation may convey a
message like, "This dilemma is frustrating but also tolerable if reduced to the absurd" (Fisher & Fisher, 1987, p. 116) or "If you
treat me in odd, crazy ways, I have the right to be just as odd" (p.
119).

The authors present an example of a school phobic 15-year-old
girl who, in their assessment, had a very symbiotic relationship
with her mother. As a consequence the daughter was driven to stay
home from school to take care of the mother. This was revealed to
the parents as follows:

> THERAPIST: Well, your daughter is indeed a very responsi-
> ble girl and she is worried about you and, would you believe
> it, she's staying home to care for you! (The therapist smiled in
> amusement.)
> MOTHER: She doesn't have to do that. She makes a mess of
> the kitchen. She doesn't have to do that. That's silly. She's
> only making trouble for me. She's no help at home! As the
> image of their "helping daughter" began to register, the par-
> ents were able to conjure up a variety of corroborative inci-
> dents. They began to laugh and a series of examples poured
> out. . . . (Fisher & Fisher, 1987, p. 117-118)

The Fishers also describe a technique for leading the parents to
see the humor in such a pattern as opposed to feeling defensive
about their contribution to the absurdity of the situation:

"Imagine that you are watching this on TV. You'd think it was VERY funny. It's a lot different when you are part of the action. It is hard to see how funny it really is." We refer to the parents' position as that of the straightman for the joke. "The straightman never laughs. . . . But if you stand on the sidelines and watch the action, you can appreciate the fun." (Fisher & Fisher, 1987, p. 118)

In addition to tactfully introducing the parents to the sense of the absurdity in the situation, the Fishers emphasized the importance of the therapist conveying his or her acceptance of the child's right to respond in absurd fashion while attempting to relieve the child of the burden of assuming an absurd role in the family. Therapy, therefore, consisted of both individual sessions with the child and sessions with the parents.

In the context of strategic family therapy, Madanes (1987) outlined a similar perspective. A symptom or problem behavior appears illogical or absurd, but the symptom is assumed to be generated and maintained by absurdity within the family system. Therefore, the therapist offers a paradoxical prescription, which though containing some absurdity itself, serves to transcend the self-defeating aspects of the existing interaction pattern and resolve the dilemma. For a dramatic and entertaining example, consider her description of the treatment of a 12-year-old boy who had been a firesetter over a 7 year interval. The behavior was even more problematic given that the child's father required a security clearance for his work, and the son had once set fire to explosives at a business party for army personnel. In the first therapy session, the boy was asked to set a fire and extinguish it and then sharply criticized, in great detail, for his lack of skill. The father was then asked to model appropriate firesetting and extinguishing behavior, and a paradoxical prescription was given: "He was directed to supervise the boy in this endeavor, setting a variety of fires with different materials in different places and putting them out. Father and son were to do this six times a day every day" (Madanes, 1987, p. 255). This continued for several weeks, the father spent more time with his son, the son asked if they could not do other more constructive things, and the therapist acquiesced. The son also seemed challenged to show the therapist that he could be competent in a number of areas and even began to do quite well in school. The therapist's prescription was certainly incongruous with the clients' expectations, contained elements of absurdity, and yet appears to have accomplished the therapeutic goal. In contrast with the preceding examples of use of humor in therapy with children, the two examples cited of humor in treating families seem to be more of an art than the more targeted uses of humor presented in earlier sections. It should also be noted that the paradoxical prescription was implemented in a family therapy treatment that took place over several weeks and therefore, though it is featured in this description, treatment must have included many other ingredients as well. Clearly, however, humor is in a much more central role in these particular family therapy approaches than it was in the psychodynamic and behavioral therapy examples previously cited.

Games and Stories

In contrast to traditional play therapy, in which play is treated primarily as a source of interpretable material, games and stories have begun to emerge in the child therapy literatures that are designed to accomplish specific goals in a humorous or playful context. These approaches emphasize humor to varying degrees, but we have chosen to be over- rather than under-inclusive in this section because the examples may show potential applications of humor that readers may be able to improve on.

One such game, designed for use with therapy groups of latency age children, is partially targeted toward modifying silly disruptive behavior, or minimizing inappropriate or undesirable instances of humor (Epstein & Borduin, 1984). The authors designed a structured group experience of 12 weekly sessions called "Children Helping Children" for children whose parents were separated or divorced. Within this program, one of the games used is "The Children's Feedback Game." Group meetings were video and audiotaped and transcribed after each session. Summaries of each week's session, describing what happened to individuals and the group were given to each child at the beginning of the next session. The group was divided into two teams, and the teams tried to earn points to earn a party for the entire group when the program ended. The leader read a description of the behavior of some unidentified child. The first task was to identify who was being described. The teams took turns guessing, earned a point for a correct guess, and could challenge if they disagreed with the other team's guess. Bonus points could be earned in four categories: feeling points were awarded when a child explained how he or she felt in response to the described behavior of another; owning points were earned when the child described correctly acknowledged his or her behavior and described how others reacted to the behavior; change points were earned by the child described if he or she suggested how to change the behavior; advice points were awarded when another child suggested how the described child might change the behavior.

Instead of correcting a child's misbehavior, the misbehaviors are frequently featured in the behavioral descriptions. The game minimized the adversarial role of therapist and child in handling disruptive behavior and focused the child's attention on the acts and feelings of him or herself and others within an enjoyable context. Although no specific examples of humor were presented, the authors did describe presenting incongruous and surprising descriptions (e.g., a description of one person's behavior that they anticipated would be misattributed to another for whom it was more typical) so that the potential for humor seems implicit in the game's structure.

In the same program, a second game is used "Could This Happen?" (Epstein & Borduin, 1985). This game was designed to ease the discussion of feelings and problems experienced by children of divorced parents. The children were presented with hypothetical situations, and they rated their probability of occurrence. Most of the items to be rated pertain to conflicts, fears, and experiences directly relevant to divorce, but some warmup items are preposterous, seemingly intended to allay anxiety in the situation and ease the child's entry into the discussion of divorce-related issues. The inclusion of later ridiculous items to be rated in this context could also serve a function of providing comic relief.

Another game incorporating purposeful humor was used by the first author to ease the process of getting acquainted with young delinquent boys in a storefront clinic setting. This game, titled "Situation Comedy" because it builds in the possibility of comedy in an otherwise awkward situation, has been described in the literature in the context of helping couples to get acquainted on a first date (Ventis, 1987). The game consisted of taking turns starting a sentence for the other person to finish as though it were his or her statement. The sentence stems may vary from ludicrous ("Freckles protect you from . . ."), to inquisitive ("My favorite sport is . . .") to more personal ("I get angry when . . ."). The person responding is only required to complete the sentence. He or she may do so honestly, humorously, or in any way he or she chooses. In the clinic in which the game was used, the boys participated as an alternative to standard probation. The game gave them an easy structure within which to meet and become acquainted with a strange adult. It created the opportunity to share humor, but imposed no pressure to be funny.

Typically, therapist and client drifted between taking turns and just talking about topics that emerged in the course of the game. The game makes it possible to question each other and engage in self disclosure, but without any pressure to respond when either person prefers not to.

Stories represent another means for using humor in children's therapy. Wenger (1982) wrote "The Suitcase Story" as an aid in therapy with children in out of home placement. The story was constructed with three goals in mind: First, to help the children express their anger; second, to help them express any abandonment fears, and third, to encourage them to discuss their longing for permanence. A suitcase was chosen as the protagonist to provide sufficient distance to permit the child to identify with the character without feeling too defensive. With regard to the expression of anger, the author noted, "In fact, not a single child listened to the story without smiling broadly upon hearing how the suitcase got even with the adults in its life" (Wenger, 1982, p. 353). After telling the story the therapist would then discuss it with the child, providing the opportunity to accomplish the goals listed in the preceding.

E. Levine (1980) reports successful treatment of childhood insomnia in a 3-year-old and a 6-year-old through indirect hypnotic suggestions embedded in personalized fairy tales. Audio recordings of fairy tales constructed using the child's favorite activities, fantasy characters, animals, colors, and foods were constructed by the therapist after discussing the most likely sources of stress with the parents.

Suggestions included comfort, happiness, relaxation, and self-confidence. Although humor is not mentioned specifically, the sample fairy tale for the 3-year-old included a "magic verse" recited by a character which was followed by suggestions concerning the reactions of the child

> Fiddlededo, Ernie and Burt
> I like blueberry frozen yogurt,
> Playing in the sprinkler,
> Going in the green truck for a ride,
> Now I feel really good inside!
> "Hmmm," said S., "that's a very funny verse. That verse has so many things in it that I like. Hmmm, if I say what I'd like each night before I go to bed, I can feel very, very good inside too." (Levine, 1980, p. 62)

The use of this story technique to present indirect hypnotic suggestions is quite similar to the use of emotive imagery by behavior therapists. In both cases, fun, humor, and a pleasant playful context are used to enhance feelings of self-efficacy, mastery, or confidence. Further, the previously mentioned guidelines for the use of emotive imagery (Rosentiel & Scott, 1977) are quite consistent with Levine's (1980) work in that she integrates so much of the child's own experience into her stories.

DISCUSSION

First, we should state the obvious. All of the examples we have described in this review are drawn from case studies. There is a need for research on the effectiveness of humor in therapy approaches with children and on whether or not there are any specific benefits associated with the inclusion of humor in existing techniques over and above the effectiveness of these techniques alone. Nonetheless, the range of applications described in this review implies considerable potential therapeutic value for humor in child therapy. Consider some functions for humor that appear to be common to several therapeutic approaches: (a) in practically any approach to therapy, humor may enhance rapport and serve to strengthen the therapeutic relationship, (b) in a variety of contexts therapists describe humor as enhancing a sense of mastery, self-efficacy, or ego strength, and (c) humor appears to help in countering fear and anxiety, associated either with the therapist and treatment, phobic stimuli, or both, and (d) humor may serve as a source of pleasure in the sometimes demanding and difficult process of therapy.

Other functions of humor are unique to specific theoretical approaches or techniques: (a) psychodynamic therapists' use of a child's spontaneous humor or favorite joke to identify and explain core conflicts, (b) the family therapists' use of an absurd or humorous prescription to counter or transcend the underlying absurdity in the family relationships, and (c) the behavior therapists' use of humor to elicit and maintain interest in information to be conveyed such as in the modeling context (this latter approach is also used to some degree in storytelling techniques).

For the future, some additional uses of humor with children in therapy seem well worth trying. The therapeutic applications of games and stories, which have been developed to help children with a few specific problems, might well be expanded for use in a wide variety of situations.

Thus far, humor has been used by behavior therapists primarily to counter fear in children. It has also been used to counter anger and aggression in adults (Smith, 1973), and adolescents (Prerost, 1984). We encountered only a single, dated reference (Redl & Wineman, 1952), however, describing the purposeful use of humor to enable hyperaggressive children to interact with others in less destructive ways. Parke and Slaby (1983) note that research with older subjects suggests that humor may mediate inhibition of aggression by eliciting positive emotional states incompatible with aggression, and/or shifting attention away from past provocations. Therefore, more effort might reasonably be directed to the use of humor in treatment of hyperaggressive children.

Another area where more extensive application of humor could be profitable is in social skills training with children. Masten (1986), in a methodologically rigorous study of humor and competence in children, concluded that humor production and appreciation may be functionally related to social interaction; an absence of humor was found to be associated with social isolation. To the extent that this is true, the modeling and reinforcement of joking behavior and humor appreciation would be desirable inclusions in social skills training to facilitate peer relationships. Although we have noted a single instance of humor used sparingly to treat a socially withdrawn child (Ross, Ross & Evans, 1971), more extensive effort seems justified in this area, not so much to teach all children to be comics, but to free such humor ability and appreciation as is present given individual differences in sense of humor.

Individual differences in humor may be important in the design and effectiveness of therapeutic interventions. Such differences may appear in early infancy (Washburn, 1929). Individual differences in personality variables relevant to humor development in childhood include introversion-extroversion (McGhee, 1986), and cognitive style (Brodzinsky & Rightmeyer, 1980). Thus far, the only accommodation to individual differences has been the association of different humor applications in therapy with different diagnostic categories and, therefore, different problems. In the future, as we know more about individual differences in humor, it may be beneficial to use different procedures for people with different personal attributes. For example, in social skills training from what is known now, it would seem counterproductive to expect an introverted individual to become a life-of-the-party type. With increasing knowledge of both humor and individual differences we should understand more about what kind of funny things should be done with whom.

REFERENCES

Bishop, B. R., & Stumphauzer, J. S. (1973). Behavior therapy of thumbsucking in children: A punishment (time-out) and generalization effect: What's a mother to do? *Psychological Reports, 33*, 939-944.

Brodzinsky, D. M., & Rightmyer, J. (1980). Individual differences in children's humour development. In P. E. McGhee & A. J. Chapman (Eds.), *Children's Humour* (pp. 181-212). New York: Wiley.

Croghan, L., & Musante, G. J. (1975). The elimination of a boy's high building phobia by *in vivo* desensitization and game playing. *Journal of Behavior Therapy and Experimental Psychiatry, 6*, 87-88.

Domash, L. (1975). The use of wit and the comic by a borderline psychotic child in psychotherapy. *American Journal of Psychotherapy, 29*, 261-270.

Epstein, Y. M., & Borduin, C. M. (1985). Could this happen?: A game for children of divorce. *Psychotherapy, 22*, 770-774.

Epstein, Y. M., & Borduin, C. M. (1984). The children's feedback game: An approach for modifying disruptive group behavior. *American Journal of Psychotherapy, 38*, 63-72.

Fisher, R. L., & Fisher, S. (1987). Therapeutic strategies with the comic child. In W. F. Fry & W. A. Salameh (Eds.), *Handbook of Humor and Psychotherapy: Advances in the Clinical Use of Humor* (pp. 107-125). Sarasota, FL: Professional Resource Exchange, Inc.

Flavell, J. H. (1963). *The Developmental Psychology of Jean Piaget*. Princeton, NJ: Van Nostrand.

Freud, A. (1936). *The ego and the mechanisms of defense*. New York: International Universities Press.

Friedman, S. (1986). *In the doghouse: Jokes about dogs*. Minneapolis: Lerner Publications.

Fry, W. F., & Salameh, W. A. (1987). *Handbook of Humor and Psychotherapy: Advances in the Clinical Use of Humor*. Sarasota, FL: Professional Resource Exchange.

Gross, S. (1985). *Dogs, dogs, dogs: A collection of cartoons*. New York: Harper & Row.

Jackson, H. J., & King, N. J. (1981). The emotive imagery treatment of a child's trauma-induced phobia. *Journal of Behavior Therapy and Experimental Psychiatry, 12*, 325-328.

Kravetz, R. J., & Forness, S. R. (1971). The desensitization setting. *Exceptional Children, 37*, 389-391.

Kuhlman, T. L. (1984). *Humor and Psychotherapy*. Homewood, IL: Dow Jones-Irwin.

Lazarus, A. A., & Abramovitz, A. (1962). The use of emotive imagery in the treatment of children's phobias. *Journal of Mental Science, 108*, 191-195.

Lazarus, A. A., Davison, G. C., & Polefka, D. A. (1965). Classical and operant factors in the treatment of school phobia. *Journal of Abnormal Psychology, 70*, 225-229.

Levine, E. S. (1980). Indirect suggestions through personalized fairy tales for the treatment of childhood insomnia. *American Journal of Clinical Hypnosis, 23*, 57-63.

Levine, J. (1980). The clinical use of humour in work with children. In P. E. McGhee & A. J. Chapman (Eds.), *Children's Humour* (pp. 225-280). New York: Wiley.

Madanes, C. (1987). Humor in strategic family therapy. In W. F. Fry & W. A. Salameh (Eds.), *Handbook of humor and psychotherapy* (pp. 242-264). Sarasota, FL: Professional Resource Exchange.

Masten, A. S. (1986). Humor and competence in school-aged children. *Child Development, 57*, 461-473.

McGhee, P. E. (1979). *Humor: Its Origin and Development*. San Francisco: W. H. Freeman.

McGhee, P. E. (1986). Humor across the life span: Sources of developmental change and individual differences. In L. Nahemow, K. A. McClusky-Fawcett, & P. E. McGhee (Eds.), *Humor and Aging* (pp. 27-51). Orlando, FL: Academic Press.

Orfanidis, M. M. (1972). Children's use of humor in psychotherapy. *Social Casework, 53*, 147-155.

Parke, R. D., & Slaby, R. G. (1983). The development of aggression. In P. H. Mussen (Ed.), *Handbook of child psychology: Vol. IV Socialization, personality, and social development* (pp. 547-641). New York: Wiley.

Prerost, F. J. (1984). Evaluating the systematic use of humor in psychotherapy with adolescents. *Journal of Adolescence, 7*, 267-276.

Redl, F., & Wineman, D. (1952). *Controls from Within: Techniques for Treatment of the Aggressive Child*. New York: Free Press.

Rosentiel, A. K., & Scott, D. S. (1977). Four considerations in using imagery techniques with children. *Journal of Behavior Therapy & Experimental Psychiatry, 8*, 287-290.

Ross, D. M., Ross, S. A., & Evans, T. A. (1971). The modification of extreme social withdrawal by modeling with guided participation. *Journal of Behavior Therapy and Experimental Psychiatry, 2*, 273-279.

Shaw, C. R. (1961). The use of humor in child psychiatry. *American Journal of Psychotherapy, 15*, 368-381.

Simons, C. J. R., McClusky-Fawcett, K. A., & Papini, D. R. (1986). Theoretical and functional perspectives on the development of humor during infancy, childhood, and adolescence. In L. Nahemow, K. A. McClusky-Fawcett, & P. E. McGhee (Eds.), *Humor and Aging* (pp. 53-80). Orlando, FL: Academic Press.

Smith, R. E. (1973). The use of humor in the counterconditioning of anger responses: A case study. *Behavior Therapy, 4*, 576-580.

Tasto, D. L. (1969). Systematic desensitization, muscle relaxation and visual imagery in the counterconditioning of a four-year-old phobic child. *Behavior Research and Therapy, 7*, 409-411.

Tolor, A. (1966). Observations on joke-telling by children in therapy. *Mental Hygiene, 50*, 295-296.

Ventis, W. L. (1987). Humor and laughter in behavior therapy. In W. F. Fry & W. A. Salameh (Eds.), *Handbook of Humor and Psychotherapy: Advances in the clinical use of humor* (pp. 149-169). Sarasota, FL: Professional Resource Exchange.

Washburn, R. W. (1929). A study of the smiling and laughing of infants in the first year of life. *Genetic Psychology Monographs, 6(5)*, 397-535.

Wenger, C. (1982). The suitcase story: A therapeutic technique for children in out-of-home placement. *American Journal of Orthopsychiatry, 52*, 353-355.

Wolfenstein, M. (1954). *Children's Humor*. Glencoe, IL: Free Press.

Yorukoglu, A. (1974). Children's favorite jokes and their relation to emotional conflicts. *Journal of the American Academy of Child Psychiatry, 13*, 677-690.

PART V:
MASS MEDIA
USES OF HUMOR

Introduction

Humor, as everyone knows, is a common form of entertainment. It is not surprising, then, that humor is often used in mass media productions, such as television, films, magazines and books. Given the concerns of the present volume, the important question is whether the entertainment-potential of humor can be utilized to help achieve desired developmental goals. Zillmann and Bryant examine the role of humor in children's educational television programs. Differences between learning in the classroom (with a captive audience) and from television at home are discussed, and special attention is given to the power of humor to recruit initial interest and hold attention in order to support learning. The impact of the kind and amount of humor employed is also discussed. The available data suggest that while children may watch a program in order to be entertained, considerable learning may be achieved at the same time.

Alberghene discusses the role that humor has played in children's literature during the past two centuries. Special attention is given to changes in attitudes regarding the value or desirability of humor in literature. Common assumptions made by writers of children's humorous literature and by critics are discussed along with issues and problems related to defining and categorizing humor. Finally, the

199

question of age differences in enjoyment of different forms of humorous literature is discussed along with the new approach of incorporating social science research on children's humor into discussions of children's appreciation of humorous literature.

Chapter 10

Guidelines for the Effective Use of Humor in Children's Educational Television Programs

Dolf Zillmann, PhD
Jennings Bryant, PhD

SUMMARY. Teaching via television is contrasted with classroom teaching, and the unique objectives to be served by educational television programs for children are elaborated. Pertinent research findings are reviewed concerning (a) the attraction of audiences in a competitive media environment, (b) post-choice attention to educational programs, (c) acquisition of educational information from these programs, and (d) the viewing experience in hedonic terms. Strategies for the effective utilization of humor as both an audience attractant and a facilitator of information acquisition are suggested. Optimal patterns for the interspersion of humor in educational programs are detailed. The risks associated with the use of reality-distorting humor, such as irony, are discussed. Finally, the implications of using ridicule as a behavior corrective are considered.

Those in the frontline of education, our teachers in immediate contact with their students, have always enjoyed the benefits of instant feedback about their efforts. By watching head positions and by checking eye contact, they could virtually see how the telling of a funny story or a joke revived attention that had faded. Uncounted testimonials to that effect do not come as a surprise. Neither do the

Dolf Zillmann is affiliated with the Department of Communication, Indiana University, Bloomington, IN. Jennings Bryant is affiliated with the Department of Broadcast and Film Communication, University of Alabama, Tuscaloosa, AL.

201

frequently attached inferences about humor's favorable impact on learning (e.g., Bradford, 1964; Earls, 1972). Revived attention is not the only factor, however, thought to help humor foster superior learning. Humor has also been thought to accomplish this effect by relaxing tense audiences (e.g., Adams, 1974) and by establishing a desirable rapport between teacher and students (e.g., Browning, 1977). The important consideration is that teachers, by using humor in a trial-and-error fashion, could correct ineffective uses and duplicate apparently effective ones. (See Bryant and Zillmann, this volume, for a discussion of effective and ineffective uses of humor in the classroom.)

The production of educational television programs for children, as well as for adolescents and adults, is an entirely different matter. First of all, there is little, if any, corrective feedback. Formative research on specific facets of programs could be performed, but rarely is. It tends to be time-consuming and expensive, and the corrective information that it might generate usually comes too late for possible program modifications. Evaluative research on completed programs also could yield useful information. But again, such information would come too late and at best could only inspire improvements in future productions. Second, and perhaps more importantly, it is a team of experts with different competencies that is in charge of the production of educational programs—not the individual teacher. This is for good reason. A myriad of novel means for presenting educational information avails itself, and the intelligent utilization of these means calls for specialists who recognize the communication potentialities of the medium. A teacher who has made the most of chalk and board, hand-held models, and a few slides would be hard pressed to conjure up innovative presentations that reach far beyond classroom experience. In contrast, the team in which educators collaborate with imaginative and technically competent writers, directors, and producers is not limited by the individual teacher's experience and, in the creation of highly informative educational programs, should be able to exploit the medium to the fullest.

Teamwork, however, creates its own problems. Especially when educational objectives are not precisely defined (and often they are not), the various collaborators tend to take off in different directions, and the educational mission may suffer greatly as a result. This is nowhere more apparent than in attempts at spellbinding, amazing, and amusing the audience. Writers and visualizers compete for originality and, seemingly in efforts to impress their own peers, occasionally create messages that amuse adults, but not necessarily children. These efforts can, in fact, become dominant to a point where educational objectives are overwhelmed, if not entirely forgotten.

In order to reduce the risk of educational programs' succumbing to creative escapades of members of production teams (escapades that may well result in highly amusing and fascinating, yet uninformative programs—rather than in programs that are both amusing and informative to target audiences), we shall put forth some recommendations. If adhered to, these recommendations should prevent grave miscarriages of educational objectives and maximize the effectiveness of entertaining, educational undertakings. Needless to say, we shall derive our recommendations from research findings. In so doing, we shall specify and separate principal objectives that must be recognized and pursued if entertaining educational programs are to be effective.

A CHAIN OF OBJECTIVES

The social and motivational conditions that influence attention and learning differ profoundly, of course, between classroom teaching and educational television. Teachers deal with so-called *captive* audiences. Their students come with the understanding that information is to be acquired and that efforts toward that end may not be all fun and games. Humor need not be used to fill the class nor to prevent students from leaving. Under these circumstances, potentially beneficial uses of humor can be concentrated at combating inattentiveness, building a favorable rapport between teacher and student, and making the intrinsically sober learning experience altogether more pleasant and enjoyable.

In stark contrast, television audiences are *elusive and fickle* (cf. Zillmann & Bryant, 1985). People tune in and out of programs at the touch of a button; and as they are mainly motivated by their desire to be well entertained, they sit ready to pass over or to abandon any program that fails to project sufficient "entertainment value." Children are no exception. They master the new TV technology (remote controls, video manipulations) at an early age and seem particularly fickle in their program choices (Heeter & Greenberg, 1985). Surely, educational programs can be prescribed by parents, and the children's consumption of educational material can be supervised. Such care is bound to be the exception, however, and the creation of educational programs for children will have to be based on the premise that only a small minority of children might be motivated to seek exposure to educational material, and that the vast majority of children is out to have fun with what is on television—as well as on videos to which they have access.

It has to be recognized, then, that educational programs for children, if not shown under captive-audience conditions created by teachers or parents, will have to compete, and successfully so, against numerous purely entertaining programs that are simultaneously available. As some cynics have pointed out, even the most ambitious, brilliantly conceived and carefully produced, thoroughly informative educational program will do little good if it fails in this competition.

The first objective thus must be the *securement of intended child audiences* for particular educational programs. This objective is actually two-pronged. *Attraction* to the screen is the initial concern. Thereafter, it is the *retention* of the attracted audience.

The securement of intended audiences is obviously a necessary condition for educational communication. By no means, however, is it a sufficient condition. Staring at the screen does not insure absorption of the information that it displays. The primary objective of effective educational communication, therefore, cannot be exposure and attention of some sort. It must be the *acquisition of presented information* by the audience. The constituent, sequenced objectives are to achieve *focused attention to the educational information*, its *comprehension*, and its *storage and retention*.

Making the learning experience a most pleasant, most relaxed, or *least stressful* one might also be considered an objective—although clearly one subordinate to the others.

It would seem unlikely that the involvement of humor in educational programs for children serves all these objectives equally well.

Research confirms, in fact, that it does not. Fortunately, findings are specific enough to allow some generalizations about which ends are best served by humor, about kinds and placements of humor that serve particular functions well, and others that do not.

THE BATTLE OF THE PROGRAMS

Competition with entertaining programs, we are told, virtually forced television educators into dedicating a good portion of their programs to humor (Lesser, 1974). Educational programs for children, such as "Sesame Street" and "The Electric Company", seem to have become success stories only because they liberally embraced humor and similar elements of entertainment. All successful educational programs for children are characterized, after all, by a lavish display of humor (Bryant, Hezel, & Zillmann, 1979).

Obvious as the audience-drawing effect of humor may be, it was conjecture that the involvement of humor is what made educational television programs competitive. Only recently has this conjecture been converted into more secure knowledge. Experimentation by Wakshlag, Day, and Zillmann (1981) has firmly established that educational programs with humor are indeed more competitive than others, and that programs devoid of humor are bound to fail in the competition with humorous programs.

More specifically, these investigators manipulated initially nonhumorous educational programs and measured children's attraction to the resulting versions of the programs. Numerous humorous episodes were inserted into the programs. They were either scattered about (i.e., single episodes were interspersed in random intervals at nondisruptive places) or they were blocked together, either being doubled up or presented in blocks of three. In the latter condition, humor came in comparatively big chunks. However, as the amount of humor was held constant, humor was encountered less frequently and "waiting times" were necessarily longer.

First- and second-grade children eventually watched these programs in free-choice situations. Ostensibly in a waiting period, they watched television—individually and without supervision. Three programs were available, and they could choose between them by flicking the familiar TV dial. The programs were, of course, those that had been manipulated. They were presented such that one was humorous and two were not. At any time, then, a humorous educational program competed against two nonhumorous ones, and the humorous program featured episodes that were presented either in fast (single episodes), intermediate (two episodes blocked), or slow pace (three episodes blocked). The children's program choices were unobtrusively monitored and continually recorded by a machine.

The findings show, first of all, that the programs, when featuring humor, were much preferred over the same programs, when not featuring humor. More importantly, they show that not all distributions of humor achieve the same effect. The infrequent interspersion of comparatively long stretches of humor performed comparatively poorly. In contrast, the frequent interspersion of brief humorous episodes did well and emerged as the winning formula. The fast-paced interspersion of humorous episodes not only attracted the children most effectively to a program, but also retained them best. Intermediate pace produced intermediate results.

The implications are reasonably clear. In free-choice situations, children sample different available television programs and are attracted to, and retained by, those that feature humor (or other immediately gratifying stimuli). The frequent placement of humorous tidbits is favored because this distribution insures that humor is encountered after the shortest waiting times. The sampling child will encounter humor sooner and be drawn into the program. The encounter of a few fast-paced humorous episodes then fosters expectations of the frequent occurrence of humor which should make the child reluctant to leave the program. On the other hand, the format in which humor is concentrated in large chunks presents extended nonhumorous segments that, if not intrinsically fascinating, are likely to inspire the search for alternative stimulation. For watching television, this means program abandonment.

What guidelines can be extracted? It can be stated that educational programs will become more competitive (a) the more humor is interspersed, and (b) the more this humor is scattered throughout the program. The funnier and the more vividly presented the humorous material, the better the results promise to be (cf. Zillmann & Bryant, 1983). It also does not seem to matter which particular kind of humor (e.g., nonsense, cynical, hostile) is being employed and whether or not this humor is related to the educational information it accompanies.

Unfortunately, the securement of the audience is not the end to be achieved by educational programs. It is the mere beginning (a start toward an end) that the massive use of humor may place information acquisition and retention in jeopardy. The uncurtailed use of humor will sooner or later lead to programs that are primarily entertaining and that carry minimal educational information. Competition with a multitude of simultaneously available entertainment choices may well leave us without alternatives. But as long as educational programs may be educational foremost, the liberal interspersion of humor must be expected to disrupt the flow of educational messages eventually, especially in preschool children whose attention span is comparatively short. It is, therefore, imperative to consider the effects of humor use on attention to, and on comprehension and retention of, educational information. These considerations, as we shall see, limit the use of humor as an audience getter. Message designers will have to respect these limits and employ alternative means to attract the child audience. Certain forms of music, for example, have been shown to serve this function rather well (Wakshlag, Reitz, & Zillmann, 1982) and, if used, would seem to make the excessive use of humor unnecessary.

LEARNING WITH A CHUCKLE

There was a time when educators thought humor and learning to be antithetical. It was feared that merriment would hamper the sober business of studying serious issues. Educational efforts directed at children were usually granted special status, and some involvement of humor has been tolerated for quite a while. But even in this realm, the wisdom of teaching in a carnival atmosphere has been questioned. McGhee (1980), for example, feared that the use of humor might create a playful frame of mind that could interfere with the acquisition of novel information mainly because it would make any rehearsal, which could be construed as effort and labor, seem undesirable or unnecessary. Such undermining of learning intentions should indeed be a concern for educators who deal with highly motivated students. The situation in educational television, however, is very different. One must start on the premise that the audience is modestly motivated, at best, to acquire educational information. It is the desire to be entertained (or possibly, to receive nurturant information) that brings the children to the screen, and learning will be more incidental than intentional. "Serious learning," desirable as it may be, might not be achievable without supervision by parents or teachers. If the involvement of humor and its kin is unavoidable, then, what effects on learning can one expect?

One argument, deriving from Schramm (1972), is that in any admixture of humor and educational information, humor will draw a disproportionate amount of attention and be, of course, most enjoyable. As the humorous portions are so very enjoyable, they will preoccupy the children. All this comes at the expense of attention to, and rehearsal of, educational material. In fact, this serious material contrasts with the funny portions, making them appear more dreadful than when not presented in connection with humor.

An alternative way of looking at the potential dilemma is to suppose that children do not abruptly switch attention on and off, dependent on the presence or absence of humor. Specifically, it is assumed that attention waxes and wanes comparatively slowly, that humor can revive fading attention, and that revived attention can carry over into nonhumorous educational presentations. In this view of things, attention by children watching television is thought to be quite imperfect. It is subject to uncounted distractions, and it is expected to fade. In fact, much of the time it should be in dire need of revival. The interspersion of humor is seen to accomplish such revival. It should return attention to the program and create vigilance that fosters superior information acquisition for subsequently presented educational information. We need no longer ponder the possibilities, however, as recent research resolved the controversy in favor of the vigilance proposal.

Studies in which educational television programs were simulated by humorous or nonhumorous slide presentations (Chapman & Crompton, 1978; Davies & Apter, 1980) indicated that humor can facilitate information acquisition in children ranging from five to eleven years of age. Studies on television programs proper have established this effect more firmly (cf. Zillmann & Bryant, 1983).

Zillmann, Williams, Bryant, Boynton, and Wolf (1980) produced various educational programs with novel contents and manipulated them analogous to the programs in the earlier described investigation by Wakshlag, Day, and Zillmann (1981). Programs on such topics as philately (i.e., stamp collecting) were either nonhumorous or liberally embellished with humor unrelated to the educational topic. Two humorous versions were produced. Individual episodes of humor were scattered about in one version (fast pace). In the other, they were doubled up (slow pace), creating longer waiting times but fewer disruptions. The study actually involved several nonhumorous versions to control for different disruption patterns. These patterns, however, were without appreciable effects.

Kindergartners and first-graders watched in same-gender pairs. The pairs' behavior during exposure was carefully monitored. "Eyes on screen"—during humorous segments and, more importantly, during the presentation of educational information—served as the primary measure of attention. But attention, or rather the absence thereof, was also ascertained in the children's interactions that were not related to educational material. Information acquisition, finally, was measured by a surprise recall test. Quite obviously, this measure addresses storage and short-term memory as well. It leaves, however, questions concerning long-term storage and retrieval unanswered.

The findings make it exceedingly clear that children, although initially paying close attention to nonhumorous and humorous programs alike, become increasingly inattentive to nonhumorous programs. In a matter of minutes, attention fades, and it keeps on dropping during the course of prolonged presentations. The findings show equally clearly that information acquisition drops right along with focused attention. Most importantly, the involvement of humor prevented such decline. It revived attention and, presumably as a direct consequence, produced superior information acquisition. Fast-paced humor interspersion was particularly effective in drawing and holding attention to the events on the screen. Put somewhat negatively, it proved most effective in preventing the inattentiveness that was observed to grow steadily when humor was not employed.

It should be noted that this facilitation of learning was observed

for humor that was *not* related to the educational message. An intrinsically uneducational sketch by a bunch of cartoon characters,
for example, was found to produce vigilance that carried over into
the presentation of educational information and thereby helped children to learn more, say, about the lives of exotic animals on stamps
from Zimbabwe. Unrelatedness apparently did no harm. Some caution, however, would seem to be indicated. If unrelated humor is
used excessively, the acquisition of educational information should
suffer considerable interference, and beneficial effects may be lost
or reverse to detrimental effects. It may be speculated that such
possible reversal is less likely if the humor employed relates to the
educational objectives or embodies them. However, the use of "integrated humor," as we shall see, is not without risk.

A subsequent investigation (Zillmann & Bryant, 1983) corroborated and expanded these findings. This time, especially produced,
nonhumorous educational programs were interspersed with humor
that varied in funniness and visual vividness. A first study was carried out with kindergartners and first-graders. It was found that nonvivid humor (i.e., humor manifest in slowly unfolding activities
and devoid of drastic, rapid stimulus changes) facilitated attention
and learning only minimally. Funniness also proved of little moment for such humor. In contrast, vivid forms of humor had strong
facilitatory effects on attention and information acquisition. Vivid
humor that was particularly funny had by far the strongest beneficial effect.

A parallel study was eventually performed with children who
were seven or eight years of age. Effects were essentially the same,
but differed somewhat for funniness. Whereas, the younger children showed little response to nonvivid humor, irrespective of its
funniness, the older children proved sensitive to funniness and
showed improved performance in response to very funny but nonvivid humor.

Other research (cf. Zillmann & Bryant, 1983) suggests that extremely funny humor might not produce the described benefits. It is
conceivable that highly original humorous material, as Schramm
(1972) had surmised, engages and preoccupies children to a degree
that nullifies the positive effect of increased vigilance. Particularly
funny, original humor did not impair attention and learning, how-

ever; and along with the more common varieties of humor it made the educational experience more enjoyable.

An investigation by Cantor and Reilly (1979) showed that the mere use of jocular language, compared with the presentation of the same educational message in equally accurate but serious style, is capable of facilitating information acquisition in sixth- through eighth-graders. This investigation also involved a variation in the relationship between humor and educational information. Humor was either unrelated to the educational message, or it was part and parcel of it. The latter is usually referred to as related or integrated humor. Counter to the expectation of superior results from integrated humor, no appreciable difference in the effect of related versus unrelated humor could be detected.

The guidelines deriving from this and related research (cf. Zillmann & Bryant, 1983) are straightforward. As the concern about possible ill effects of humor that is unrelated to the educational information that it accompanies proved groundless, such humor can be involved rather liberally. (The drawbacks of excessive usage have been indicated earlier.) Humorous episodes should be interspersed frequently throughout educational programs, but they should come in small packages. Care should be taken, however, to place the humorous episodes in ways that least disrupt the informational flow of comprehensive educational messages. Vigorous humorous presentations should be given priority over subdued ones. Ideally, the humorous episodes should be moderately funny. Highly original humorous presentations should be treated with caution. The latter amounts to saying that all forced efforts toward originality of the humor in educational television are misplaced. Humorous originality, if achieved, may well delight writers, directors, and producers, even teachers and parents, but it has not been found to aid educational missions. In fact, as we shall now see, it occasionally places these missions in jeopardy.

THE IRONY OF IRONY

Cantor and Reilly (1979), in the aforementioned study, examined the failure to obtain superior results with integrated humor more closely. Tracing the effect on all educational items individually, they discovered that the use of irony proved counterproductive and nullified the beneficial effect of other forms of integrated humor.

The educational program that they used presented life-styles and culture of a fictitious South American tribe. Irony took linguistic form and was created by exaggerating characteristics of people in the direction contrary to the facts. For example, the extreme short-ness and lightness of these people was seriously talked about as follows: "They are very small people by our standards. The aver-age male is four foot two and weighs approximately 80 pounds. The women average three foot eleven and weigh approximately 70 pounds." In the humor transform, this became: ". . . The average male is a towering four foot two and weighs approximately 80 pounds. The women average three foot eleven and tip the scale at 70 pounds." The careful listener should have no trouble spotting the contradictions, recognizing the humorous intention, and infer-ring the actual circumstances by removing contradictory informa-tion. Most children failed to do this, however. Apparently, their attention was less than perfect, contradictions went unrecognized, and faulty impressions were not corrected. In later efforts at recall-ing the information, the humorous distortions ("towering men" and "women who tipped the scales") seem to have come more readily to mind than the specific facts that were distorted by them. This points, of course, to a general problem with integrated humor: The humorous stimuli are likely to be better recalled than the non-humorous educational information that they accompany or with which they are intertwined. In case, these two types of stimuli con-tradict one another, confusion is the likely result. Not all forms of integrated humor, however, entail distortions or contradictions. In-tegrated humor that amplifies an educational point, for instance, does not invite confusion. If anything, it is likely to assist the re-trieval of the educational message proper (because the potentially superior recall of the humorous stimuli can be expected to trigger the recall of the nonhumorous stimuli associated with them). The risk of confusion thus should be limited to humor that features dis-tortions of educational information.

The implications of the use of irony and other forms of informa-tion-distorting humor in educational television were more fully ex-plored in an investigation conducted by Zillmann, Masland, Weaver,

Lacey, Jacobs, Dow, Klein, and Banker (1984). A program was especially created in which a storekeeper and a customer discuss and demonstrate the properties of unfamiliar, exotic Hawaiian fruits. Information about the properties — such as sweetness, stickiness, toughness, prickliness, or juiciness — was either correct or distorted. Moreover, distortion was either consistent with a particular fruit property or contrary to it. For example, in the condition devoid of humorous distortion and two protagonists verified the claim that a soursop is very juicy by squeezing a small glassful of juice from it. In the other conditions, they consistently distorted or exaggerated this claim by squeezing a pailful of juice from the little fruit — shown with all the trappings of slapstick comedy; or they produced irony by agonizingly squeezing the fruit for a mere drop of liquid — again with all the indicated comical embellishments. In addition to these program versions, additional ones were created in which the humorous distortions were corrected by the protagonists' verbal clarifications.

Children from kindergarten and from the first and fourth grades eventually evaluated the funniness of these programs and responded to a surprise recall test. This test focused on what they had learned about fruit properties. Tests were administered both pictorially and verbally. The children's impressions of the soursop's juiciness, for example, were measured in response to a scale showing a drop, a tablespoon, a small cup, a mug, a pitcher, and a pail. The experimenter asked in addition: "How much juice would a soursop make? Only a drop, a tablespoonful, a small cupful, a mugful, a pitcherful, or a pailful?"

The findings leave no doubt about the fact that humorous distortions tend to go unrecognized and foster confusion. Humorous exaggeration left children with exaggerated perceptions, and the use of irony led to perceptions that were distorted in the opposite direction. Presumably because of the vividness of the images manifesting the humorous distortions and the images' superior accessibility in memory (cf. Fiske & Taylor, 1984), verbal corrections proved utterly ineffective. Their effect was actually negative in that they spoiled enjoyment. The programs featuring humorous distortions were more enjoyed than the distortion-free program, but only when the distortions were not corrected.

It had been expected that kindergartners and first-graders would fall prey to humorous distortions. The fact that fourth-graders were misled, and equally strongly so, came as a surprise. It had been thought that these older children would have developed the cognitive skills to recognize and promptly correct humorous distortions. The findings do not necessarily mean that they have not developed these skills, but would suggest that under conditions of less-than-perfect attention these skills, should they exist, are not utilized.

In order to clarify this situation, a follow-up study was conducted with fourth- and eighth-graders (Weaver, Bryant, & Zillmann, in press). The expectation that eighth-graders, finally, would be skilled, however, enough not to be misled by humorous distortions proved erroneous. The study fully replicated the findings of the initial one for fourth-graders and extended them to eighth-graders. The only difference between the two grades was that the younger children found the programs featuring uncorrected distorting humor funnier than the older ones. Humorous exaggeration and irony, then, have been found to be educationally counterproductive for children ranging from kindergarten to eighth grade.

It has been observed that children have generally more difficulty with irony than with other forms of humor (McGhee, 1979). Some scholars (Helmers, 1965) have set the age at which full comprehension and appreciation of irony is achieved as high as eighteen years. This would seem, however, to be overly conservative. There are simple uses of irony that do not appear to pose problems even for the youngest of children. For example, when Fozzy Bear on "Sesame Street" totally bungles an assignment and Kermit quips: "Great job, Fozzy, great job!" not too many preschoolers will detect much nurturance in the comment. Similarly, as a child introduces his pet dog as "a real killer" and the dog is then seen being terrified by a kitten, not too many first-graders should have missed the point. On the other hand, most college students might not spot the irony in the presentation by their professor who, believing to have explained (erroneously so) why certain research demonstrations are scientifically unsound, exclaims: "Now, that's what I call great research!"

The message in these illustrations is that distortion-based humor can only be enjoyed when the distortion is readily recognized, and that recognition of distortions depends on prior knowledge of the undistorted circumstances. If the students understood their professor's attack on the research that he then characterized as "great stuff," they can spot and enjoy the irony in the exclamation. Likewise, if toddlers understood the inconsistency in praise for bungling, they then might be amused by Kermit's quip.

It is the requirement of prior knowledge about the phenomena at the heart of irony that has grave implications for the use of irony in educational television. Educational efforts are meaningful only if the phenomena that they convey are novel. Surely, there is room for repeated presentations to insure that what used to be novel has become familiar. But the conveyance of what is well known already hardly qualifies as educational effort. It is, nonetheless, under the latter circumstances where irony flourishes. And it is under truly educational conditions that irony is bound to fail, creating bewilderment at best and utter confusion at worst. Moreover, when correct information is presented and then challenged by irony or other distortions, the contradiction or inconsistency will tend to be resolved in the direction of whatever is more vivid — and the humorous distortion usually is.

Consider an example from "Sesame Street". It was designed to inform children about safety afforded by wearing seatbelts in cars. The segment features two characters flying an airplane. Both characters buckle up, and they are seen flying about. When the plane turns upside down, they are seen hanging, as if by rubber suspenders, way out of the cockpit. Once the plane returns to normal position, they are drawn back into their seats. The humor in this demonstration of seatbelt safety is both well integrated and distorting. Seatbelts are safe because they do not give. Rubber belts would be of little use. In fact, they would be extremely unsafe. Yet, there is humor in their ironic use, the kind of distorting humor that is easily created and that producers of children's educational programs, although they must realize that the humorous information is incompatible with the educational information to be provided, apparently find irresistible. But what does this use of humor do to educate children? Those who already knew that seatbelts do not stretch may have been amused, but they certainly did not learn anything that they had not known before. Moreover, those who might have benefited from a demonstration of what seatbelts actually do in times of trouble might think of them now as devices that prevent kids from leaving planes and cars.

Many educators (e.g., Singer, 1980; Singer & Singer, 1979) have criticized educational television for its use of "adultish" humor, but it has not been insinuated that the humor is overly hostile or sexy. The criticism is directed at writers and producers who, it seems, create humor to impress their peers rather than to teach effectively. Humor is often way above the children's heads. It is not at the children's level. To keep it at this level is obviously not easy, especially with regard to irony. But writers and producers, if they want to be effective educators, must resist temptations and learn to pass up the jokes that come so very easily with the mere distortion of educational information.

What, then are the guidelines? Irony and other distortion-based forms of humor are a risky proposition, indeed, and their use should be kept to a minimum. This recommendation stems from the fact one never knows just who will be watching any given program. Children or adolescents with a firmly established understanding of the events that are distorted should be able to enjoy the humor resulting from this distortion without becoming confused. However, those lacking such an understanding may simply become confused, so that learning is actually disrupted instead of supported. The only safe strategy, thus, is to avoid distortion-based humor altogether.

LAUGHTER AS A WHIP

Laughing at others' ineptitudes and misfortunes, especially when these others are disliked and seen deserving of such fate, has always been a source of much merriment to onlookers (cf. Zillmann, 1983). Merriment of this kind permeates throughout all cultures and domains of human endeavor. As a source of merriment, it abounds on educational television as well (Bryant, Hezel, & Zillmann, 1979). Being laughed at, after showing awkwardness, ignorance, or other forms of ineptness, is an entirely different matter. The laughter of others directed at self is a most chilling experience, particularly when these others are those one wishes to have for friends. Being laughed at or *ridiculed* is undoubtedly a noxious experience that is to be avoided, and deliberate ridicule must be considered a form of punishment. Many educators may well condemn the use of such punishment in educational television (and elsewhere) as cruel, undesirable, and perhaps more importantly, unnecessary. Others may accept its use as a corrective, especially when the ridicule is not directed at the person whose behavior is to be influenced, but at a fictitious character instead. Other-directed ridicule is, after all, indirect or vicarious punishment without the sting of personal experience, and one might therefore deem it acceptable as an educational corrective.

Notwithstanding, justifiable misgivings about the educational use of punitive laughter, ridicule has been employed quite regularly in educational television, either as a corrective or simply to enhance humorous situations. Bill Cosby, for instance, is known for the line: ". . . so that other kids won't laugh at you and say you're silly." The context is always: Do it right. Don't bungle it. Otherwise, the technique is to threaten ridicule for failure. More characteristic is the use of ridicule amongst characters, such as Ernie's raucous laughter and lighthearted, presumably funny insults in response to Bert's "childish" (i.e., to be corrected) behavior or clumsiness.

Is the witnessed ridicule of others, especially of peers, capable of influencing and modifying children's behavior in desirable ways? To our knowledge, only one investigation has addressed this question and offers some guidance. Bryant, Brown, Parks, and Zillmann (1983) created a program in which a puppet played in unique ways with a novel toy and another puppet made various comments about the play. Of interest here is the discouragement of a particular way of playing with the toy. This discouragement took three forms. The playing puppet was either unambiguously instructed not to play in this manner with the toy (command), politely informed that this was not the way to play with it (suggestion), or ridiculed for playing with it in this way. The children, four- and six-year-olds, eventually found the novel toy amongst their own toys, and their playing with it was recorded. Specifically, the extent to which the children imitated the discouraged behavior was assessed.

The investigation also involved conditions in which the behavior to be modified was encouraged or neither encouraged nor discouraged. Compared against these controls, all forms of discouragement appeared to be effective. However, they were differentially effective. Four-year-olds responded most strongly to the command, presumably because it was least ambiguous. No difference between the effectiveness of ridicule and pleasant suggestion was observed in this group. The six-year-olds did not at all react in this fashion. They were least responsive to the command. Pleasant suggestion proved to be somewhat more effective in altering their specific play behavior. But the impact of ridicule was by far the strongest. These older children were most reluctant to play with a toy in ways that prompted the ridicule of another player — in fact, of a puppet protagonist on a television screen. Their imitation rate was less than half of that in the other conditions (command and suggestion).

This initial investigation suggests that ridicule, as an educational corrective, is ineffective for preschool children. In view of the moral considerations that were discussed earlier, its use is of dubious value and should be minimized. In contrast, ridicule proved highly effective for first-graders and, presumably, would be effective from there on out. Its desirability as a corrective technique has to be judged in moral terms. It would seem that corrective ridicule could be embraced as an educational technique only when the ends justify the inherently punitive means and when alternative means are no less punitive.

CONCLUSION

Table 1 summarizes the principal findings on which the discussed guidelines are based. The reader who would like to learn more about the pertinent research is referred to a more detailed review by Bryant, Zillmann, and Brown (1983) and Zillmann and Bryant (1983) as well as to the technical papers cited in these reviews.

Table 1
Findings Pertaining to the Effective Use of Humor
in Children's Educational Television Programs,
Grouped by Objective

Attracting and Holding Audiences

    (a) Incorporation of humor, whether or not related to educational information, has beneficial effects.

    (b) Amount of humor is unrestricted; the more humor, the stronger the effect.

(c) Scattered distributions of humor produce better effects than clustered distributions of the same amount of humor.

Acquisition of Educational Information

(a) Interspersion of unrelated humor, if not excessive or disruptive, has beneficial effects.

(b) Scattered interspersion of unrelated humor produces better effects than interspersion of the same material in clusters.

(c) Visually and auditorily vivid presentations of unrelated humor produce better effects than nonvivid, subdued presentations of such humor.

(d) Incorporation of highly original humor may not yield beneficial effects.

(e) Incorporation of humor that is related to educational information and that challenges or distorts it, as in irony or humorous exaggeration, tends to confuse and can have detrimental effects.

Relaxed and Joyful Learning

(a) Merriment from humor renders the learning experience more pleasant, irrespective of the effect of humor on information acquisition.

(b) Humorous forms that presuppose knowledge that children have not yet acquired, fail to produce merriment and, hence, do not make the learning experience more pleasant.

Behavior Correction

(a) Witnessed ridicule of behavior is ineffective in preschool children.

(b) In school children, witnessed ridicule of behavior is a more effective corrective than witnessed commands or witnessed suggestions.

REFERENCES

Adams, W. J. (1974). The use of sexual humor in teaching human sexuality at the university level. *The Family Coordinator, 23*, 365-368.

Bradford, A. L. (1964, September). The place of humor in teaching. *Peabody Journal of Education*, 67-70.

Browning, R. (1977, February). Why not humor? *APA Monitor*, 32.

Bryant, J., Brown, D., Parks, S. L., & Zillmann, D. (1983). Children's imitation of a ridiculed model. *Human Communication Research, 10*, 243-255.

Bryant, J., Hezel, R., & Zillmann, D. (1979). Humor in children's educational television. *Communication Education, 28*, 49-59.

Bryant, J., Zillmann, D., & Brown, D. (1983). Entertainment features in children's educational television: Effects on attention and information acquisition. In J. Bryant & D. R. Anderson (Eds.), *Children's understanding of television: Research on attention and comprehension* (pp. 221-240). New York: Academic Press.

Cantor, J., & Reilly, S. (1979, August). *Jocular language style and relevant humor in educational messages*. Paper presented at the Second International Conference on Humor, Los Angeles.

Chapman, A. J., & Crompton, P. (1978). Humorous presentations of material and presentations of humorous materials: A review of the humor and memory literature and two experimental studies. In M. M. Gruneberg, P. E. Morris, & R. N. Sykes (Eds.), *Practical aspects of memory* (pp. 84-92). London: Academic Press.

Davies, A. P., & Apter, M. J. (1980). Humor and its effect on learning in children. In P. E. McGhee & A. J. Chapman (Eds.), *Children's humor*. New York: Wiley.

Earls, P. L. (1972). Humorizing learning. *Elementary Education, 49*, 107-108.

Fiske, S. T., & Taylor, S. E. (1984). *Social cognition*. New York: Random House.

Heeter, C., & Greenberg, B. (1985). Cable and program choice. In D. Zillmann & J. Bryant (Eds.), *Selective exposure to communication* (pp. 203-224). Hillsdale, NJ: Erlbaum.

Helmers, H. (1965). *Sprache und Humor des Kindes*. Stuttgart, Federal Republic of Germany: Ernst Klett.

Lesser, G. (1974). *Children and television: Lessons from Sesame Street*. New York: Random House.

McGhee, P. E. (1979). *Humor: Its origin and development*. San Francisco: W. H. Freeman.

McGhee, P. E. (1980). Toward the integration of entertainment and educational functions of television: The role of humor. In P. H. Tannenbaum (Ed.), *The entertainment functions of television*. Hillsdale, NJ: Erlbaum.

Schramm, W. (1972). What the research says. In W. Schramm (Ed.), *Quality in instructional television*. Honolulu: University Press of Hawaii.

Singer, J. L. (1980). The power and limitations of television: A cognitive-affective analysis. In P. H. Tannenbaum (Ed.), *The entertainment functions of television*. Hillsdale, NJ: Erlbaum.

Singer, J. L., & Singer, D. G. (1979, March). Come back, Mister Rogers, come back. *Psychology Today*, pp. 56; 59-60.

Wakshlag, J. J., Day, K. D., & Zillmann, D. (1981). Selective exposure to educational television programs as a function of differently paced humorous inserts. *Journal of Educational Psychology, 73*, 27-32.

Wakshlag, J. J., Reitz, R. J., & Zillmann, D. (1982). Selective exposure to and acquisition of information from educational television programs as a function of appeal and tempo of background music. *Journal of Educational Psychology, 74*, 666-677.

Weaver, J. B., Bryant, J., & Zillmann, D. (in press). Effects of humorous distortions on children's learning from educational television: Further evidence. *Communication Education*.

Zillmann, D. (1983). Disparagement humor. In P. E. McGhee & J. H. Goldstein (Eds.), *Handbook of humor research: Vol. 1. Basic issues* (pp. 85-107). New York: Springer-Verlag.

Zillmann, D., & Bryant, J. (1983). Uses and effects of humor in educational ventures. In P. E. McGhee & J. H. Goldstein (Eds.), *Handbook of humor research: Vol. 2. Applied studies* (pp. 173-193). New York: Springer-Verlag.

Zillmann, D., & Bryant, J. (Eds.). (1985). *Selective exposure to communication.* Hillsdale, NJ: Erlbaum.

Zillmann, D., Masland, J. L., Weaver, J. B., Lacey, L. A., Jacobs, N. E., Dow, J. H., Klein, C. A., & Banker, S. R. (1984). Effects of humorous distortions on children's learning from educational television. *Journal of Educational Psychology, 76,* 802-812.

Zillmann, D., Williams, B. R., Bryant, J., Boynton, K. R., & Wolf, M. A. (1980). Acquisition of information from educational television programs as a function of differently paced humorous inserts. *Journal of Educational Psychology, 72,* 170-180.

Chapter 11

Humor in Children's Literature

Janice M. Alberghene, PhD

SUMMARY. This article surveys research on children's literature and humor by professionals in the field of children's literature. Although the researchers' interests are diverse, they are in at least implicit agreement about two aspects of their research: the early history of humor in children's literature and the kinds of questions that need to be addressed. This chapter, therefore, begins with an overview of pre-twentieth century books which indicates the main lines of development of humor in children's literature. The second half of the chapter considers the questions and presuppositions that have shaped the study of humor in children's literature to date. Presuppositions about both humor and the nature of the child have often excluded from discussion humor which is thought to be too anarchic, too critical of society, or too revealing of the darker side of human nature, but the best of the research respects the child as an active reader and respects humorous stories as having something to say.

The great American humorist, James Thurber, wrote for children as well as for adults. His children's books were a success with their intended audience, yet judging from one of his letters to the critic Elliott Landau, Thurber did not consider himself an expert on humor and children: "there have been a great many times when I haven't had the vaguest idea of what the hell they were laughing about." At the same time, however, Thurber acutely observed that children "have a lot of secret areas of laughter, such as the giggles," and he confided his "doubt that anything giggled about by

Janice M. Alberghene is affiliated with the Department of English, Bowling Green State University, Bowling Green, OH.

223

children is actually very funny" (Landau, 1962, p. 163). In the three decades since Thurber mentioned his doubts, few critics of children's literature have matched his skepticism, but a number have echoed his bewilderment even as they have explored the terra incognita of children's humor.

Reasons for bewilderment abound. Discussing humor is a tricky business, due only in part to the difficulty of being interesting while explaining why something is funny. An equally important obstacle concerns the widespread misconception that humor is not significant, does not *mean* anything — is *only* a joke. Moreover, the problems that attend any discussion of humor are compounded when children's literature becomes the focus of scrutiny; it too suffers from the misconception that it does not mean much, that it is "only a story." Despite all these difficulties, the body of criticism about humor in children's literature offers more insight than problems. This article surveys that research not only to establish the extent of its inquiries to date, but also to suggest where it might go next.

The concerns of critics of children's literature range from the "Rabelasian" humor of picture book artist Tomi Ungerer to the usefulness of humor in children's literature as a deterrent to war. Although this diversity of interests sometimes leads the critics to widely differing conclusions, they are in at least implicit agreement about two aspects of their research: the early history of humor in children's literature and the kinds of questions that need to be addressed. This chapter, therefore, begins with a short overview of pre-twentieth century humor and then goes on to consider the questions and presuppositions that have shaped the study of humor in children's literature to date. Readers should note that although I have tried to indicate main lines of inquiry and major developments in the history of humor, this chapter by no means exhausts the topic, nor is that its intention.

THE EARLY HISTORY OF HUMOR
IN CHILDREN'S LITERATURE

Perhaps one reason the history of humor in children's literature inspires little controversy is because that history is so brief. Children's literature itself is a relatively recent phenomenon. Scholars continue to push back its origins as they examine the oral tradition, medieval manuscripts, and, in one particularly adventurous instance, four thousand year-old clay tablets from the Sumerian renaissance (Adams, 1986), but historians of children's literature generally look back no further than the eighteenth century to find the origins of children's literature as we know it today. The editors of *From Instruction to Delight: An Anthology of Children's Literature to 1850* provide an apt summary of the historians' position:

> Prior to the middle of the eighteenth century . . . the emphasis fell heavily and deliberately on instruction—so much so that before 1744 there were, properly speaking, no children's books. In that year John Newbery produced *A Little Pretty Pocket-Book*, which heralded the beginning of *delight* and, along with the ubiquitous chapbooks, ushered in a new era in children's reading. . . . by 1850 there had emerged a literature whose unashamed *raison d'etre* was to give pleasure to children. The Golden Age had dawned. (Demers & Moyles, 1982, p. xi)

Given the emphasis on enjoyment, it is not surprising that the nineteenth century is also seen as marking the real flowering of humor in literature for children. Earlier comic texts, often in the form of the cheap, folded paper booklets known as chapbooks, were borrowings from adult (or age-undifferentiated) sources such as the oral tradition with its "drolls" or humorous folk stories and adult literature such as *Gulliver's Travels* and *Don Quixote* from which boasting stories and comic adventures were excerpted. Mother Goose rhymes appeared in print at least as early as 1744, but like the folk tales, these humorous rhymes now associated with childhood had their origins in an oral tradition and did not distinguish stories for children from those for adults. A small number of jest and joke books were printed for children in the eighteenth century, but these aside, one early historian of children's literature concluded that "to poke fun in an offhand manner at little boys and girls seemed to have been the only conception of humor to be found in the children's books of the period" (Halsey, 1911; rpt. 1969, p. 108). This assessment might be a trifle harsh; contemporary critic Samuel Pickering notes that eighteenth-century biographies of inanimate objects such as *The History of a Pin* "tickled the funny bone several times during its [the pin's] course of adventures" (1981, p. 102).

The nineteenth century opened with humorous narrative verse in the tradition of Mother Goose, but *Old Dame Trot and Her Comical Cat* (1803) and *The Comic Adventures of Old Mother Hubbard and Her Dog* (1806) were soon joined by Sir William Roscoe's *The Butterfly's Ball and the Grasshopper's Feast* (1807). This rhymed fantasy written for the entertainment of the author's young son was so successful in appealing to a wider audience that imitations like Mrs. Dorset's *The Peacock at Home* (1808) were not far behind (Bingham & Scholt, 1980). Perhaps more significant than these imitations, however, is the fact that Roscoe's book was the first title in a *series* of books for the beguilement of the young. This is not to suggest that a torrent of humorous books soon followed, but that as children's literature became less overtly didactic and more overtly entertaining, more humorous books were specifically written and published for children.

Textbook writers and writers of histories of children's literature generally cite the following handful of nineteenth-century books as that century's high points of humor: *A Visit from St. Nicholas* (1823), Lear's *Book of Nonsense* (1946), *The English Struwwelpeter: or Pretty Stories and Funny Pictures for Little Children* (written in 1844; English translation in 1848), *Alice's Adventures in Wonderland* (1865) and *Through the Looking Glass* (1872), *The Adventures of Tom Sawyer* (1876), *The Peterkin Papers* (1880), *The Adventures of Pinocchio* (1883, English translations in 1891, 1892). All of these books are still read today, and with the possible exception of *The Peterkin Papers*, are considered to be classics of children's literature. For example, the authors of *Fifteen Centuries of Children's Literature* dub Clement Moore's poem about jolly gift-giving St. Nick "the first American 'classic' poem for children" and call Lear's *Book of Nonsense* "one of the first children's books without instruction or moralizing" (Bingham & Scholt, 1980, pp. 168, 180).

The claims made for the classics of Lewis Carroll and Mark Twain are much grander. Beverly Lyon Clark's article on Carroll from *Touchstones: Reflections on the Best in Children's Literature* begins by noting that *Alice's Adventures in Wonderland* "ushered in what is generally considered the Golden Age of children's literature in English" (1985, p. 44). Lucia Binder goes a step further. She acknowledges the importance of Lear's *Book of Nonsense* but states that with *Alice*, "Lewis Carrol [sic] not only created the genre of fantastic tales but also a new humorous trend: nonsense" (1970, p. 11). Binder also cites Twain as an innovator: "This [*The Adventures of Tom Sawyer*] may well be the first instance where the word 'humour' is justified within the context of children's books, humour as an expression of a serene outlook on life and the world based on wisdom" (p. 13). Writing in 1947, sixty years after the fact, Alice M. Jordan, "the acknowledged dean of New England Children's Librarians," (Andrews, 1963, p. 2) nevertheless musters considerable indignation when she considers that "few New England boys knew Tom Sawyer" until 1880, four years after the book narrating his adventures was published. Moreover, "Even then Mark Twain's riotous humor was scarcely appreciated. It was an exceptional public library where Tom Sawyer was allowed in the hands of children . . ." (Jordan, 1947; published 1963, p. 15).

Lucretia P. Hale's stories about the quirky and impractical Peterkin family met with a warmer initial reception. Madelyn Wankmiller's profile of Lucretia P. Hale quotes one contemporary reviewer as saying, "You declare the book [*The Peterkin Papers*] is too silly for anything; you vow that you will not laugh at what is so absurd; yet you stick to the book and shake your sides, and hope dear Miss Hale will live forever" (Wankmiller, 1957, published 1963, pp. 248-249). Wankmiller herself calls Hale's creations "the first American nonsense stories, the forerunners of *Mr. Popper's Penguins* and *Homer Price*" (p. 248), while Huck credits the stories with providing the forerunners of modern eccentric women characters such as the British Mary Poppins and the American Amelia Bedelia (Huck, 1987).

It is instructive to pause a moment here to consider why the Peterkins were well received by their contemporaries, whereas *The Adventures of Tom Sawyer* triggered considerable negative response. The key to this lies in its giving offense to genteel sensibilities; Lucretia P. Hale was "dear Miss Hale" to her nineteenth-century reviewer, but the satire and sensational adventures of *Tom Sawyer* were more than enough to prevent its author from being called "dear." Hale's humor is actually very conventional in that it depends upon the reader's being amused by her characters' ignorance, not defiance, of social conventions or common sense solutions to everyday problems. Twain's humor has a lot more bite; it satirizes and calls into question many of the conventions and assumptions Hale's stories reinforced.

That humor is even more biting in *The Adventures of Huckleberry Finn* (1884), a book Huck doesn't mention in the 750 plus pages of *Children's Literature in the Elementary School* (1987). Bingham and Scholt caution that the "themes, situations, and dialects make *Huckleberry Finn* difficult for children," (1980, p. 217), and it is probably this difficulty, rather than a desire to censor, that accounts for its omission. Late nineteenth and early twentieth-century critics left no doubt, however, as to their motivation. The editor of *Century Magazine* omitted some of the material Twain sent him when he published extracts from the book, but the Concord, Massachusetts library went a step further and banned it, and in 1905, more than twenty years after the book's publication, the Brooklyn Public Library called *Tom Sawyer* and *Huckleberry Finn* "bad examples for ingenuous youth" and banished them from the children's room (Nilsen & Donelson, 1985, pp. 517, 518). *The Adventures of Huckleberry Finn* has since become a perennial on censorship lists, so the example from 1905 is noteworthy less as an instance of censorship of *Huck Finn* than as demonstrating *Tom Sawyer's* falling prey to guilt by association after the publication of *Huck Finn*. As the century progressed, *Tom Sawyer* met with fewer and fewer objections, but this should not be interpreted as a permanent abandonment of the impulse to censor.

The Adventures of Pinocchio is a case in point. Paul Heins has written that the creator of Pinocchio, Carlo Collodi (pen name of Carlo Lorenzini) "really wanted to impress on them [children] the importance of school, the merit of an honest occupation, and the virtue of good human relationships; but with a sudden quirk of genius he borrowed the mask of comedy and covered the face of didacticism" (1982, p. 200). Heins's assumption that the "mask of comedy" sugar coats the pill of didacticism for *child* readers is one which most critics share, but much less is made of the fact that the "mask of comedy" can have a similar function for adult readers as well. It can allow them to focus on the book's humor and "accept" the book as amusing while dismissing the notion that the book might have anything substantive (and potentially discomforting to adult authority) to say to child readers. Adults in this situation in effect censor *their own* reading of the children's book through a determinedly sunny reading or interpretation of the text. Some humorous texts, *Pinocchio* for example, pose too substantive a challenge for mental editing; nothing less than actual revision and adaptation will suffice.

Richard Wunderlich and Thomas J. Morrissey's study of *Pinocchio's* fate in the United States points out that while *Pinocchio* is well-known, what many Americans actually know are later adaptations by other writers, not Collodi's original with its "egotistical and infuriating" Pinocchio. The Pinocchio they know is "either innocuously mischievous and therefore cute — or innocent and trusting and therefore lovable" (1982, p. 209). Although Wunderlich and Morrissey are concerned with *Pinocchio* per se, not the broader issue of humor and children's literature, their thesis concerning *Pinocchio* has implications beyond this book. Before we look at these implications, however, we need to look at Wunderlich and Morrissey's thesis in more detail. As they explain:

> In our view, the social definition of childhood has changed since the 1880's, and *Pinocchio* has been changed to accommodate it. . . . Collodi's original has often been rejected because it portrays an older view of childhood — a view defining children as little adults or adults-in-becoming. Such a definition, however, allows children to have emotions and concerns which contemporary psychology attests they actually do have.
>
> Unfortunately, for a long time beginning in the earlier part of this century, the more unacceptable psychological realities — such as hatred, jealousy, unbridled aggression, sexual desire — were considered exclusively adult characteristics. (p. 205)

Unacceptable psychological realities are the stock in trade of many humorists; they say what society would censor or reject if it were expressed in any other form. But there are limits to what is acceptable as humor, even though those limits are rarely articulated and are always subject to the social context in which the humor is expressed. When that context features children, psychological reality often gives way to the impulse to censor. As Wunderlich and Morrissey point out, *what* is censored depends on the society's particular definition of childhood.

This is not to deny that societies are made up of individuals, individuals whose views of childhood frequently clash, but the point Wunderlich and Morrissey make applies on the individual level as well: unspoken ideas about the nature of childhood play a large role in determining what both a society and an individual consider appropriate for children. Since humor often deals with what is usually unspoken and/or repressed, discussions of children and humor sometimes mask the real issues and objections when a text is pronounced unsuitable for children.

Such masking is by no means the exclusive prerogative of earlier eras. We shall see it in a moment when we look at reactions to *Struwwelpeter*, just as we'll see it later on when we look at discussions of contemporary humor for children. It is important to recognize masking when it occurs, not simply as a matter of curiosity, but because it confuses the terms of discussion. What is really an ideological judgement sometimes poses as an aesthetic judgement, while what is actually a moral judgement sometimes poses as a psychological observation. These confusions only further complicate the study of children's literature and humor.

Adult reactions to *Struwwelpeter* illustrate some of the confusions that can result from mistaking the terms of discussion. No doubt many of the adults who have objected to this book have done so for reasons that are perfectly straightforward. They believe that children would be frightened by the book's "cautionary tales in verse about Shock-Headed Peter, who wouldn't comb his hair or cut his nails, Harriet who played with fire, and Augustus who would not eat his nasty soup until he became 'thin as a thread/and the fifth day was dead'" (Huck, 1987, p. 114). They would be surprised to hear the critical pronouncement that Dr. Heinrich Hoffman's cautionary tales "were meant to frighten children into good behavior. Instead, they loved the pictures and gruesome verse," presumably as much as contemporary children love the comic-gro-

tesque verse of their literary heirs, Shel Silverstein and Jack Pre-
lutsky (Huck, 1987, p. 115). How could children *love* gruesome
verse? This is a reasonable question as it is one which gives rise to
the response that indeed not all children love the book; some do find
it as frightening as the concerned adults fear they might.

The real problem here is not whether or not children have loved
the book. To the contrary, it is still in print, has gone through
dozens of English editions, and has been translated into thirty-one
languages (Demers & Moyles, 1982; Sutherland, 1986). The problem is the supposition that these cautionary tales "were meant to
frighten children into good behavior." This assessment of Hoffman's intent echoes an ambiguous assessment (it is not clear whose
intent is described) which appears in a respected history of children's literature: "These rhymes . . . were intended as awful warnings in their native Germany but in England and the United States
have never been considered as anything but wildly hilarious"
(Meigs, 1969, p. 263). Describing the rhymes as "meant to frighten"
or as "awful warnings" assumes, perhaps unconsciously, that Dr.
Hoffman, the pediatrician who wrote *Der Struwwelpeter* for his
three-year-old son, was either a sadist or a subscriber to rigidly
Calvinist views of the child and the need for stern measures to gain
the child's salvation. We have already seen that beliefs about the
nature of childhood influence what is thought to be appropriate in
humor for children. With *Struwwelpeter*, we see that assumptions
about the *author's* concept of childhood or about the culture in
which he wrote can also enter into assessment of the author's
humor.

In contrast to the priori assumptions, a careful look at *Struwwelpeter*, in particular at the introductory leaf to the fortieth English
edition, suggests that Hoffman was more interested in laughing than
in frightening the child into good behavior. Here Hoffman explains
that he came to write the story as a Christmas present for his three-
year-old after searching in vain for

a picture-book, which should be adapted to the little fellow's
powers of comprehension. But what did I find? Long tales,
stupid collections of pictures, moralizing stories, beginning
and ending with admonitions like: "the good child must be

truthful", or: "children must keep clean", etc. (Hurlimann, 1968, p. 57)

If Hoffman's own words don't convince the adult reader of his playful and satiric intent, a glance at *The Daisy: or, Cautionary Stories in Verse Adapted to the Ideas of Children from Four to Eight Years Old* (1807), the book he parodied, should remove remaining doubts (Demers & Moyles). The reader could, also, turn to later parodies of cautionary tales (such as Hilaire Belloc's *Cautionary Tales* [1907] or Maurice Sendak's *Pierre: A Cautionary Tale in Five Chapters With a Prologue* [1962]) to see Hoffman as one of the forefathers of a tradition which laughs at heavy-handed literary didacticism.

It is then more accurate to say that *Struwwelpeter* may have been *used* by some adults to frighten children into good behavior, but such was not the author's intent. Why the book has been used that way is open to speculation. Jack Zipes's analysis of *Struwwelpeter* refers to "a peculiar hostility to children (what Germans call *Kinderfeindlichkeit*) which has been a disturbing element in the history of German civilization" (Zipes, 1976, p. 165).[1] At any rate, a children's book like *Struwwelpeter* which humorously mocks adult authority is sure to prompt adult misreadings which repress the mockery and, as a consequence, the story's humor.

Although twentieth-century assessments of Hoffman's intent have often been unduly harsh, *Struwwelpeter* is at least mentioned by many of the textbook authors and authors of histories of children's literature. Wilhelm Busch's *Max und Moritz* (1865) is, however, ignored by many of these same authors even though Busch's book is just as important in terms of the history of humor in children's literature; it is an "inspired story in pictures . . . [that] depicted for the first time a crazy series of pranks which children would find well worth copying" (Hurliman, 1968, pp. 161-162) and an inspiration for one of the most important developments in children's humor, the comic strip.

The irony is that these two reasons for the book's importance are also reasons for its being ignored. Most adults feel that children can think up enough pranks without getting additional hints from their reading (never mind that Max and Moritz's eventual death might forestall the young reader from following their example). Likewise, for some adults who are professionally involved with children's literature, Busch's relationship to the comic strip gives rise to equal cause for dismay (Bader, 1976). His influence on the earliest American comics ("the yellow journals") has been well-documented; *Max und Moritz* served as the direct model for Rudolf Dirks's *The Katzenjammer Kids* (Taylor, 1972). This association is enough reason for some authors to omit him from their textbooks and histories; they don't consider comic books to be Literature with a capital "L," so they give this important form of children's humor scant consideration.

While Busch's association with comics might be sufficient to explain his omission from some texts, it's also true, as Taylor notes in reference to whole corpus of Busch's work, that Busch "has something to offend everyone" (1972, p. 80). His use of stock characters is particularly disturbing because literal readings of his work lead to the conclusion that Busch shared or was trying to propagate the negative stereotypes embodied by those stock figures. Whether his work should be understood literally or viewed as satire, Taylor cautions that it is nevertheless almost impossible for post-Holocaust critics looking backward at the conclusion of *Max und Moritz* ("the social misfits" are shoved into ovens and ground up in mills) "to reproduce Busch's original intent" (p. 87).

Given the difficulties of divining Busch's original intent, and the likelihood of his being misinterpreted by young readers whatever his intent, *Max und Moritz* would seem to be a book well worth forgetting. To do that one would fall prey to one of the confusions endemic to many discussions of children's literature: the failure to see the difference between paying attention to a book and examining it critically versus recommending it for child readers. More importantly, dropping problematic texts from histories and textbooks intended for adult readers distorts the record and causes further misunderstandings. Books appear to be new developments or fail to be recognized as such, or their very nature is misunderstood because what came before them has been lost or suppressed. As we shall see when we turn our attention to the comments of modern and contemporary critics of children's humor, the fate of *Max und Moritz* is symptomatic of a larger tendency to suppress or dismiss from critical discussion humor which is thought to be too anarchic, too critical of society, or too revealing of the darker side of human nature. Since children don't read criticism of children's literature, these suppressions often made in their name "protect" an audience different from the one intended. They protect *adults* from having to consider issues akin to those which the critic Walter Arndt identifies Busch as having satirized: "the repression of children (and other rebels)" by the middle class and "the amoral nature of 'the child,' formerly and officially conceived of as innocent" (Arndt, 1982, p. 212).

Although it is possible to construct an overview of critical consensus on the high points of nineteenth-century humor for children, consensus on twentieth-century humor is provisional and fragmentary. It could hardly be otherwise when there are so many more books. More books means more room for tastes to differ, but the whole project is complicated by the fact that here, as with nineteenth-century literature, one looks in vain for comprehensive histories of humor in children's literature. This is probably attributable in large part to the priority given to tracing the evolution of children's literature from texts devoted to instruction to texts intended for amusement and pleasure. Texts that please or amuse (in the sense of "interest") the reader are not necessarily comical, so the history of what is specifically *humorous* has been subsumed by the larger question of didacticism versus delight.

With the exception of a few brief articles or chapters surveying humor in children's literature, studies of humor and children's literature have gone in one of three directions. The first of these, the scrutiny of comic books, has been well documented elsewhere, and for this reason, as well as for the practice of consigning comics to the realm of popular culture (rather than literature) is outside the scope of this chapter. The other two directions may more properly be called approaches since they have either: (a) focused on a single author or handful of books, or (b) focused on the nature of humor and/or the nature of children's responses to humor without looking in detail at the books which occasion these responses. Consensus cannot be said to emanate from these studies either, but the issues which have emerged repay scrutiny. It is to those issues that this discussion will now turn.

ASSUMPTIONS ABOUT CHILDREN'S LITERATURE AND HUMOR

James Smith, one of the few critics to devote a textbook chapter to surveying children's literature and humor, begins his discussion by enumerating "unexamined assumptions about children's literature" and ends it by listing unexamined assumptions about children and humor. As he himself states, "The central implication of this chapter is that our adult thinking about humor in children's literature is generally very sloppy and vague" (1967, p. 222). This is a serious charge, but it is partly corroborated by my chapter's earlier discussion of how *some*, not all, of the criticism of nineteenth-century children's literature was influenced by assumptions about the nature of childhood. Smith (who was writing over two decades ago) did not indite all adult thinking about children's literature and humor as his use of the word "generally" ("generally very sloppy and vague") implies some exceptions to the rule, but it is useful to keep his critique in mind when evaluating other critics' contributions to the study of humor in children's literature. Many later critics have noted some of the same unexamined assumptions, and in the process of examining them, suggested alternative ways of thinking about humor in children's literature. The work of still other critics, however, shows that these same assumptions are still embedded in their thinking about the topic.

Smith's own assumption (an examined one in his case) is that humor "is and should be a part of children's literature" (p. 222). This can be characterized as a sensible, moderate position especially when contrasted with the extremes of the first three of the unexamined preconceptions he notes: (a) "children and laughter are just about synonymous . . . so children's literature becomes almost identified with funny literature," (b) "humor is some absolute quality which a children's book either has or doesn't have," and (c) "we assume there are no significant differences among the things that different children laugh at" (pp. 203-204).

Smith also categorizes four perspectives on children's humor. While the first of these no longer has much currency in critical circles (although it may hold true for some pedagogical and parenting styles), the remaining three, particularly the second, are by no means absent from critical discussion. The most ideological of the perspectives maintains that life is a serious business; humor is, therefore, either inappropriate, sinful, or a waste of time that should be spent cultivating useful habits. A second perspective is also concerned with inappropriateness, but the target here is not all humor, but a particular kind of "subtle" humor which supposedly cannot be appreciated by the child. (This perspective will be referred to in a later section of this chapter.) Yet, another perspective defines "good" humor for children as that which both adults and children find humorous. And finally, there is the hands-off approach which Smith calls "unanalytic." The assumption is that children long for humor and should be given all they want without a lot of adult fuss about what kind of humor it is (pp. 219-222).

Each of the perspectives, even the hands-off approach (i.e., "I wash my hands of the worry"), betrays distrust of humor. Children's book author Sid Fleischman echoes other humorists when he comments that many people feel that comedy can't be taken seriously, but he takes the perception a step further when he says, "The trouble seems to stem from a traditional judgement that humor is unpredictable. What some find funny, others may not." To that Fleishman rejoins that "the premise is faulty. Why must we like the same books, the same paintings, the same music, the same humor?" (1976, p. 469). James Thurber's rejoinder takes a slightly different tact. He felt that children's taste often runs to the "grisly," and that if children's humor is unpredictable, it might be because "Not many adults have the kind of total recall that lets them remember what was funny to them as children" (Landau, 1962, pp. 162-163). Thurber is seconded by Phyllis Fenner a children's librarian who observed that adults "are less tolerant of their [children's] humor than of any other characteristic" (1960, p. 3832).

Certainly nothing less than an unwillingness to take children's humor seriously would explain the condescension and damning with faint praise evident in one widely-used textbook on children's literature. There we read that not only the young child has a "somewhat primitive sense of humor" (Huck, 1987, p. 416), but also that many humorous books are not desirable reading material as they "serve the useful function of getting children 'hooked' on books so that they then move on to reading better literature" (Huck, 1987, p. 512). The flip side of saying that humorous books for children are acceptable until something better comes along is to insist that an undeniably good humorous book for children is not really a *children's* book; it is a book for adults. Nilsen and Nilsen note this phenomenon in connection with literature for adolescents (1982), but it applies to books intended for their younger siblings as well.

DEFINITIONS OF HUMOR

All definitions of humor in children's literature are not as slippery as the one which redefines good children's humor as adult humor, but the range of definitions critics have offered testifies to a widespread belief that humor defies attempts to pin it down. Translator Anthea Bell, for example, feels that humor "transcends frontiers — or perhaps, rather, slips past or under or over them when solemnity and pretentiousness aren't looking" (Bell, 1985, p. 9). Her universalist view of humor sees it as "easily recognizable, [but] extraordinarily difficult to define" (Bell, p. 13).

Critics of children's literature have approached the difficulty in a number of different ways. One of the more popular approaches has been to draw distinctions between two closely related terms. Thus Lloyd Alexander opposes wit and humor ("laughter of the mind" vs. "laughter of the heart"), high comedy and black humor (life is laughable vs. life is absurd), and comedy and tragedy, although he, like a number of other critics, stresses that comedy and tragedy differ "not so much in vision as in method" (Alexander, 1970, pp. 13-15). He shares Fleischman's belief that "Comedy is tragedy; but it is tragedy in motley" (Fleischman, 1976, p. 469.). For yet another critic, this definition also distinguishes that which is humorous from that which is merely funny (Landau, 1962). Whatever distinctions the critics draw, however, they are agreed in linking the truly humorous to "right thinking" (Bell, 1985, p. 10) and "the ultimately prevailing goodness which, in its turn, is equated with happiness" (Cart, 1987, p. 49).

DEVELOPMENTAL STAGES AND KINDS OF HUMOR

It is only a short step from defining terms for the discussion of humor to thinking about kinds of humor and questioning who is likely to appreciate which kind(s). These questions are so central to the study of children's literature and humor that they have occasioned considerable commentary, much of it shaped by the literary critics' and librarians' attempts to apply the methods and insights of the social sciences to their topic. For reasons of space, I mention this work only briefly, since the reader can turn elsewhere in this volume for reviews of work in the social sciences. Please note, however, that the "developmental" literary studies in my bibliography are marked with an asterisk for the reader's convenience. Note too, that with the exception of Monson's work, those studies most heavily indebted to the social sciences were published before 1970 (i.e., before the serious empirical studies of children's humor that began in the 1970s).

Readers who glanced at this section's heading may have wondered what was meant by "Kinds of Humor." One of the ironies of the attempt to be scientific while studying humorous literature is the confusion of terms it spawned. For example, Robin Bateman reported, "There *seem* [my italics] to be six different sets of circumstances in literature which provoke mirth in the youth, and the response to them varies with age and with intelligence" (Bateman, 1967, p. 154). These "sets of circumstances" include: the funny incident, incident entanglement, the comic pictorial image, the sense of superiority, ludicrous nonsense, and subtlety. The first three and last two categories are stimuli to an effect, laughter, but the fourth category is itself an effect, the *sense* of superiority. Bateman then appears to redefine the "sets of circumstances" in the summary which concludes her paper, but it should also be noted that her conclusions merit further investigation, in particular her noting the young child's strong response to comic pictorial images evoked by words.

Moreover, Bateman's confusion of categories pales before Kappas's inventory of types of humor. Like many other commentators, Kappas believes that incongruity is the basis for all humor, but she nevertheless divides humor into ten categories, one of which is incongruity. The other nine are a jumble of causes, intentions, forms, and techniques: surprise, slapstick, the absurd, human predicaments (including the humor of superiority and degradation), ridicule, defiance, violence, and verbal humor (Kappas, 1967). Other critics, such as Smith (1967) and Monson (1979), have narrowed their lists to half this length. Smith's list of four might be said to be the archetypal list of indispensible categories: physical humor, humor of situation; humor involving the play of language; and humor of character, including "humor of human folly" (Smith, 1967).

The attention paid to categories stems from the need to create a yardstick against which to measure the development of the child's sense of humor. The presupposition (largely unexamined) is that certain categories of humor are less sophisticated than others. Although there are variations among the critics, an archetypal hierarchy abstracted from their individual hierarchies would look much like the archetypal list in the preceding. Slapstick and other forms of physical humor are at the bottom of the hierarchy, then nonsense and situational humor followed by word play, wit, and satire (in that order), and finally the high comedy of human folly. As one might assume from the attention paid to the hierarchies, they are seen to measure more than just the development of a sense of humor. Depending on the critic, the child's standing on the scale also measures his or her cognitive, emotional, or moral development, and sometimes all three.

Kappas, for example, constructs detailed portraits of five-, nine-, and fourteen-year-olds to illustrate her thesis (widely shared by other critics) that the "overall pattern [of development] is one of a progression expansion of the child's sense of humor into more and more areas of emotional and intellectual experience until he becomes increasingly adept at utilizing humor for his own ends" (Kappas, 1967, p. 69). Dianne Monson's more recent work updates Kappas; Monson refers to contemporary research in the social sciences such as Paul McGhee's studies that relate humor to maturity and moral development and to his theory of fantasy-assimilation (Monson, 1979).

Mostly separate from these discussions is another set of "developmentalists," those critics and writers interested in the development of the child's literary competence and ability to appreciate different types of humor in literature. Their lists of kinds of humor emphasize books and literary genres, and their questions search for the child's place in the critical milieu. Thus Beverly Cleary writes:

> Fortunately . . . we have a variety of humorous books for children, for the sense of humor of authors is as varied as the sense of humor of readers. Sid Fleischman spins tall tales and period adventure stories; John Fitzgerald tells funny small-town stories in the tradition of Mark Twain; Ellen Raskin capers through madcap fantasy; Arnold Lobel is a master of gentle, whimsical stories and fables; and I happen to enjoy, in reading and writing, domestic comedy about the sort of people I have known and care about. (Cleary, 1982, p. 556)

In a similar vein, DeLuca and Natov note, "Like adult comedy, comedy in children's literature includes farce, high comedy, and satire, each presenting the writer and critic with problems: the writer creates what he or she must; the critic admires or disparages the result, but where does the child fit in?" (DeLuca & Natov, 1977, p. 5). DeLuca and Natov believe that the child "fits in" in more places than many people imagine; even though "a whole level of understanding may be beyond the grasp of most children," exposure to the best of high comedy and satire helps children develop aesthetic awareness and stirs an "intuitive support for their own natural sense of honesty, justice, simple common sense, and for their desire to trust their own instincts and imagination" (DeLuca & Natov, 1977, p. 7).

The approach taken by DeLuca and Natov (1977) and Cleary (1982) highlights the role of the *humorous text* in fostering development. Recognition of humor in literature depends upon familiarity with the conventions of how stories are told, and in particular, with how funny stories are told. Familiarity with these conventions comes only with exposure to the stories themselves. But more than mere "familiarity" operates here; what Joan Blos (1979) notices about books for young children applies to books for their older siblings as well: "Also successful are the books whose structures and patterns lead young children slowly through the steps of a joke" (Blos, 1979, p. 38). Books for older children elaborate the process; their structures help the child learn to recognize and enjoy more sophisticated forms of humor.

SOPHISTICATED FORMS OF HUMOR

At this point in the discussion, it is important to recall two of the frequently encountered "unexamined assumptions" or perspectives that Smith identified: the assumption that children and laughter are almost synonymous and the belief that subtle humor is inappropriate for children. These assumptions are often found together. Combined, they promote the view that children's humor and humorous books for children are simple and obvious. In diametric opposition are those discussions which examine word play, allusion, the blending of the serious and the comic, and black humor.

While none of the critics maintain that epigrams have three-year-olds rolling in the aisles, most critics agree that children enjoy playing with words from an early age. Their enjoyment starts with the way words sound, progresses to puns,[2] and culminates with appreciation of repartee and allusion. Adults, however, often fail to recognize young people's mastery of the latter: "High school literature teachers lament the fact that most of their students fail to grasp allusions to classical literature. This doesn't mean that they don't understand the process of allusion" (Nilsen & Nilsen, 1982, pp. 59-60). The same students have no difficulty grasping one rock song's allusions to another song, but the adult observer might not recognize this as allusion because the *content* of the allusion is not highbrow and the observer's own lack of familiarity with the content may short circuit recognition.

Recognition of the child's literary competence is also short circuited by the adult's faulty memory. Cleary (1982) reports that what adults see as purely comic may be seen as both serious *and* comic by the child. Although the reasons the child finds the story both sad and comic stem from his or her present inability to master completely a situation similar to the one the story portrays (Cleary, 1982), the child's ability to call the story both funny and sad means that the child can entertain two opposing ideas at the same time, one of the prerequisites for mature reading as well as for mature thought. That the child's reading is a mature reading, not a misreading, is indicated by Cleary's account of learning that her books were both "funny and sad" after receiving many letters from children which used this phrase: "The words, at that time never used by adults in reference to my books, began to haunt me. Funny and sad, or even funny and tragic, describes my view of life" (Cleary, 1982, p. 558).

USES OF HUMOR AND HOW HUMOR WORKS

Cleary (1982) follows her account of her young readers' letters with a theory about why children laugh and why children need humorous books. She says they "enjoy feeling superior to their younger selves [represented by a character in the story] and are relieved to know they have grown." Moreover, humorous books don't just reassure the child; "books that help children laugh at their younger selves are the books that help them survive" (Cleary, 1982, pp. 561-562). Like Cleary, most of the critics who write about the uses of humor include at least a passing reference to its being helpful for survival, with "survival" referring variously to intra-psychic, interpersonal, or global concerns. They also discuss educational benefits ranging from humor's hooking reluctant readers into sitting down with a book to humor's transforming young people from passive to active readers. In fact, when the critics start to discuss the uses of humor and how humor works (the two topics are closely linked), they make enough claims to cover rehabilitating forms of humor that would seem suspect or at the least low-brow in another context.

Numskull stories, for example, tell children that "blunders lead not to irreparable harm but simply to embarrassment, and at best to growth and self-knowledge" (DeLuca & Natov, 1977, p. 5). Even macabre and grotesque humor finds defenders, and the defense is predicated on the very reasons critics like Rossana Guarnieri find such forms of humor inappropriate for children. Guarnieri is repelled by these "media for getting rid of aggressions or overcoming complexes" (Guarnieri, 1970, p. 10). On the other hand, Steinfirst

(1980) uses the work of psychologist Martha Wolfenstein to discuss the child's needing humor in order to deal with his or her feelings of hostility, sexual curiosity, and inferiority. Steinfirst (1980) concludes somewhat startlingly that children's books aren't bold enough to help out in this department (evidently she is unfamiliar with Siegel's defense of author Tomi Ungerer's "Rabelasian" humor, or with Raymond Briggs's *Fungus the Bogeyman*, a book as appetising as its title) and that children will have to take care of their needs by telling dirty jokes to each other (Steinfirst, 1980).

CONCLUSIONS

We have come full circle then, from humor in children's literature as a cure-all, to humor in children's literature as a pale substitute for the jokes children tell each other. Clearly, much remains to be done in the study of children's literature and humor. The current body of research offers a number of seminal articles, but no definitive (even if temporarily definitive) studies of the history of humor in children's literature, or of the issues that should be raised, or of the methodologies that might be employed. The best work to date respects the child as an active reader and respects humorous stories as having something to say. In the past, this work has been enriched by insights from other disciplines, but now much more can be accomplished with the resources that have recently become available. Humor in children's literature is alive and well and flourishing, but it can always use a little more critical fertilizer and interdisciplinary pollination to spur new growth and quicken our appreciation of cherished perennials.

NOTES

1. Zipe's comment appears in a review essay (*Down with Heidi, down with Struwwelpeter, three cheers for the revolution: Towards a new socialist children's literature in West Germany*) in which he discusses the work of contemporary German children's authors whose work definitely *does not* reflect hostility to children.

2. Folklorist Alvin Schwartz (1977, Children, humor and folklore, *Horn Book 53* [June], 281-288) reports that children's joking involves considerable word play.

REFERENCES

Adams, G. (1986). The first children's literature? The case for Summer. *Children's Literature, 14*, 1-30.

Alexander, L. (1970). No laughter in heaven. *Horn Book, 46* (February), 11-19.

Andrews, S. (1963). Biographical note on Alice M. Jordon. In S. Andrews (Ed.), *The Hewins lectures, 1947-1962* (p. 3). Boston: Horn Book.

Arndt, W. (Ed. and Translator). (1982). *The genius of Wilhelm Busch*. Berkeley: University of California Press.

Bader, B. (1976). *American picturebooks: From Noah's ark to the beast within*. New York: Macmillan.

Bateman, R. (1967). Children and humorous literature. *School Librarian, 15* (July), 153-161.

Bell, A. (1985). Translating humor for children. *Bookbird*, March, 8-13.

Binder, L. (1970). Humour in children's books. *Bookbird*, December, 8-14.

Bingham, J., & Scholt, G. (1980). *Fifteen centuries of children's literature: An annotated chronology of British and American works in historical context*. Westport, CT: Greenwood.

Blos, J. (1979). Getting it: The first notch on the funny bone. *School Library Journal, 25* (May), 38-39.

Cart, M. (1987). A light in the darkness: Humor returns to children's fantasy. *School Library Journal, 33* (April), 48-49.

Clark, B. L. (1985). Lewis Carroll's *Alice* books: The wonder of wonderland. In Perry Nodelman (Ed.), *Touchstones: Reflections on the best in children's literature (Volume 1* pp. 44-52). West Lafayette, IN: ChLA Publishers.

Cleary, B. (1982). The laughter of children. *Horn Book, 58*, (October), 555-64.

DeLuca, G., & Natov, R. (1977). Comedy in children's literature: An overview. *The Lion and the Unicorn, 1*, 4-8.

Demers, P., & Moyles, G. (Eds.). (1982). *From instruction to delight: An anthology of children's literature to 1850*. Toronto: Oxford University Press.

Fenner, P. (1960). Funny, is it? *Library Journal, 85* (October), 3822-3824.

Fleischman, S. (1976). Laughter and children's literature. *Horn Book, 52* (October), 465-70.

Guarnieri, R. (1970). Humour and society. *Bookbird, 8* (March), 10-13.

Halsey, R. V. (1969, reprint of 1911 ed.). *Forgotten books of the American nursery*. Detroit: Singing Tree Press.

Heins, P. (1982). A second look: the adventures of Pinocchio. *Horn Book, 58* (April), 200-204.

Huck, C. S., Hepler, S., & Hickman, J. (1987). *Children's literature in the elementary school (4th ed.)*. New York: Holt, Rinehart & Winston.

Hurlimann, B. (1967, 1968, translation of 1959 ed.). *Three centuries of children's books in Europe*. Cleveland & New York: World Publishing Company.

Jordan, A. M. (1963, publication of 1947 Address). From Rollo to Tom Sawyer. In S. Andrews (Ed.), *The Hewins lectures: 1947-1962* (pp. 3-21). Boston: Horn Book.

Kappas, K. (1967). A developmental analysis of children's responses to humor. *Library Quarterly, 37* (January), 67-77.

Landau, E. D. (1962). Quibble, Quibble: Funny? Yes; Humorous, No! *Horn Book, 38* (April), 154-164.

Meigs, C., Eaton, A. T., Nesbitt, E., & Viguers, R. H. (1969). In C. Meigs (Ed.), *A critical history of children's literature: A survey of children's books in English* (Rev. ed.). Toronto: Macmillan.

Monson, D. L. (1979). *A look at humor in literature and children's responses to humor*. (ERIC Document Reproduction Service, 22 pp., ED 162 285).

Nilsen, A. P., & Donelson, K. L. (1985). *Literature for today's young adults (2nd ed.)*. Glenview, IL: Scott, Foresman and Company.

Nilsen, D. L. F., & Nilsen, A. P. (1982). An exploration and defense of the humor in young adult literature. *Journal of Reading, 26* (October), 58-65.

Pickering, S. F., Jr. (1981). *John Locke and children's books in eighteenth-century England*. Knoxville: The University of Tennessee Press.

Schwartz, A. (1977). Children, humor, and folklore. *Horn Book, 53* (June), 281-287.

Siegal, R. A. (1977). The little boy who drops his pants in a crowd: Tomi Ungerer's art of the comic grotesque. *The Lion and the Unicorn, 1*, 26-32.

Smith, J. S. (1967). The hoot of little voices: Humor in children's books. *A critical approach to children's literature* (pp. 203-224). New York: McGraw-Hill.

Steinfirst, S. (1980). More about the funny bone: A response. *School Library Journal, 26* (January), 42-43.

Sutherland, Z., & Arbuthnot, M. H., with chapters by D. L. Monson & D. M. Broderick. (1986). *Children and books, (7th ed.)*. Glenview, IL: Scott, Foresman and Company.

Taylor, R. L. (1972). The ambiguous legacy of Wilhelm Busch. *Children's Literature, 1*, 77-92.

Wankmiller, M. C. (1963, publication of 1957 Address). Lucretia P. Hale and *The Peterkin Papers*. In S. Andrews (Ed.), *The Hewins lectures, 1947-1962* (pp. 235-249). Boston: Horn Book.

Wunderlich, R., & Morrissy, T. J. (1982). The desecration of *Pinocchio* in the United States. *Horn Book, 58* (April), 205-212.

Zipes, J. (1976). Down with Heidi, down with Struwwelpeter, three cheers for the revolution: Towards a new socialist children's literature in West Germany. *Children's Literature, 5*, 162-179.

PART VI: CHAPTER COMMENTARY

Introduction

This final section discusses the contribution made by each of the chapters in this volume. No attempt is made to summarize the contents of the chapters; rather, selected issues, research findings, or points of view are discussed which are either controversial or particularly deserving of special emphasis. Both positive and negative forms of criticism are offered, as the case seemed to the editor to merit.

Chapter 12

The Role of Humor in Enhancing Children's Development and Adjustment: Chapter Commentary

Paul E. McGhee, PhD

The present volume was designed to draw attention to the importance of humor in children's lives. Humor is intrinsically enjoyable, of course, but it can make important contributions to children's overall adjustment and development in many ways. We have seen in the preceding chapters some of the ways in which humor can add to children's intellectual, social and emotional development. Thus, when used effectively, humor can help stimulate new learning and creative thinking, and it can help children adapt to both short- and long-term stress. Its built-in appeal can also be used to attract and sustain interest in such growth-promoting mass media productions as educational television and books. The humor children initiate themselves helps them become more competent in social interaction and enables them to better cope with the daily stress associated with growing up.

The present chapter reexamines basic issues or views presented in each chapter. In each case, key points are emphasized, questioned or elaborated upon as the case seems to merit.

Paul E. McGhee is affiliated with the Laboratoire de Psychologie Differentielle, Université de Paris V, Paris, France, and the Department of Human Development and Family Studies, Texas Tech University, Lubbock, TX.

249

BARIAUD:
THE FISHER-PRICE TOY CONCEPT
APPLIED TO HUMOR

Most adults know that if you're going to buy a child a toy, it's important to be sure that it matches the child's age-level. Many toys and games include this information on the package, so it is easy to make selections that are appropriate for the child's social skills, intellectual ability or physical coordination. Children not only play with such toys longer before tossing them into the closet to be forgotten; they also presumably enjoy them more and make progress in their social, intellectual or motor development as a result of playing with them.

Studies of humor, as Bariaud notes, also suggest that humor is enjoyed more when it is at the "right" level; that is, not too easy, but not too difficult either. To be maximally funny (other things being equal), cartoons, jokes and other forms of humor need to be moderately engaging of the child's current level of intellectual abilities. But the humor needs to be quickly understandable, and not require the child to work too much to figure out why it is funny. This being the case, adults wishing to use humor to support the achievement of some developmental goal (e.g., learning or better adjustment) will be more effective if they know in advance the level or kind of humor that is most likely to be understood and enjoyed by the child. One purpose of Bariaud's chapter, then, is to provide age norms for the humor of children and adolescents in order to help those wanting to use humor in various applied contexts to be more effective in their efforts.

Bariaud notes the problems that theorists and researchers have had in conceptualizing and studying humor; nearly all those who have attempted to study or discuss it have emphasized its complexity. Thus, for example, there is still no agreement on just how humor should be defined or on the most valid means of measuring degree of humor comprehension or appreciation. Yet, each of us generally has no difficulty in knowing whether something is funny or not, or whether one event is funnier than another. The best conclusion we can draw at this point is that humor usually (some would say always) involves the playful consideration of some form of (generally, but not necessarily, resolvable) incongruity. This incongruity may center around the physical world, social customs, abstract values, or any other context in which our prior experience produces within us a particular set of expectations or a knowledge structure related to the events, objects, or ideas in question. In other words, humor involves the playful distortion or reorientation of the known world.

But this characterizes only the cognitive side of humor. Bariaud is careful to point out the equal importance of the affective aspects of humor. Much of her own work is designed to demonstrate how the emotional salience of the content of a cartoon or joke plays the key role of determining not only the level of humor appreciation, but the way in which the humor is understood and appreciated, as well. There seems to be little doubt that it is the emotional aspect of humor that makes it such a rich and enjoyable experience.

Like Ziv (see his chapter in this edition), Bariaud considers the intent to amuse to be central to a definition of humor. In everyday life, we commonly encounter unexpected and incongruous events which trigger laughter in us. For Bariaud, such events are comical, but not humorous. My own view concerning this issue is that while it is important to distinguish between intentional and unintentional sources of laughter and humor, the underlying cognitive and emotional processes are sufficiently similar that they should both be considered as humor. From the humor recipient's point of view, I see little difference in the essential nature of the experience when the humorous event is known to be either intended or accidental. Bariaud argues that there is humor only when someone creates an incongruity with full knowledge of its power to amuse at the time of its creation. But while social communication and a shared sense of complicity certainly enrich humor, is there really a lack of humor in their absense? In my view, "comical" events are best thought of as a subset or a particular form of humor, rather than being a nonhumorous form of experience. In a comical event, the observer actively "creates" the incongruous event that is the basis for humor. The observer could then share the event by pointing it out to someone else. While this disagreement may seem to be a peripheral one, it points out the difficulties investigators have had in reaching agreement upon the basic nature of the phenomenon they are studying. It is not necessary to resolve this issue, however, in order to accomplish the goals of the present volume.

The bulk of Bariaud's chapter focuses upon theoretical views and research findings related to the humor of preschool and elementary school children. The views and data discussed provide the reader with an excellent summary of the major findings concerning children's humor up to adolescence. This should provide the reader with a sufficient understanding of children's humor to permit him/ her to effectively incorporate humor into children's lives along the lines discussed in this volume.

BRYANT AND ZILLMANN: HUMOR IN THE CLASSROOM— IS THERE A LESSON TO BE LEARNED HERE?

In anticipation of the first International Conference on Humor and Laughter in Cardiff in 1976, I distributed a questionnaire to those presenting papers at the conference and asked them (among other things) to list the areas of humor they thought were most important to study (McGhee, 1976). The most frequently mentioned topic was the role of humor in learning. The chapter by Bryant and Zillmann indicates that we have come a long way in answering certain questions along these lines, but the link between humor and learning is more complicated than anticipated.

Bryant and Zillmann draw attention to an important discrepancy between research findings and articles written by and for teachers. While the research findings are generally mixed and full of qualifications, the professional "trade literature" is much more unhesitatingly positive about the place of humor in the classroom. How are we to explain this discrepancy? Bryant and Zillmann note that the criteria for accepting articles in trade publications are very different from those of research journals. The latter require observation under controlled or known conditions and the use of procedures which allow generalizations to be made within certain specified limits. Since it is very difficult to know the pertinent values of all the variables we have reason to believe would contribute to classroom learning, the research process is inevitably a slow one which must qualify its conclusions. When numerous studies consistently produce the same finding, we can feel more comfortable about generalizations. A teacher writing for other teachers simply needs to have personal success in using humor in order to write a glowing article about the value of humor. Teachers who have tried humor and met with disaster in the classroom are not likely to write an article going into the details of their failure; and even if they did, it is unlikely that such an article would be accepted for publication. Thus, articles in trade publications are likely to give an unrepresentative view of teachers' actual experiences with humor, and they cannot help us sort out what does and does not work. On the positive side, however, these articles are very valuable in drawing attention to teachers' experience in the classroom, and to their belief that humor really does make learning more interesting/enjoyable and that it facilitates retention.

Let's assume that teachers who make strong claims about the effectiveness of their own use of humor in the classroom are right. This suggests that these teachers have (through trial and error or intuition) hit upon a successful combination of those factors that are constantly being qualified by researchers. Humor really does work—for them! The teacher who finds a method that works is likely to have trouble understanding all the controversy. It is likely that the spontaneous use of humor is a natural and common form of behavior for this person even outside the classroom, so that its use within the classroom is simply an extension of his or her normal style of interacting with others. A teacher who has never developed spontaneous humor skills can expect to encounter difficulty in making humor work in the classroom. Such a teacher who tries to copy the methods of the successful humor user may find those methods to be disastrous.

Individual differences in teachers, then, may prove to be one of the most important factors determining humor's effectiveness in the classroom. Among comedians, it is common knowledge that success (in this case, getting laughs) depends entirely upon "delivery" and "timing." Since a teacher in front of a group of students is in one sense a performer, there is every reason to believe that these two factors are equally important in the classroom. It is very difficult, however, to do experimental research on delivery and timing; so it is not surprising that we know nothing about their importance in a scientific sense. We could determine the strength of the "teacher-effect" by presenting teachers with identical lesson plans, including instructions on the humor to be added, when and how to include it, etc. Every attempt would be made to have each teacher teach the class in exactly the same way. Any differences in learning, interest or enjoyment of the class might then be attributed to the differences in actual execution of the humor by different teachers. (The problem here, of course, is that any observed differences could also be due to teacher-differences in execution of parts of the lesson plan that are unrelated to humor.)

Attentive teachers should be able to make reliable judgments about the impact of classroom humor on interest in and enjoyment of course work. Judgments about its impact on learning cannot be trusted since it would be impossible to sort out the role of humor from the role of endless other factors that influence learning. However, if humor does increase interest and enjoyment, teachers can feel reasonably confident (within the limitations specified by Bryant and Zillmann) that enhanced learning will accompany this interest.

Under what conditions should teachers be concerned about humor interfering with learning? Again, research findings do not yet permit a definite answer to this question. Several conditions, however, are likely candidates for failures: (a) unskilled use of humor by the teacher, (b) humor which is either too simple or incomprehensible, and (c) too much humor. In the case of the latter, lack of careful monitoring of humor in the classroom may change the mood of the majority of students into one of play and silliness, a mood which should be incompatible with attention and learning.

Teachers who have reason to doubt their ability to use humor effectively may choose to seek out special training designed to enhance their spontaneous humor skills. Junior high and high school teachers would be especially good candidates for such training, since, as Bryant and Zillmann point out, the higher intellectual abilities of their students make it much more difficult for the average teacher to come up with humor that will be well-received. Elementary school teachers are probably more enthusiastic about using humor in the classroom precisely because it is easier to make it work in this respect with younger children. There is every reason to expect humor to be equally effective at higher grade levels, but teachers may have to make a greater effort to increase their own humor skills so that humor has a fair chance to work in the classroom.

WILLIAMS:
METAPHORS FOR LEARNING –
CHILDREN ARE SPONGES

This is the only chapter in this edition which does not focus on humor. It was included because of my own view that both humor and metaphor may be considered forms of intellectual play (see McGhee, 1979), and because the use of each in the classroom can bolster traditional approaches to teaching. The selective use of humor and metaphor by teachers can help sustain interest in the material to be learned and enhance its retention.

Williams notes the general consensus that new material to be learned must inevitably be linked to what is already known. Metaphors and humor simply facilitate this process, albeit in very different ways. In most cases, humor plays an indirect role of keeping the person's interest so that the real information to be learned is attended to. In some cases, of course, as is common with political cartoons, humorous depictions of events may cause us to see them in an entirely new light. The contribution of humor to learning is more direct here, as it is with metaphor.

At first glance, learning via metaphors does not appear to be that different from other forms of learning. That is, as Williams notes, "something that the student does not yet know or understand is compared to something else that the student already understands well." What is different about metaphors is that some aspect of one domain is equated with a component of another in a way that is inappropriate or incorrect, at a literal level. Thus, children are not really sponges, but the metaphor invites us to find meaning in the statement by applying what we know about sponges to children. Once we extend the quality of absorption to children (i.e., in terms of their ability to absorb information they are exposed to and make it a part of themselves), we have a new way of viewing children. Williams notes that metaphors can be used both to expand our knowledge of a subject, as with the children-sponge example, or to more quickly learn something about a completely new subject.

This chapter is an especially important one, in that teachers have generally failed to capitalize on the power of metaphors as facilitators of learning, perhaps even moreso than in the case of humor. Williams discusses several theoretical rationales for why metaphor should be an effective educational tool, and then he presents research findings which demonstrate its effectiveness. In the last half of the chapter, he provides explicit guidelines for teachers to follow in order to maximize the effectiveness of the metaphors that they build into their teaching. The careful integration of both humor and metaphors into teaching may prove to be more effective in enhancing learning than either approach alone.

Finally, there is reason to believe that creativity and the ability to produce and understand metaphors are closely related (see Kogan, 1983). Since metaphors involve seeing meaningful links across categories normally considered unrelated, a more creative person should see these links more easily. More important for teachers, however, is the likelihood that using metaphors as instructional tools will also help stimulate the development of creativity in children (in the same manner as that described by Ziv in this volume in connection with humor). Thus, metaphors can help teachers achieve two valued goals at the same time.

ZIV:
A HUMOROUS PATH TO THE DEVELOPMENT
OF CREATIVE THINKING?

A frequently heard complaint concerning our educational system is that it gives inadequate attention to the development of creative thinking capacities. While most teachers and educational researchers agree that it is important to nurture creativity, it has never been clear how one might go about this or how one should decide if an approach is working. Ziv notes that researchers have increasingly come to equate creativity with divergent thinking over the past 25-30 years. But it does not necessarily follow, he observes, that individuals obtaining high scores on divergent thinking tasks will produce more creative products in the arts, science, or in any other field. We continue to know very little about the combination of motivational, personality and other factors that combine with creative thought capacities to yield those rare individuals who produce works agreed upon by society to be highly creative.

It should be safe to assume that creative insights are an essential prerequisite to any subsequent production of complex creative products. A person who lacks the ability to forge new ways of seeing things, to find innovative but meaningful connections between concepts or events which initially appear unrelated, is virtually certain (barring chance factors) to fail in creative endeavors, regardless of how much time and effort is put into them. This being the case, any experiences which nurture the development of creative thought capacities mark an important step in the right direction. Thus, the finding (reported by Ziv) that exposure to humor increases scores on divergent thinking tasks is very promising.

But what do these studies really tell us? Positive correlations between scores on a humor measure and scores on a test of creativity, of course, provide no support for the view that it is one's enhanced humor abilities which cause one to be more creative. It is just as likely (if not more likely) that it is one's heightened creative insights which enable one to both create enjoyable humor and understand the humor of others. The other findings presented by Ziv are more problematic. These findings show that exposure to humorous recordings or videotapes before taking a creativity test leads to heightened creativity scores. Similarly, asking subjects to respond humorously on a creativity test produces higher creativity scores.

Ziv concludes from these studies that "There is . . . convincing evidence that increased exposure to humor can enhance the level of one's creativity." It is difficult, however, to accept the conclusion that such brief exposures to humor actually led to increased creative capacities. Such capacities are presumably only gradually developed during childhood. Rather, such short term exposure to humor probably simply help create a relaxed and playful context in which already existing creative abilities can be used at a level closer to their "potential." Rather than increasing creativity, then, the humor experiences provided by Ziv may have merely allowed for a more accurate estimate of subjects' level of creativity. In other words, his conclusion is best restricted to test performance.

It is worth emphasizing, however, that the basic idea represented in his conclusion is a sound one. That is, a child who is regularly exposed to humor over a period of months or years can be expected to acquire heightened divergent thinking skills precisely because humor involves the same form of bisociation assumed to character- ize all creative thought. Cartoons and jokes provide the child with altered ways of seeing familiar objects and events, and these alter- ations should be just as effective at creative bisociative thinking habits as exposure to nonhumorous (but meaningful) alterations of the familiar. The fact that requests to answer humorously produce more frequent responses judged to be creative is consistent with the notion that the quality of "divergentness" in one's thinking is more important than whether this divergentness is channeled into a hu- morous or nonhumorous direction.

Singer (1973) and Feitelson (1972) suggested that early creativity may be expressed in make-believe play. According to Singer, "Make-believe play in childhood is probably best regarded as one aspect of the general capacity for divergent production. . . . In this sense it has clear links to what later emerges as creativity in the young adult . . ." (1973, p. 255). Consistent with this view, John- son (1976) found measures of divergent thinking in preschoolers to be a stronger predictor of engagement in fantasy play than were measures of convergent thinking. McGhee (1979) proposed that children's initial humor emerges out of and takes the same basic form as pretend play. In combination, these views suggest that chil- dren who spend more time in pretend play during the preschool years, and who acquire a more active interest in humor during childhood and adolescence, may be expected, as a result of these activities, to acquire higher levels of creative abilities than their less playful and less humor-oriented peers.

McGHEE:
THE FUNNY SIDE OF SOCIAL COMPETENCE

McGhee discusses a broad range of social functions served (ei- ther for the individual or the group) by humor, and proposes that skill at effectively inserting humor into ongoing social interaction be viewed as a form of social competence. Some supportive data are cited, but virtually no attempt has been made to study this rela- tionship among children. Even the limited data reported for adults are not totally convincing. That is, the two studies cited using college students relied at least partly on self-reports of wittiness or frequency of humor initiation. Even the observed humor initiation data obtained by Turner (1980) led only to the conclusion that individuals considered to have higher levels of interpersonal competence initiate humor more often than their less competent peers.

All of us have encountered chronic joke-tellers whose humor just didn't seem to work very well, and who certainly did not strike us as people with high levels of social skill. However, this is actually consistent with the moderate size of the correlations obtained in these studies. Thus, some individuals initiate humor frequently, but would not be considered to be highly socially competent. Others who have clearly developed superior social skills have done so without relying on humor. There are undoubtedly many paths toward becoming highly skilled at social interaction, and the skilled use of humor is only one of them.

No pertinent longitudinal studies have been completed, but it seems likely that college students who have adopted humor as a major part of their style of interpersonal interaction began to do so at some point in their childhood. One generally does not suddenly become an effective humorist as an adolescent; there must be a reasonably lengthy period of practice and building up skills at delivery of jokes, humorous stories or spontaneous wit.

So what's different about the child who comes to place heavy reliance on humor in interacting with others? A number of correlational studies have now painted a coherent picture of the child who becomes a frequent initiator of humor. By the time he or she enters school, the budding humorist tends to be (a) more talkative, (b) show more advanced language development and communicative skills, (c) have more energy, (d) be more dominating and aggressive (assertive) toward peers, and (e) show more concern about receiving positive reactions from others, including heightened seeking of attention, recognition and affection or emotional support (see McGhee, 1980). The fact that humor initiators tend to be more popular than their less humorous peers suggests that their attempts at humor are providing them with the very attention and emotional support they want. Individuals lacking these qualities may develop high levels of social competence, but they are likely to do so without being able to use humor when the situation seems to call for it.

Given the social uses of humor described by McGhee, there is little doubt about the value of developing effective humor skills. For those children who initially lack such skills, the provision of "humor training" might enable them to become more assertive and self-confident in their interactions with others, help them acquire new friends, and generally make them more effective in achieving social goals.

MARTIN:
"LOOKING ON THE LIGHT SIDE" —
OR THE FUN SIDE OF COPING

Martin is careful to point out at the beginning of his article that a broad range of coping skills is needed to deal effectively with the many stresses that confront most children and adolescents in growing up. Humor is just one such skill, and is probably most effective when combined with others.

The belief that humor serves important coping functions has been a popular one throughout most of this century. While Freud (1905) and others have offered explanations of how and why humor helps us cope, and while Wolfenstein (1954) and others have discussed the age at which children should become capable of using humor for this purpose, Martin correctly notes that we know surprisingly little about whether humor really helps us cope and (if it does) just how it does so. Martin and his colleague Herbert Lefcourt were among the first to attempt to systematically study humor's effectiveness in dealing with stressful events. In general, the research findings support the view that people who have better developed humor skills and who more often include humor in their daily lives are better at coping with stressful events. At this point, it is not clear whether those with a better developed sense of humor actually experience less stress in their lives, or whether they simply work through their stress more quickly because of their humor skills. It may be that both effects occur. That is, the person who is accomplished at seeing "the light side" of stressful events may, as a result, find the event less stressful to begin with. This reduced level of stress may make it easier for the person to "pull himself out of it" by either initiating or exposing himself to additional mood-changing humor. In any case, it is important to note that even being exposed to humor initiated by someone else may help moderate the adverse effects of stress among those who are not themselves naturally inclined to find humor in the midst of stress. This effect should be weaker, however, than when the person under stress manages himself to find a humorous side of his plight.

The regulation of one's mood via humor may eventually prove to be the major factor responsible for humor's ability to facilitate coping. That is, people who frequently build humor into their everyday lives may establish a protective layer of positive emotion or outlook which is simply incompatible with anger, depression, loneliness, etc. On the other hand, an effective coper may simply have learned that a positive mood can gradually be substituted for a negative one by creating or exposing oneself to humor. Our present state of knowledge doesn't permit us to say whether humor is directly related to the source of distress and produces more effective coping than humor which is totally unrelated to the stress.

While the data reported by Martin were obtained with college students, comparable outcomes should occur with school-aged children and younger adolescents. The person who can find real humor in the midst of stress should be a person who has a strong sense of humor in general, and a college student with well-developed humor skills has presumably gradually developed these skills throughout childhood. It is very difficult for most of us to experience humor in a strong negative emotional state, and it is unimaginable that this ability would suddenly appear in late adolescence without some prior development along these lines. Future research needs to focus on the age at which the type of findings reported by Martin first appear.

Assuming that humor can facilitate coping with daily stress among children in the same manner that has been demonstrated for adults, what can parents and others do to help children acquire such coping skills? As Martin points out, parental modeling of effective coping skills under stress (without denying or minimizing the importance or seriousness of the source of stress) may be the most important way of influencing children along these lines. Such modeling not only shows the child that humor does help in coping; it also gives the child concrete ideas about just how to go about using humor for this purpose. The problem here, of course, is that most parents are probably not very skilled themselves in using humor for coping. They may still support the development of coping skills, however, by maintaining a pattern of frequent playful interactions with the child. This would both indirectly support the child's general development of his sense of humor (since a playful frame of mind is a prerequisite for humor), and give parents a foundation for subsequent effective assistance at helping the child see the light side of a stressful event.

There is clearly an art to using humor under conditions of stress, and this art is presently poorly understood. Parents and other adults working with children need to be careful in initiating humor or exposing children under stress to humor, lest the child feel that his stressful circumstance is not being taken seriously. Given that a prior foundation of playfulness and humorous interaction has been established with the child under nonstress conditions, the possibility of this reaction by the child would be minimized; under these conditions parents could monitor their humor-related efforts to find out what works and what doesn't work in terms of helping the child cope.

A final note of caution should be added here. Given our present state of knowledge of how humor facilitates coping, it should not be viewed as a tool to be relied upon by itself. That is, humor should be seen as a supplement to other active means of dealing with stress, not as a replacement for them. A child who is limited to humor as a means of coping may appear to handle the stress well in the absense of any real coping.

D'ANTONIO: KEEPING CHILDREN "IN STITCHES" IN HOSPITALS

There is no doubt about the fact that hospital stays are sources of stress for children. Thus, if humor is capable of relieving emotional stress, this would be the ideal place to demonstrate it. D'Antonio discusses some of the fears expressed by children in hospital settings, along with the way they view common hospital events. Perhaps the most striking part of this article is the examples of humor initiated by children themselves in the midst of their anxieties and uncertainties. While no data are available regarding the percentage of children who joke or clown around under such conditions, or the characteristics that distinguish those who use humor in this setting from those who do not, some children are clearly quite accomplished at mastering (or trying to master) their stress by poking fun at various elements related to it. This is consistent with the view that humor can serve children under stress conditions just as well as it serves adults.

Our concern, then, needs to be directed toward the children who enter the hospital lacking such skills. The key question is whether the provision of humorous TV programs, films, or humorous interactions initiated by hospital staff can help reduce stress related to the hospital stay. To my knowledge, no one has yet attempted this on a systematic basis. As with educational and therapeutic uses of humor, successful outcomes can be expected in hospital settings, but care needs to be exercised in the approach adopted by staff members. The child must not get the message that his circumstances are not being taken seriously. As noted in the previous section, adaptation to the hospital environment should be improved if the child himself is encouraged to poke fun at hospital routines, his own appearance, etc.

It is especially important to note the integration of play and humor proposed by D'Antonio. Humor is best enjoyed and most likely to be produced when in a playful frame of mind. Thus, the establishment of special play settings in the hospital or the encouragement of play activities by the staff may be expected to yield an environment which is more conducive to the production of stress-related humor by the child.

The importance of opportunities for play by children in hospital settings has only recently begun to receive attention (see Bolig, 1984). Given the close link between humor and play, the findings and issues raised in connection with play have clear implications for the use of humor in hospital settings. For example, it is well-known that play is more likely to occur in familiar, "safe" environments than in novel and threatening ones. Hospital environments, then, should not be very conducive to play. While there is no way to eliminate most of the unique features of hospital "equipment," the presence of familiar toys, games, teddy bears or other known and loved objects could help create a corner of familiarity which would support the development of a mood for play. The provision of a play room is a step in the right direction, but this allows the child only a brief opportunity to play before going back to his own room. The gains to be achieved by a play room should be maximized if the play materials were available in the child's own room.

A great advantage of humorous over nonhumorous forms of play is that the child needs neither supporting objects nor a special space for engaging in the activity. He needs only the will and the ability to create humor on the spot in order to receive a therapeutic boost out of the stress that engulfs him. If nurses were trained to joke with children and to support the child's own humor in the midst of their normal hospital routines, this would provide a means of helping children cope with hospital-related stress which would be cost-efficient and (hopefully) bring some pleasure to nurses as well. In short, keeping children in stitches with humor should help minimize the stress encountered while waiting for their stitches to be removed.

NEVO:
EXTRACTING HUMOR FROM DENTAL ANXIETY

Nevo first documents the extent of anxiety associated with visits to the dentist's office, and then briefly notes the kinds of attempts that have been made to alleviate this anxiety. Adopting Ventis' (1973; see also Ventis & Ventis, this edition) proposed systematic desensitization approach using humor, she outlines possible ways for dentists to reduce anxiety with doses of humor. As she notes, there is some evidence that using humor to produce positive affective responses which are incompatible with anxiety or anger does, in fact, reduce the extent of the negative emotional state. Since the specific source of the anxiety (e.g., heights, dogs, enclosed spaces, dentists, etc.) should have no bearing on the effectiveness of a systematic desensitization approach, there is every reason to expect humor to be effective in reducing dentist-related anxiety. My own discussions with dentists suggest that while many have long relied upon talking to the client as a means of distraction, there is growing receptiveness to using humor to achieve the same goal.

At this point, there are few guidelines at present regarding how to achieve this goal most effectively. The most important advice may be to simply monitor the client's reactions in order to see what works best. In the case of children, of course, dentists need to have a sense of the child's developmental level of humor before making attempts to be funny (see chapter 1). As with other contexts in which humor is used for some applied purpose, dentists must take care not to go too far with their humor (e.g., by constantly making humorous remarks). That is, the child has a serious purpose for being there, and the available cues most be consistent with an image of competence and professionalism. Otherwise, efforts at humor may backfire and serve to increase the child's anxiety (e.g., because the dentist is not really paying attention to what he's doing).

Finally, dentists need to remember their own experiences of having their mouth full of strange utensils. Nothing is more frustrating than a dentist who asks questions while you are incapable of an intelligible syllable, let alone answering. While (modified) laughter may be possible under these conditions, it may also be uncomfortable. Thus, dentists need to carefully time their occasions for joking so that the child is able to laugh without a mouthful of strange objects, or without concern about getting his tongue caught in the drill.

VENTIS AND VENTIS: HUMOR IN THERAPY— "THAT'LL BE 5 CENTS PLEASE"

It has always been difficult to do research on the effectiveness of any form of therapy using experimental procedures and "objective" measures. Even if agreement is reached on whether a therapy program has been effective, it is rarely clear why it worked. Therapy which includes humor is no different. Was it effective primarily, or even partly, because of the use of humor in the treatment program? In virtually all cases, the inclusion of humor constitutes just a part of an ongoing therapy program. So we have no way to determine exactly what role the humor played in the client's subsequent improvement. The important point, however, may be that therapists are increasingly becoming convinced that humor is an effective tool in therapy. Since the therapist is in the best position to make this judgment, the best that the rest of us can do for the time being is to assume that they are right. Humor's ability to facilitate coping in a broad range of contexts has been stressed at several points in this volume. It would be surprising if it were not also effective in therapy.

Most of the recent work on humor and therapy has concerned adults, but (as Ventis and Ventis note) considerable work has been done with children as well. A key distinction concerns whether the humor is initiated by the child or by the therapist, although it is not clear whether therapeutic benefits are greater in one case or the other. While many therapists use the child's spontaneous humor during therapy mainly as a means of gaining insight into the child's problems, most would also agree that it can also be directly beneficial to the child.

If humor initiated by a child or adolescent in therapy is therapeutic, why is this the case? While various reasons are proposed in this chapter, the notion of mastery is especially worth underscoring. Psychoanalytically-oriented therapists have long held that humor helps both children and adults master their anxieties and fears (see Levine, 1977, for a discussion of this issue). An effective "coper" is a person who has problems, but is not overcome or debilitated by them. This person has a range of coping skills and draws on the combination of behaviors that has worked best in a given kind of situation in the past. Some children learn on their own that joking or otherwise poking fun at things related to their anxiety or conflict creates a form of distance between them and the problem. The circumstance somehow seems less menacing when viewed from this distance, perhaps especially because of the playful frame of mind which accompanies real experiences of humor. For some children, this playful distancing may, in itself, be enough to reduce the stress. For others it may provide a comfortable vantage point from which to take other steps to really deal with the problem. In either case, the problem is mastered (or coped with) because it no longer "runs" the child.

Paradoxically, however, some children and adolescents give the impression of hiding behind their humor. That is, the humor produced appears to simply lead them to avoid the source of their problem by keeping it at an unthreatening distance. For these children, humor does not work as a coping tool (at least in the sense of helping them master the source of their stress, as noted in the preceding). Quite the contrary, it interferes with real adaptive coping. High stress may be avoided, but the child remains dependent on humor to keep the source of stress at a safe distance. These children clearly need other kinds of coping skills to deal with their stress. At this point, it is not understood why humor is able to promote effective coping in some children but not in others. Therapists clearly need to be sensitive to where the child's own spontaneous humor falls along this continuum in order to treat the child most effectively.

For most of us, it is precisely the areas related to our stress that are most difficult for us to be playful about or joke about. In one sense, then, humor is not available to us at the time when we need it the most. Thus, it is entirely appropriate for therapists to serve as "stress gurus" who help us see humor in some aspect of our problem. If a therapist can teach children skills at humorously reframing parts of events or conditions surrounding their anxiety, anger or depression, this should help provide them with a new coping skill which will be at their disposal when subsequent high stress events occur.

A therapist's use of humor may also play the valuable role of "breaking the ice," of creating a comfortable and trusting context in which other aspects of treatment can be more effectively undertaken. The usual caution needs to be exercised, however, by therapists who initiate humor in the presence of children and adolescents experiencing high stress. As Ventis and Ventis note, the inexpert use of humor may lead the child to feel ridiculed or that his situation is not being taken seriously. Unfortunately, at this point, we have insufficient knowledge to spell out the steps which therapists might take in building humor into their therapy with children. What works with one therapist with a particular child might not work for another therapist with a similar case. Therapists can best learn how to use humor effectively in therapy by first learning from other therapists what has worked for them in particular cases, and then inserting humor into their own therapy. In so doing, the therapist needs to be fully armed with a knowledge of the kinds of humor that correspond to the child's developmental level, and be sensitive to the impact of the humor on the child. Therapists must themselves learn when to use or not use humor, what kinds of humor to use, whether or not the humor should strike close to the real sources of stress, and when to simply abandon the use of humor in favor of other approaches.

ZILLMANN AND BRYANT: HUMOR AS THE KEY TO INTEGRATING LEARNING AND ENTERTAINMENT IN EDUCATIONAL PROGRAMMING

Zillmann and Bryant draw an important distinction between learning in the classroom and learning from television: namely, that the former involves a captive audience while the latter does not. Thus, the role of sustaining interest via humor is clearly more important in the case of educational television than in the classroom. People of all ages generally seek entertainment from television, not new knowledge. It is for this reason that humor and other basic entertainment devices have come to play such a dominant role in programs which have primarily educational goals. While many children and adults clearly seek out and enjoy opportunities for learning which lack an emphasis on humor and entertainment, the television industry has increasingly operated on the assumption that if television is to be used to achieve educational goals, learning must be fun!

In sharp contrast to such programs as "Ding Dong School" in the 1950s, "Sesame Street" marked the first real attempt to use humor and other highly polished entertainment techniques (e.g., music) to achieve educational goals. As Zillmann and Bryant point out, however, the producers of "Sesame Street" initially only assumed that humor would work. Even though it quickly became evident that frequent viewing of "Sesame Street" does increase learning of the basic concepts the programs are designed to teach, it was impossible to determine the extent to which the addition of humor contributed to or detracted from learning. It is only in the past decade, with the research of Zillmann and Bryant and a few other researchers, that we have been able to provide some definite answers to questions about just what humor can and cannot accomplish in the domain of educational television.

Zillmann and Bryant summarize experimental evidence which shows that: (a) children are more likely to watch humorous than comparable nonhumorous programs in free-choice situations, and this effect is greatest when brief humorous episodes are sprinkled throughout the program rather than being concentrated in one part of the program; (b) this attention-holding power of humor is enhanced with funnier and more vividly produced material, but does not depend on the kind of humor used or the extent to which the humor is meaningfully related to the material to be learned; (c) information from humorous programs is remembered better than information from comparable nonhumorous programs, even if the humor has no meaningful link to the target information; (d) the positive effects of humor on learning are enhanced by increased funniness and vividness (or pace) of the humor; (e) excessive use of humor in educational programs should be avoided; and (f) exaggeration, irony and ridiculing forms of humor should be avoided.

The finding that exaggeration and irony were not effective in facilitating learning, and that they even created confusion is especially important to note. Since, as Zillmann and Bryant indicate, each of these forms of humor require thorough familiarity with the exaggerated or ironic elements, they can only be used when it is certain that the humor will be understood. If confusion and uncertainty were created in connection with the humorous elements, this could serve as a mental distractor and actually reduce learning and retention. Since we have no control over who watches various programs, it is inevitable that many viewers will fail to grasp the intended humor. This could be due to mere lack of sufficient familiarity with the content or, in the case of irony, to the fact that it is just too intellectually demanding. Irony is sufficiently difficult for even adolescents to understand, and it is probably best completely avoided in programs with learning as a primary goal.

Given the high amount of time that most children spend watching television, it is essential that a balance be struck between the educational and pure entertainment functions of television viewing. Ideally, many programs would be available (each with special appeal to children in particular age ranges) in which a true merging of these two functions occurs. Humor may be the best vehicle for accomplishing this integration. With well-balanced servings of humor, learning stops being viewed as learning (often translated as work) and simply becomes fun.

ALBERGHENE:
ONCE UPON A TIME . . .

It was noted in the introduction to this volume that research on humor has only recently begun to be "taken seriously." Alberghene notes that the same can be said about humorous literature written for children. And yet, it seems clear that humor plays a major role in recruiting interest and maintaining attention to children's literature. While the historical summary provided in the first half of this chapter is fascinating reading for anyone interested in children and their humor, our discussion here will be restricted to issues related to more current forms of humorous literature written for children.

Given the nature of the other chapters in this volume, one of the most interesting issues discussed by Alberghene concerns the way in which writers of literature for children view humor intended for their readers. Many (if not most) appear to have written on an "intuitive" basis, lacking a clear sense of how the humor enjoyed by children might vary at different ages. This has not really been a problem, however, since once a humorous story or book is written, the age-appropriate audience is eventually drawn to it.

Some individuals in the field of children's literature hold startling views about children and their humor. For example, in a statement credited to James Smith, it is noted that "we assume that there are no significant differences among the things that different children laugh at." One of the most fundamental results of research on children's humor indicates that children at different ages are capable of understanding and appreciating different forms of humor. Since even casual observation of children points to this conclusion, we must assume that Smith was referring to children of a given age level. Even within the same age level, however, individual differences in what is seen as funny (or in the degree of funniness) abound in children, just as they do in adults. There may well be greater similarity than difference across individuals at a given age level (especially prior to adolescence), but this overriding similarity (presumably reflecting similarities in cognitive level and general experience in the world) should not be taken to mean that children of a given age do not differ in what they laugh at (see Bariaud, 1983, and this volume).

Alberghene notes another perspective which "defines 'good' humor for children as that which both adults and children find humorous." This is a puzzling view, since, if anything, the opposite must be true. Humor which is thoroughly enjoyed by adults is likely to be too sophisticated for children to understand, or to call upon domains of knowledge not yet acquired by children. If the difficulty level is, in fact, appropriate for children, then it is virtually certain that it is the heightened sexual, aggressive or otherwise "tendentious" content of the humor which makes it enjoyable to adults, and this should be sufficient to make it a questionable candidate for children's literature. In any case, even if children and adults do laugh at the same story or event (as was the case for "Laugh-in," the comedy TV program in the 1960s), it is very unlikely that the humorous event is viewed in the same way. In this respect, the humor responded to by children and adults is not really the same, even though it appears to be. Literature or any other form of humor which is genuinely appreciated by both adults and children can always be expected to have varying "levels" of humor suitable to different levels of intellectual functioning.

It is not surprising that no definition of humor has been agreed upon in children's literature. After years of effort, social scientists have similarly failed to reach agreement. There appears to be neither any necessary (although some continue to view such factors as incongruity, sense of superiority, or aggression as necessary) nor sufficient conditions for humor. It is reasonable to continue our efforts in both literature and the social sciences in the absense of an agreed-upon definition, however, since both children and adults have no difficulty in recognizing when they find something funny. Thus, we can examine differences in children's enjoyment of humorous literature even though we cannot really say what it means to find something humorous.

Along these lines, some individuals in children's literature continue to attempt to classify the number of "kinds of humor" that exist. While this is always an interesting exercise, it has become increasingly clear that the number and kinds of categorizations made generally says as much about the person doing the classifying (e.g., their ability to make distinctions, their theoretical interests, etc.) as it does about the material being classified. Also, the specific categories specified must to some extent depend on the particular examples of literature chosen for analysis. In any case, while we can expect agreement on many categories, we are unlikely to ever reach agreement upon a complete list of categories.

It is noteworthy that literary critics and librarians have begun to "apply the methods and insights of the social sciences" to discussions of children's literature. Any piece of literature is clearly a highly complex product, so that even if a child does say that he enjoyed it or found it funny, it is impossible to know just what was enjoyed, or why. The adoption of social science methods should help provide these answers. At present, there remains a major gap between the forms of children's humor studied by psychologists and others and the more complicated genres and contexts of humor found in literature. At best, those in the field of children's literature can consult research on children's humor for guidelines regarding what should and should not appeal to children of different ages. It is not until humorous forms of literature are themselves systematically studied, however, that we will begin to make real progress in our understanding of children's appreciation of humor in literature. In the absense of such an approach, teachers and literary critics will continue to know which stories and books children enjoy, but they will learn little about why they are enjoyed or about the role played by humor in determining the level of enjoyment experienced.

CONCLUDING REMARKS

A volume devoted to practical applications generally rests upon a sound framework of firmly established knowledge. Our understanding of children's humor clearly has not reached this point, although some topics have been much more thoroughly studied than others. While a considerable amount of research has been completed upon the nature of general developmental changes in humor, very little effort has been made to study important dimensions of individual differences in children's humor. Investigators will continue to expand and refine their understanding of children's humor in these two general directions, but it is now clear that we need not wait until a full understanding of their humor is achieved in order to use humor to help support positive forms of development and adjustment in children. The present volume has demonstrated how humor can be used to promote learning and creativity, instill an interest in literature, facilitate social development, and facilitate emotional adjustment and development within the context of the normal daily stresses associated with growing up and of occasional high stress situations such as hospitals and dentists' offices. There is also research in progress which (at least among adults) supports the view that there are physical benefits to be derived from vigorous humor-induced laughter. Many of us have long had the conviction that humor and laughter are somehow good for us. As we continue to learn more about the various cognitive, social, emotional and physiological factors associated with humor, the evidence (when pertinent) has almost always been consistent with this view. Thus, the best advice continues to be to incorporate humor and laughter into our lives when we can. This is doubly important for children, since the child who becomes especially appreciative of humor, and skilled at producing it, has an entire lifetime to relish the benefits and enjoyment it brings.

REFERENCES

Bolig, E. (1984). Play in hospital settings. In T. D. Yawkey & A. D. Pellegrini (Eds.), *Child's play: Developmental and applied* (pp. 323-343). Hillsdale, N.J.: Erlbaum.

Feitelson, D. (1972). Developing imaginative play in preschool children as a possible approach to fostering creativity. *Early Child Development and Care, 1,* 181-195.

Freud, S. (1960). *Jokes and their relation to the unconscious.* New York: Norton. (Originally; *Der witz und seine beziehung zum unbewussten.* Leipzig: Deuticke, 1905.)

Johnson, J. E. (1976). Relations of divergent thinking and intelligence test scores with social and nonsocial make-believe play of preschool children. *Child Development, 47,* 1200-1203.

Kogan, N. (1983). Stylistic variation in childhood and adolescence: Creativity, metaphor, and cognitive styles. In P. Mussen (Ed.), *Handbook of child psy-*

chology, Vol. III: Cognitive development (pp. 630-706). (Vol. III edited by J. H. Flavell & E. M. Markman.) New York: Wiley.

Levine, J. (1977). Humor as a form of therapy: Introduction to symposium. In A. J. Chapman & H. C. Foot (Eds.), *It's a funny thing, humour* (pp. 127-137). Oxford: Pergamon.

McGhee, P. E. (1976). The humor questionnaire: An analysis of humor researchers' views of appropriate directions for future research. Paper presented at the meeting of the First International Conference on Laughter and Humor, Cardiff.

McGhee, P. E. (1979). *Humor: Its origin and development*. San Francisco: W. H. Freeman.

McGhee, P. E. (1980). Development of the sense of humour in childhood: A longitudinal study. In P. E. McGhee & A. J. Chapman (Eds.), *Children's humour* (pp. 213-236). Chichester England: Wiley.

Singer, J. L. (1973). *The child's world of make-believe*. New York: Academic Press.

Turner, R. G. (1980). Self-monitoring in humor production. *Journal of Personality, 48*, 163-172.

Ventis, W. L. (1973). A case history: The use of laughter as an alternative response in systematic desensitization. *Behavior Therapy, 4*, 120-122.

Wolfenstein, M. (1954). *Children's humor*. Glencoe, IL: Free Press.

Index